The Consequence

Gerald Jones

For my children Leanne, Clare & Mark

God came down to gather flowers
On the way, he gathered ours.

Aberfan Oct 21st 1966

Acknowledgements

Although this book was started many years ago,
it is only in the past couple of years that, through
Kevin Wilson's help and inspiration, I have been
able to complete this book.

Many thanks to:-
Newtown Library.
Wrexham County Borough Museum.
Ian Williams, for his help in the computer department.
Beryl Jarman, who likened me to Michelangelo when
painting the Sistine Chapel; *'When will it be finished?'*

Rufus Fairweather & Fleur Richards for their comments
and encouragement.

And to the people who have read this book before
publication for their comments, good and bad.
I thank you.

Cover picture courtesy of Brian Cooper.

The Prologue

"Set your nets at the back of that tree, Jack," shouted Jim, pointing to the exposed roots of a wind-blown elm. "We should get a couple out of this warren and Bill, shift that bloody dog out of that hole." Bill looked at the rabbit hole the terrier had marked; he could just see his back legs through the dirt he was kicking out.

'He was a good dog, that one,' thought Bill, 'hardly ever made a mistake; he knew if the warren held rabbits or not'. He walked forward, the snow crunching under his boots. Kneeling down in front of the hole, he got hold of the dog by the back legs and dragged him out, then netted up, knocking the wooden peg in with a stone, as the frost had made the ground too hard for it to be pushed in by hand.

"Make this the last one," said Jack in a pissed off tone. "It's getting late and I don't fancy digging the ferret out if it kills in."

Jim never said a word as he took the ferret out of its box. Bill looked at the ferret. A real mean one she was; she had bitten everyone that had handled her, everyone except Jim of course; if she had bitten him it would have been the sharp end of a spade that would have ended her life. He glanced at Jim as he fed the ferret down a different hole that was part of the same warren. Then, as he and Jack had finished netting up, the ferret came back out of the rabbit hole and, for a few seconds, stood at its entrance with its nose in the air. Then it turned and disappeared to do what its natural instincts were telling it to do.

Jim stood up; he was a big man - six foot two and built like a sawmill. He was standing there with rolled-up sleeves even on a day like this. Just to look at him sent a shiver through Bill. Jim was twenty-nine years of age, ten years older than Jack and seven years older than Bill. Jim Pryce was a tree feller, cutting down huge oaks that would be sent to local mills providing timber for the building industry. He was the father of three children, and his priority in life was to them and his wife, Violet. When not working, he could be found in his garden or in the fields, walking the hedgerows around his home, ferreting for rabbits with his friends. Jim, he was really a quiet man, a thinking man insofar as when he spoke, you listened.

Jack, on the other hand, was loud and showy and an unknown observer would have called him a clever little bugger. Little, being the operative word, for Jack was only five foot five inches tall but he was fit, strong and fast, making him a fine adversary for anyone thinking that he would be a pushover in any pub fight. Jack was a farmworker, a man of the land, a man to stand his ground.

Bill Jones, also a farmworker, was a man of principle whose word was his bond. He was the only child of Albert and Jessie Jones and, as an only child, his mother was always fearful of losing him. From the day he had been born, Jessie had prayed that God would watch over him. Bill's character was evident in the way he had been brought up, but he also had a mind of his own and sometimes he would do and say things that were not to her liking, but she respected his motives, realizing that he was what God had given her. Bill's friendship with Jim and Jack Davies went back many years. Jim was a neighbour and their relationship was family-like, even to the point that Jim's children would call him Uncle Bill. His friendship with Jack had always been there, and although Jack was three years younger, it was in school that their bond really set in. Bill was Jack's protector, fending off bullies who would try to take advantage of Jack's diminutive size. He was, and always would be, Jack's hero.

"How many nets have we down?" shouted Jim.

"Seven," said Jack with his ear pressed into the snow, listening to the thumping and scurrying that was going on under their feet.

"Any second now," said Bill as he intently watched the three nets that he had placed five yards away from where Jim had loosed the ferret. Jack moved like lightning as the first rabbit, squealing in terror, bolted into the net in front of him. This was the best part of ferreting, getting ready for the rabbits to run into the nets. The boys could hear them running as the ferret got closer to the rabbits; their hearts started beating faster as they looked from one net to the other, anticipating which net they would dive on first. Then it happened when they were least expecting it, yet at the very moment they were expecting it. For a split second, they were standing looking and not moving. There, in front of them, a rabbit bolted into the net but as the boys had made sure that the string on the outside of the net ran freely, there was no chance that it could escape. In seconds, they had to get the rabbit out of the net, kill it and replace the net, in case another rabbit decided to come out of the same hole.

The snow had started to fall again as they gathered up the nets. The ferret was in its box and the four rabbits they had out of that warren were lying side by side, by each one's head a patch of red snow, blood spreading like ink on blotting paper. Daylight was fading and it was getting colder. The wind had changed and was now blowing more easterly. Still, it had been a good afternoon; nine rabbits in total and only one 'dig out.' Bill gathered his share of rabbits and, with his penknife, cut behind the sinew of each rabbit's back leg just above its foot, so that the other foot could be threaded through, thus making them easier to carry. He noticed the others were ready for off. Jim took his cap off and brushing away the snow said, "Okay boys, let's go."

So, there they were, three long-time friends, making their way home from this snow-covered Mid Wales hillside, little knowing that the rabbits they had killed today and all the rabbits they had ever killed were to be, in a strange way, the saviours of their minds in the years to come.

1

They could hear the whistle blow from over a mile away, everyone looking down the track.

"It's an 89 0-6-0", said a voice amongst the twenty or so young men who were standing on the station platform.

"And how the hell do you know that?" asked Jim, looking for the smartass that could tell what train it was without even seeing it.

"By the sound of its whistle." Everyone looked at Skinny Steve.

"Every class of train has its own sound and I'm telling you, it's a Jones Class 89," he paused; "Any bets?" he asked confidently. No one said a word.

"He's a clever shit," Jack said as he picked up his suitcase. "They sound all the same to me."

It was Saturday the 13th of February when Bill opened a letter from the Ministry, a letter he was expecting. It had been a week since he had stood alongside Jim and Jack at the recruitment office at 38 High Street, Welshpool, seven days since enrolment forms B2513 were placed in front of them and whereupon their details and signatures were to be recorded. Without even thinking,

Bill pointed out the space on Jim's form where he had to sign his name, as his name was the only thing he was capable of writing. The recruiting officer looked up but said nothing; it wasn't the first time he had seen men unable to read and write. Jim, after signing his name, slid the paper over to Bill to finish filling it in for him. He then stood back, his position in the queue taken up by a young man who didn't look old enough to be there. He heard the recruiting officer ask his age; there was a muffled reply, then he heard the officer telling him to go home, have a birthday, and to come back tomorrow. Another B2513 was placed in front of Bill and without the slightest hesitation, he dipped the pen provided into the inkwell and started to fill in his form. Bill folded the piece of paper with all of Jim's details needed to fill in his form and slipped it into his trouser pocket.

With the medical over and their taking the oath of allegiance done, they stepped outside and caught the next train to Montgomery Station, walking the last two and a half miles home.

On the 27th of January, under the provision of the Military Service Act 1916, it became clear that all men between the ages of 18 and 41 would be deemed to be enlisted for the period of the war. There were provisions for men who may be exempt by local tribunals from joining the army, men more useful to the nation in their present employment; men who were ill or infirm, men in whose case military service would cause serious hardship owing to exceptional financial or business obligations or domestic position, and men who conscientiously objected to combatant service.

Posters proclaiming the military's intentions and the implementation of same were nailed to every pub wall in the country, and other places where young men would meet. It was then strongly rumoured that, within a few months, married men would also be conscripted and there was nothing said about this not being the case. On the bottom of the poster that was nailed to the wall outside the Llandyssil pub was printed in bold lettering,

"DO NOT WAIT UNTIL MARCH 2nd - ENLIST VOLUNTARILY NOW"

It was this last statement that brought it home to Bill. He had searched his conscience since Britain had declared war on Germany over a year and a half ago and in that time a lot of men had died in Europe. In Gallipoli, the 7th Battalion Royal Welch Fusiliers had lost over half their men; that was his Battalion, Montgomeryshire men, some not even twenty years of age killed, their pictures in the local papers telling of the gallantry and fearless actions of which these boys were capable.

He and Jack didn't join in the first rush of volunteers as there was almost a frenzied march to the recruiting offices across the country. "We will see what happens", they thought. Even some politicians reckoned that it would be over by the first Christmas. As it was, time went merrily along until reports of the slaughter started to come through. Then there were the men who didn't want to go to war. In the County Times, there were countless stories of men who chose to go to a tribunal, changing their jobs to ones that would get them out of having to join up.

Then, at the start of the New Year, women whose sons were on the front line started to look at young men who walked the streets, asking why they were not in the army. And it became not uncommon for men to open letters, addressed to them, which contained a white feather, a sign of cowardice. This sort of intimidation never happened to Jack or Bill, but they knew that sooner rather than later it would. So, when the new regulations were about to come in, the boys, including Jim, who was married with three children, decided to volunteer before the 2nd of March, as to volunteer would sound a little better than being conscripted. As Jim had said, "If I have to go to war I will go with my friends."

Jack and Jim received their call-up papers the same day as Bill, along with their train warrants. They were to join, as they had requested, the 1/7 RWF and their instructions were to present themselves, along with said papers, at Park Hall training camp on February 25th, 1916 at 2.30 pm. On the Saturday, three days after receiving their papers, Jim, on his way to the village shop, was surprised to see that four men in army uniform had set up a recruiting station on the village green; just a couple of fold-up tables and two chairs.

"Expecting a bit of a crowd?" he asked as he saw the pile of forms, ones that he recognized on one of the tables.

"A bloody waste of time," said a soldier with a cigarette stuck to his lip.

"I don't know why they send us out to small villages like this, as most of the lads that sign up go to Newtown or Welshpool to do it."

"And you, sir?" asked a lad seated at the table.

"Me?" Jim replied with a smile. "I signed up in Welshpool last Wednesday."

"My point exactly," said the man with the cigarette in his mouth, "and your mates?"

"They signed up with me," Jim said as he turned and walked to the shop.

On entering the bar in the only public house in the village, Jack bent down and stroked Shy's head, running his hand from his wet nose along his flank to the tip of his tail.

"Remember, Michael, if you go before your dog, I want him." Michael looked up from his seat by the fireplace.

"So you keep telling me," said Michael in his soft Irish voice. "But from what Bill has been telling me, it will be you that won't be around for a spell, as it will be for Egypt that you will be bound."

"We don't know that for sure," interrupted Jim who had called into the pub after his visit to the shop and was standing with his back to the bar. And then, in the same breath, he asked the landlord to pour a beer for Jack, reaching into his trouser pocket for some money and placing it onto the bar.

"Now, you know I can't take your money for Jack's drink, Jim. We went through all this some time ago, and the no-treating order laid down that any drink was to be paid for by the person supplied. I know from time to time I forget myself, but with strangers around like the boys on the village green, I can't take chances. Anyway, the law will be back to normal after the war, I'm sure." As the landlord spoke, Jack was already placing money on the bar for his own drink.

"Many people on the green, Jack?" enquired Bill.

"Two or three men talking to the recruiting officers, and a bunch of kids kicking a ball about." "There won't be many taking the King's Shilling today," said Bill as he placed a big log on the fire.

"Now that's something, this King's Shilling business - just when are we likely to get it?"

"Now the answer to that question, Jim," interrupted Michael, "is quite simple - you won't get it. The practice of giving the King's Shilling ceased thirty-six years ago in 1879, but the term 'to take the King's Shilling' is still used, meaning that you have sworn allegiance to the crown and that you are now a member of the British Armed Forces."

"So, we won't get a shilling?" said Jim.

"Not from the government, you won't." Michael paused, "I have known you boys for all of your lives, and believe it or not, the thought of you going to war has disturbed me. But the thought of you not going to war would have disturbed me more. I know that a lot of people of the village think I am a little odd and, over the years, they may have been justified in thinking that in the way I have kept myself to myself, never really asking for anything and never really giving in return. Maybe I have reasons to be the way I am. Then I ask myself whether my reasons for relating to people the way I do are justified in the first place? The answer: probably not, so gentlemen," Michael stood up and delved into his coat pocket, "I am giving you the King's shilling."

Jim, Bill and Jack looked at each other in disbelief. This wasn't the Michael Barry Gill that they had known all their lives; the, indeed odd, Irishman that children would taunt and run away from. This was the voice of an intelligent and caring man, with thoughts going around in his head that no one could guess. There had been rumours that told of a young man leaving Ireland because of the potato famine, who sailed to America and fought in the American Civil War, but these were old rumours and had been forgotten and had only resurfaced now that Britain and its Empire had declared war on the German nation.

"You can't do that, Michael, it's not right," said Jim. Michael stood with his arm outstretched; in the palm of his hand, there were three silver shillings.

"Take one each," he said. "I may be too old to fight, but that doesn't stop me having an interest in the young men from my village who are willing to go to war knowing that they may not come back. And you, Jim," who almost stood to attention when addressed, "you are the oldest and probably the wisest; you look after these two". Then, turning to Bill and Jack, "I'm not saying that you should do everything Jim tells you, but just to think about what he says. And with that, I might sit down, but first I will shake your hands and wish you well, as we may never meet again." With that, Michael sat down in his chair. Jim and Jack said their farewells and left. Outside, Jack shook his head. "What the hell was all that about, Jim? Do you think we have misunderstood Michael for all these years?"

"No," said Jim in deep thought.

"No, we haven't misunderstood him, I think he has misunderstood himself and now, as an old man, let's hope he still has time to be the Michael he used to be, or the one he always wanted to be. Either way, he has bloody well impressed me."

Bill sat down by Michael; neither spoke.

"Well," Michael said after a pause that was just long enough to be acceptable to both.

"Well, what?" Bill answered back.

"Well," he said, lowering his voice, "that little speech, that little speech of mine."

"Ah," Bill said, sitting up in his chair and with a smile that filled his face, "your Gettysburg Address." Michael looked at Bill, all expression draining from his face, and then grabbing Bill's arm and through a beaming smile of his own, exclaimed, "And whatever made you think of the Gettysburg Address?"

"Well," Bill said as Michael let go of his arm, "I believe it was a speech of historical importance in American history and your address at the Upper House could be seen as just as important to one, namely Michael Barry Gill, and those that witnessed it. So, I raise my glass to you, Michael, and I hope we all find what we are looking for."

Outside on the village green, the boys had picked up their ball and gone home. There was no one at the tables other than the recruiting officers, and they looked like they wished they were somewhere else. Then, from the blacksmith's shop, emerged Megan Davies, the blacksmith's sister, with her sister-in-law, Rose. They walked toward the tables and picked up four mugs and an empty plate and, as they talked, the pub door could be heard closing. On looking up, they could see Michael and Bill were fastening their overcoats. Shy ran over toward Megan, who bent down and ruffled his head with both hands.

"Hello Shy," she said as Shy insisted she gave him more of the same. "You like me doing that, don't you?"

"I see you have a friend there, Megan," said Bill. Megan looked up and smiled. Megan then asked Bill if he could spare a moment. At this point, Rose took her leave and, carrying two mugs and the plate, walked the stone's throw to her home, her heavily pregnant frame making her walk look awkward and cumbersome. Michael, while talking to the recruitment officers, noticed Megan approach Bill.

"So, you will be leaving on Wednesday, Bill?" she said as she stood in front of him. Bill shrugged his shoulders.

"We have to do the right thing, Megan." "Yes, I know," she said hesitantly, then looking into his face, she took a step forward and placed her hand on his forearm.

"I was wondering if it would be alright if I were to write to you and the boys while you are away, to give you the local news, that sort of thing." Bill was pleasantly surprised by Megan's offer and placed his hand on hers as she was about to let go of his arm.

"Megan, I would appreciate that very much and will look forward to your letters." As Megan stood on tiptoe, she kissed Bill on the cheek and whispered, "Look after yourself, Bill." After letting go of his arm, she grabbed the two remaining mugs off the table and ran home.

Within twenty minutes, the village green was empty, and although it had been a dry day and was still only 3.30 pm, Michael wondered if it was the chill in the air that had sent everyone indoors, and was thinking to himself that that would be the best place to be.

"Before you go away, Bill, I was wondering if you could call and see me as I feel I need to explain a few things," Michael said.

"I could call Tuesday afternoon if that would be alright," replied Bill, "but I don't think you have anything you need to explain to me."

"Well maybe and maybe not, but Tuesday afternoon will be fine." Then, as they parted company, Michael said,

"Tell your Mum and Dad I said hello."

"Will do," answered Bill. "See you Tuesday."

2

A powdering of snow fell on the Tuesday night, dusting the landscape with its effervescence. Bill slept well considering the upheavals that the day would bring. Jessie had already packed a small suitcase.

"You won't need a lot," she said, "and once you get your army uniform, you will not be putting your suit on again until the end of the war."

It had been a hard two weeks for Bill's mother ever since the boys had gone to Welshpool to sign up. She knew this day would come, and worse still would come the day they would go away proper. As it was, Park Hall camp wasn't that far away and maybe they would have some leave during their time there. She thought of Mary, Jack's mother, and Violet, Jim's wife, and how hard it was going to be for her and the three children with Jim not being there. But she also knew that the women of the village would rally around and help out as best they could, as they had done since the start of the war when the first sons of the village had left. Now it was her turn to feel the anguish and solitude of other mothers. Bill's father had already gone to work; it was not in his nature to show any kind of emotion, even to the point of shaking his son's hand. He just slapped him on his back and said,

"I'll be gone in the morning. Good luck and look after yourself."

Jack got up late, dressed and went downstairs. The house was empty except for his mother, who had placed a bowl of bread and milk on the table.

"Sit down and eat that," she said, "you still have two hours to go."

"I know," he said, "it's all the hanging around I can't stand."

"What time are you meeting the boys?"

"Half eleven," he said looking at the clock that hung on the wall above the fireplace. He finished his bread and milk then looked across the table and saw his suitcase standing by the front door. There was a name tag tied to the handle with a piece of string. He stood up and went into the back kitchen for his boots.

"You've polished them," he said.

"Did them first thing this morning," she said, casually raking the fireplace then, using an ash pan and brush, she swept up the ash and placed it into a small bucket.

Jack had tied his boots and went outside, the cold air hitting his lungs as he stepped out onto the road. The fine snow that had fallen during the night would soon be gone, he thought. Then, looking up the road, he noticed movement outside the blacksmith's shop. David, the blacksmith, was looking at the shoes of a pony, and Jack thought how secure David's future was compared to his own. There was no malice in his thinking; in fact, there had been a lot of misfortune in that family. It was only now in the last year or so that the long hours and hard work that he, Rose and Megan had put into their blacksmith's business was finally paying off. Jack stamped his feet; he was impatient, he wanted to go, he was eager to meet his future.

Bill didn't have to wait long before he saw Jim coming down the road. His distinctive gait emphasized the lurch of his body. His suitcase, Bill noticed, was strapped to his back, giving freedom to his arms. Their meeting was, in a way, a sense of relief.

"This is where it all begins," said Bill as he fell into step with Jim. "This waiting around all bloody morning has driven me up the wall." Jack was on the village green and joined them as they walked past the closed door of the pub on their way out of the village. Nothing much was said, each one having thoughts of their last goodbyes to the ladies in their lives and for Jim's children, who were far too young to understand the significance of his leaving, his kisses and goodbyes meaning little if anything at all.

Half a mile further on, they came to a crossroads; to the right, the hill road to Montgomery, to the left the village of Abermule and straight ahead, the road to Montgomery station and beyond. Setting the pace, Jack strode out in front, but after a while, Bill and Jim had made up lost ground with the three of them walking under Montgomery Station bridge together.

Voices could be heard as they trod the gravel path lined with the mandatory white fencing that had become uniform to all railway stations. Then, as Bill opened the small wicket gate that led onto the platform, a big cheer went up from the twenty or so lads that were on the platform.

Comments such as "The Llandyssil lads are here to save us all" and "Look, it's the three musketeers" were heard. A lot of the lads were from Montgomery itself and then there were some from other villages, but pretty much all of them lived within a radius of three to four miles. The main topic of conversation was understandably the war, the conflict in Europe and the disaster that was Gallipoli, but from now on they agreed all things would be different. There was an air of excitement on the platform. Bill looked from one small group of men to another, trying to gauge their enthusiasm. Some were full of it, others just sat on their suitcases without saying much at all. There were men of all shapes and sizes, some he didn't doubt would make fine soldiers but there were others he feared for and as he looked at them, he began to realise that this situation was repeating itself all across the country where other young men were on other platforms, catching other trains that would take them all away from their homes and into war.

When the train pulled into the station, Skinny Steve was the first to confirm his assumption that the train was again a Jones Class 89. Of course, there had to be someone who would try to undermine his knowledge of this train by asking where the name "Jones" came in.

"It was the designer," shouted Steve, "Herbert Jones, the man who designed the engine." As the train stopped and the doors opened, someone else shouted, "And how heavy is it, Steve?"

"Do you want it in short tons or long tons?" Steve answered back.

"For God's sake just get on the bloody train, Steve." Even as the doors were closing, the same voice could be heard saying,

"How the hell does he know so much about trains?"

"He lives next to a railway line," said someone else.

Bill walked the corridor of each carriage and noticed that practically all compartments had someone in them. Suitcases were being placed under seats or in the string luggage racks above their heads. He made it to the last carriage just in time to see the guard hanging out of the door waving his green flag and blowing a whistle. The train shunted forward catching everyone by surprise, then, on regaining their balance, it shunted forward again, then again and again, each time encountering less resistance on the track as it gathered speed. The engineer sounded the train's whistle, no doubt to the satisfaction of Skinny Steve. His love of trains wasn't that difficult to understand; with the train now up to speed, the whole thing took on a new dimension, it became a living thing. The comforting sway of the carriage, the chatter of the wheels as they ran over points and expansion gaps between the lengths of the steel tracks, clickety-click, clickety-click, its very sound synonymous with travel and adventure.

Having momentarily lost Jim and Jack, Bill now stood at the open window of the door that the railway guard was hanging out of. The smell of soot and smoke from the train drifted in; he inhaled the acrid cloud as he looked upon the fields and woods as they passed him by.

A covey of partridge, startled by the train, caught his eye as they flew low and in unison over a hedge and across a field, coming to rest at the foot of a large oak tree. Its foliage, which had grown and shown itself last April, had disappeared, each leaf turning differing shades of red and brown before falling, nudged by the wind and rain, letting go of the branches that had held them during the summer months. Bill noticed some red squirrels running along one of the oak's branches as he felt a tap on his shoulder.

"Hello, Bill," said a voice behind him; on turning he saw the smiling face of Ian Brown.

"Hello, Ian," he said, "I haven't seen you in months."

The remainder of the journey was spent in the company of his friend from Abermule. Ian was the son of the Reverend Walter Brown and, at nineteen, he was three years younger than Bill, slightly built and with a mop of curly brown hair. Originally from Manchester, he had arrived with his parents some twelve years earlier after the death of the Reverend Colin Williams. The poor man had had the misfortune to have been killed by a kick to the head from his horse, whilst trying to get the beast into the shafts of his trap.

Ian was an intelligent and knowledgeable young man and for that reason, along with his indecisiveness, the local lads used to poke fun at him and were successful in making him feel an outsider. Bill had a personal liking for him; he had a quality he seldom found in others. Ian was a good person, never big-headed or a show-off, but always a mine of information. Even as a young lad, Bill knew that Ian was not a country boy and never would be, but he tried.

On many occasions, during the summer months when they were younger, Bill and Ian would often call on each other and lay nets to catch rabbits or spear trout that swam amongst the roots of trees that had grown into the pools of crystal water. Ian would talk on subjects that were familiar and known to Bill, but even then, Ian was reluctant to talk of anything other than rabbits, pigeons or ferrets and, as important as these things were, he did not want to give Bill the impression that there were other things out there to be considered. That was until the day Bill asked Ian about his interests. He knew Ian liked to read a lot, but just what did he like to read about?

"I'm not telling you," he said. "Anyway, you will only laugh."

"And why should I laugh?" protested Bill, "Why do you think that, just because you are interested in a subject, that subject may not interest me?" Ian then told him of his liking for the works of Shakespeare and Greek mythology.

"Well," said Bill, "I'm not sure about Shakespeare, but Greek mythology sounds interesting. You will have to tell me about it one day."

The train stopped at a few more stations, including Welshpool, before it terminated at Oswestry. At each stop, more young men would climb aboard, uncertainty showing in the eyes of some and the devil may care in the eyes of others. Jim had found two empty seats when he had got onto the train at Montgomery station.

"We'll sit here," he said to Jack as the train shunted forward.

They didn't talk as the train rattled and swayed on the iron tracks that were spiked down onto Australian Jarrah sleepers. Jim looked around; most men, he noticed, wore their Sunday best: suits, white shirts, ties and overcoats, everyone carrying a small suitcase or kitbag. Those who could not find a seat stood and steadied themselves by holding onto leather straps that hung in the carriages. The smell of cigarette smoke lingered in all the compartments; occasionally, a window would open and a blast of cold air would disperse the smell only to replace it with smoke of a different kind. Nearing their destination, Jim looked again at the young lad that had sat opposite him during the journey.

"And what do you do for a living?" he asked as he finally caught his eye.

"I work as a clerk in Lloyds Bank in Welshpool, sir," said the young lad. Jim was pleasantly surprised to hear the young lad call him 'sir' but he realised that he was a number of years older and it was only good manners to call one's elders 'sir'. Still looking at him, Jim asked, "Are you any good at your job?"

"I'd like to think I'm damn good at my job, sir," the lad nervously replied with a grin.

"Then do yourself a favour, son, and join the Army Pay Corps; that way you will stand a better chance of seeing your mother again after all the shit that is about to happen has happened. There are many ways of serving your country, young man, so find a way that is acceptable to the army as well as being acceptable to yourself."

The young lad smiled as Jim finished speaking.

"You're the second person to have suggested that to me," he said, "and I think I might enquire as to your suggestion."

Jack, having heard the conversation above all the other noise going on, had already made a mental note of the young man sitting opposite. He noticed that there wasn't much of him; even with his posh suit on he wouldn't have weighed more than eight stone and he wouldn't have weighed any more soaking wet. Jack noticed the cut of his suit, the trilby he wore, the knife-edged creases and the turn-ups on his trousers. Jack looked at his shoes, brown with a shine that you only saw in shop windows. Jack imagined him to be a mirror image of his father.

"And your father?" Jack said.

The young lad turned his head slightly on hearing Jack's voice.

"My father," he said, smiling, "he works in the same bank."

The train stopped with a shudder, the sound of metal on metal as the wheels of the locomotive braked and abruptly came to a halt. Immediately, there came the sounds of whistles being blown, doors being opened and slamming against the sides of the carriages as men streamed out, pushing and shoving their way onto the station platform, to the sound of hissing steam being released from chambers within the train. There were men in army uniforms with stripes on their shoulders, strutting up and down the platform bellowing out orders. Higher-ranking officers with their peaked caps and Sam Browne belts looked on. Seemingly unconcerned, they stood lazily tapping their legs with their swagger sticks.

Bill looked around him; there must have been hundreds of men on the railway platform. Confusion seemed to be as much a part of the question as it was the answer. He heard Skinny Steve shouting that some bastard had pinched his case and the one that he was carrying wasn't his. The army men with the stripes on their shoulders were still screaming orders, trying to get some semblance of order, pushing men into line but not all facing the same way; men just did what they were told to do and in no time, they were falling in, three abreast and marching off the platform. As they did, Jones Class 89 gave them a blast of its whistle.

Bill Jones, along with two hundred and fifty or so new recruits, walked through the gates of Park Hall Training Camp at 3.30 pm and the sergeants marshalled them into lines with shouted instructions. What sun there was that day had gone and early evening light was setting in. Their standing on the parade ground in orderly lines reminded Jack of his school days, lining up on the playground at the start of assembly. All were gathered together for a common purpose and what is our purpose, thought Jack, already knowing the answer.

They were split into groups of thirty, then marched towards rows of billeting huts. Luckily, the boys were not split up and they entered hut number 36. They quickly grabbed beds next to each other near to the centre of the hut, Jack's bed being four down from the cast iron stove that stood in the middle of the building.

"A comforting thought on cold nights," said Jim, as he threw his suitcase onto the bed.

Bill, shoving his suitcase under his bed with his foot, gingerly sat on the edge of his bed, then, with more confidence, started to bounce up and down, the iron bed with its set of springs holding firm.

"There must be a few thousand of these," Jack said as he lay fully stretched out on his. He didn't even bother to take off his shoes, although, in all fairness, he had them hanging over the end.

"Clean sheets," he said; "they must have been expecting us."

"A lot of men left here the day before yesterday; once they have finished their training, they are shifted off and a new lot like us are brought in to start ours," said Jim.

Before light the following morning, *reveille* sounded and would do so every morning thereafter. After a cup of tea, beds were made and a quick clean-up of the hut was undertaken. All new recruits were then gathered on the parade ground and, in three rows, were marched to the army stores to pick up their uniforms, webbing, identity disks, boots and whatever was required to clothe a soldier of the King's Army.

Back in the huts, men were stripping down to their long johns and unceremoniously throwing their civilian clothes into their suitcases.

"Won't be wearing that lot for some time," said a chap in the next bed to Bill. He introduced himself as Terry Smout from Dolfor. There was a lot of shaking of hands and introductions in those first few days at Park

Hall, but Jack admitted that, like a lot of people, his memory for names was not good. There were many faces that he did know and some he knew the names of, but he didn't think too much about it. As Jim sat on his bed to tie up his bootlaces, he grinned. This, he thought, was the first pair of new boots he had had in a long, long, time, and they didn't fit.

"It's not the boots," said Jack, "it's your feet that are the wrong size." Then, as he bent his head forward, the identity disks that hung on a piece of string around his neck swung into his vision. He looked at them, then he held them up. The brown disk had eight sides with two holes at opposite ends, the string around his neck passing through one of these. To the other hole, another cord secured the other disk, which was red. Both disks having identical information stamped onto their compressed fibre composition, he noticed his service number, surname and initials, regiment and religion. The need for the red disk to be independent of the cord around his neck, so he was told, was that in the event of a soldier being killed or having otherwise died, the red disk could be taken and recorded, leaving the brown disk around his neck for other purposes. As Jim held his identity tags in his hand, he had just one concern, and that was he hoped to Christ that, during his stay in the army, he would not be left with just the brown tag around his neck.

Bill, being the last one out of the hut, closed the door behind him. In front, walking toward the parade ground, were thirty men now in military uniform. He looked at them; how different they looked. He was sure some of them looked taller and straighter than they did before they entered the building behind them; he even felt different himself. Was it the uniform that made him feel like he did? No other reason came to mind.

A sea of khaki now made its way towards the parade ground, with other men from other huts converging too.

Even the backs of their uniforms told a story. As they were changing into their uniform, a burly, ageing sergeant had stepped through the door of the hut, and as he walked amongst the young soldiers, he started to tell them of the unusual feature on their uniform.

"This regiment," he said, "was distinguishable from others by the unusual feature of the flash, five overlapping black silk ribbons that hang from the back of their tunic collars."

Some of the lads stopped what they were doing and sat on their beds listening to what the sergeant had to say. These ribbons were seven inches long and each one had a v- shape cut into the ends of them.

"The flash," he informed them, "was a legacy of the days when soldiers wore pigtails, their black hair standing out against the red tunics that were worn at the time. Then, when soldiers' hair was cut shorter, the flash came into being."

At 06:30hrs, all men would be out on the parade square learning to march. They would be out there for hours, forming squares and about turns. They were taught how far to the horizontal they were to swing their arms when marching; they were told when and where to snap to attention and obey commands without hesitation or question. Lunch was between 12.15 and 14:00hrs, followed by more drill till 16:15hrs, when relief came in the form of an announcement stating they were dismissed for the day, other than those who were unlucky enough to be detailed off on a working party.

3

At home, Megan spat on the hot flat surface of the iron she was holding. It sizzled to her satisfaction; she then set about ironing David's white Sunday shirt. It was the first of many items that were piled in the wicker basket. As she placed that garment across the ironing board, she wondered if she would finish them all in time to give Mrs. G a hand to clean the Rectory kitchen. Mrs. G was the cook there and, apart from her kitchen duties, she seemed to run everything and everyone at the Rectory; nothing happened there without Mrs. G knowing about it.

It was in the afternoon on the first Monday of every month that Megan would help Mrs. G in giving the kitchen a good scrub down. Mrs. G had been at the Rectory for many years and had seen vicars come and go. It had got to the stage where it seemed that it was Mrs. G who vetted new incoming vicars, and not the vicars that vetted the Rectory staff. Megan had been giving Mrs. G a hand doing various chores for almost two years, and not once did Mrs. G ever give away her age; Megan guessed her to be around sixty-five. In the beginning, when the fourteen-year-old Megan started work in service at the Rectory, she worked as a scullery maid and found that Mrs G was very strict, having a colourful vocabulary and a venomous tongue to go with it. However, over the two years Megan had been helping out, she had found that Mrs. G's bark was worse than her bite and it was only three weeks ago that Mrs. G had confided in Megan, telling her that she was one of the best workers she had ever had. So much so, that Mrs. G had even found extra work at the Rectory for Megan. For this, Megan was most grateful. Although the money was a pittance, Megan didn't complain. She knew she was being exploited, but she was young, strong-willed and independent; life was better now than it had ever been.

Megan had had her fair share of hardship in her young life, losing her mother as she gave birth to a stillborn baby girl when Megan was eight years of age, and then her father dying of pneumonia two years later. Megan had cried her tears and even now, with her nineteenth birthday just two weeks away, she could still recall her father's deep, rough poetic voice. And as he lay dying, she remembered him telling her not to cry, and with his big blacksmith's hands stroking her hair he said again, "Don't cry, my princess, don't cry."

But she did cry, for he was her life. She cried for weeks after his death. It was only her brother, David, who could ease the pain of her distress. It was after the funeral, when they stood alone in the kitchen of their blacksmith's home, that David draped his nineteen-year-old arms around his sister. He despaired at her uncontrollable sobbing and it was then that he swore he would carry on his father's business. Many had doubted his ability to do so. Many had offered him permanent farm work but now, with tears running down his cheeks and onto the head of his only family, a broken-hearted ten-year-old girl dependent on him for everything, his mind was made up. He would work and live for her well-being and, God willing, one day laughter would come into her life, as up until then there had been precious little of that. Megan also remembered that day and, despite the passing of the years, the memory of her father would remain forever in her heart.

As she folded his shirt, she could see tear stains on a similar one, one that had long since been discarded. Then, as she held it to her face and smelled its warm freshness, she thought of the night of her father's funeral when she crawled into her brother's bed and asked him to cuddle her, as her father often did. His first instinct was to reject her request as it would be improper for her to share his bed, but as these were circumstances that were put upon them, he relented and let her stay. On that first night, he held her with compassion and a fatherly instinct that was years beyond his age. Megan slept in her brother's bed for one week after that, then she only agreed to sleep in her own bed on the condition that it was in his room. This he agreed to and it was a month later, when Megan had regained enough confidence, that she closed the door to David's bedroom and moved back into her own room. Two years after that they left their father's blacksmith's shop in the village of Llandinam and took over the blacksmith's shop in Llandyssil.

4

Michael Barry Gill, in his seventy-ninth year, was dying and he knew it. He sat back in his chair and closed his eyes. The warmth from the fire comforted him as he brought back images of his life. He sought out memories, memories that had for so long been in the shadows of his mind. He remembered being told that he was the youngest of seven children. His mother had died in 1845 when he was six years of age. Two of his sisters had died before he was born, whilst his other sister and brother had died within twelve months of each other when he was nine. The Irish potato famine was responsible for the deaths and displacement of tens of thousands of people, and Michael Gill's family was among them. Their father had found work when he could but, in the end, was unable to pay the rent and the family were evicted from their home. He had taken his children to County Mayo to live with an aunt, then he went away to find work and was never seen again.

Michael had, as a child, witnessed starvation and death and, like many his age, hunger had become a way of life. The numbers of dead grew into their thousands and landowners such as the Earl of Lucan, who, it is was said, owned a total of 60,000 acres, were not concerned with the welfare of people who lived on their estates. Those people, like everyone else, were evicted, even to the point of some having their squalid little homes pulled down with them still inside.

Their salvation was to emigrate. Thousands went across the Irish Sea to England and thousands caught ships from Ireland to sail to Canada. In the early years of the famine, ship owners capitalised on the mass exodus of people by supplying inferior ships to dubious shipping companies. It seemed that the wellbeing of the passengers came second to the profits of the shipowners and the companies that ran them. These ships were unsuitable for the journey and, until stricter regulations came into force, the owners were more interested in the number of people that got onto their ships than got off them at their final destination.

The percentage of deaths on board these ships was high, mainly due to malnutrition, fever, typhus, and cholera. As if the journey wasn't bad enough, at the end of their voyage, healthy people were put into quarantine along with everyone else, including those already infected, resulting in these unfortunates being buried in the land that was going to save them.

After a few years, these coffin ships, as they were called, were being replaced by better and more robust vessels. The shipping agents were beginning to realise their failings. The more responsible ones recognised that to increase their share of passengers, they had to come up with something that would be irresistible to the masses, namely, the dramatic reduction of deaths on board ship. By far the most popular country that appealed to most famine survivors was America. This was a six-week voyage and the cost was not only in money. Most would leave loved ones and possibly never see them again, although many were young enough to think they would. Few would achieve anything other than to live, and a few, just a few of them, would aspire to the heights of their dreams.

Michael, together with his brother and sister, survived the famine by living on their wits, through good fortune, stealth, cunning and a fair amount of thieving along the way. Michael remembered his brother telling him when he was fourteen that he would not let another member of his family die. It was at this time that Michael had decided to leave Ireland and go to America. But first, he had to learn to speak English, as Gaelic was not the language that was to get him where he wanted to be.

Michael opened his eyes, stood up and went to his bedroom. He opened the drawer of his bedside table, took out an old biscuit tin, placed it on his bed and opened it. Inside were a few odds and ends, things he had put away for reasons that now were unclear even to him. Then he carefully took out a folded silk handkerchief. In the right-hand corner, embroidered in a pink silk thread, was the letter 'M'; it was the first letter of his mother's name, Molly. This was the first time he had held or seen it in thirty years. "Molly," he said softly, tears welling up in his eyes, "I can't even remember your face." He gently folded the handkerchief and placed it back inside the tin.

Michael put another log on the fire. He was tired, but his need to recall his story was compelling. He looked into the flames and thought of the two Megans in his life; Megan, the blacksmith's sister and his Megan... the only woman he had ever loved.

It was that look on her face, he thought, and the way she placed her hand on Bill's forearm. He shook his head somberly, his mind racing back over the intervening years. He had stood not two yards from them on the village green, over four years ago, on the day the boys went to war. He had overheard her ask if it would be alright if she wrote to the boys while they were away. But it was the way she looked at Bill. He recognised that look; he had seen it before in America, in a shabby apartment room in lower Manhattan, on his own Megan's face. He closed his eyes, seeing her pale crestfallen face in such detail that he raised his hand as if to touch her. He recalled the look in her sad brown eyes. She had placed her hand on his forearm as she thanked him for the money he had given her, money that would get her out of the mess she had found herself in. The gratitude was in her voice and hope was in her eyes.

On the morning of the 8th of September, 1857, in the port of Fenit near Tralee, the ropes that had held the *Lady Russell* were released and she was free to sail the Atlantic, her destination America. Two hundred and sixty-one passengers had braved the cold grey morning and stood on deck to wave to whoever had come to see them off. One young man standing on deck didn't look at the crowd of well-wishers, he stood with his back to them and gazed into the horizon. Michael Barry Gill was eighteen years old. The Irish potato famine was over but the repercussions of it lasted many years. Of the two hundred and sixty-one passengers on board, most were under the age of thirty, the vast majority being single and over half of them were women. The journey to New York would take about forty-seven days and young Michael Gill was to relish every day. The *Lady Russell* moved silently in the water. Above him, in the rigging, the shouts of the crew could be heard unfurling sails that, God willing, fair winds would fill. She slipped out of the harbour, gliding past the lighthouse on Sapphire Island, then out into the open sea. He looked back to see the hills around Fenit and Tralee slowly fading from view. The low grey dismal clouds that hung over them must have fitted perfectly the mood of some of the passengers who, for better or worse, had made the same decision as himself. Michael said goodbye to a country that he felt had given him nothing but misery and suffering. For the last four years, he had worked hard and for long hours to be able to see and feel this moment.

Standing by his bed, Michael bent down and stroked the head of his best friend. Shy looked at him in the darkness, knowing that he too must lie on his bed till morning. Michael took off his socks, boots and trousers; the latter he hung over the iron bedstead that many years before had been the property of old Ned Penny until his demise. He got into bed and pulled the bedclothes over himself. Although he still had his shirt on, it bothered him not at all as there was no one to reprimand him for what he thought was a logical thing to do on cold nights; he thought no more about it.

He lay on his back and stared into the blackness, casting his mind back to his voyage to New York, as uneventful as it was in terms of death, disease, or disasters. Nothing since had made him feel more alive than standing on the bow of the *Lady Russell*, with his eyes closed, feeling her power forward, her hewn bow cutting through waves that made her rise, fall and shudder. Clasping the ship's ropes to steady himself, the relentless rush of wind flayed his hair and blasted his face, near taking his breath away, as did the ocean's salted air, like an elixir hitting his lungs, making him feel like he could live forever.

This was a new world for the young Irishman. There were sights that he had been told about that he would now see. New words and phrases had entered his vocabulary from listening to the crew as they went about their rushed business. He wondered if it was mandatory that they did what they did as fast as they did; their shouts and gestures, curses and banter. It seemed they all knew what to do, what was expected of them, and the mayhem was for the benefit of the passengers.

He marvelled at the sight of whales blowing spent air that looked like fountains coming out of the sea; the size of these creatures he could barely comprehend. He would spend hours leaning on the ship's timber railings, watching dolphins swimming alongside, leaping out of the water and clearly enjoying the chase. He noticed the ease with which they would glide above and below the surface of the sea and, when breaking clear of the water, would create a faint slipstream in their wake.

Was Michael Gill a sociable person? He considered himself not to be and it wasn't because he wanted to be like he was. He concluded a long time ago that his childhood, or the lack of it, had something to do with the way he ended up. Just how did he end up?

"I'm not a bad man," he said to himself, "on the contrary, I haven't stolen any bread since I was ten years of age, and thirteen when I last pinched some swedes from a farmer's tump." Then there were the chickens; he smiled when he thought about the chickens. He and his brother were part of a gang of men working on a big cowshed, one that was being built by, as they put it, the bastard of a landlord who had thrown them out of their house. Toward the end of the famine and after it, livestock had become a landowner's cash crop, and people became a commodity that was detrimental to their balance sheet. The chickens were kept in a shed with a wired chicken run, sixty yards from the manor house, alongside the horse stables. It became the duty of one of the stable lads to count them in each night. During the day, the chickens were let out of the pen to roam and roam they did. A week before, the hens started to go missing, while two foxes were seen in a field adjacent to the shed. Adequate precautions had been taken in not letting the hens out of their run during the day. After a few days, with no sign of any foxes, they were let out again. This time Michael watched their every move.

One day after lunch, he noticed two of them go into the field just below where he was working. They disappeared over a brow and into a ditch, no doubt looking for water. After a while, he noticed that only one had come back. At this particular time, he was working on his own, so unbeknown to anyone, he went to look for the missing hen. He found it, stuck headfirst up a clay land drain pipe. Making sure he could not be seen, he pulled it out and quickly removed its head from its body, pulling out a few of its feathers and scattering them, adding its head to the scene. He hastily washed his hands in water from the ditch, tucked the hen under his jacket and made for the roadside hedge about fifteen yards away. The hawthorn hedge made good cover for him as he pushed the hen through the hedge at its base. Making sure he covered the hen with leaves, he felt confident that tomorrow night's tea would still be there to pick up on his way home from work. The chicken feathers and head were soon discovered, prompting an immediate hunt for the foxes responsible. It took two weeks to find and kill the foxes perceived to be responsible for taking the four chickens. The foxes may have had one, but Michael Gill had taken the other three.

He thought again about his social failings, if that's what they were. It wasn't a major problem in his life, but from time to time he would dwell on the positive and negative side of his personality. Even now, at the age of seventy-nine, he thought it ridiculous that he should even be thinking about his personality. Yet, here he was doing just that.

At mid-morning on the 22nd of October, the *Lady Russell* sailed into the port of New York, passing the lighthouse on Sandy Hook, the Islands of Fort Wood and Ellis on the left and Governor's Island on the right. She docked in berth three, lower Manhattan docks, Manhattan. All passengers were directed to Castle Garden processing station, where their health and general condition was assessed. Shortly after, Michael found himself standing on West Street, which also acted as the wharf running parallel to the docks. He found it strange at first, standing on solid ground again, the motion of the ship still in his head, so communication between his legs and his head was a little slow.

A week prior to him standing on West Street, Michael had been on deck listening to stories of a seaman's life, told by one of the crew he had got to know well, when a well-dressed man and a lady whom he presumed to be his wife, albeit looking much younger than the gentleman, approached. They stood to one side, as the seaman finished talking, excusing himself, saying he had things to do.

"Going to show off in the rigging," Michael joked, as he started to climb the ropes.

"You would make a good sailor," the seaman shouted back with a laugh.

"Not thinking of changing your profession, are you?" the well-dressed gent said, smiling as he approached.

"I beg your pardon?" Michael was bemused as to the question.

"I'm sorry," the man said, as he offered his hand, "Let me introduce myself. My name is Gordon Doyle, of Doyle and Simpson and this is my wife, Margaret." Michael shook his hand. "Pleased to meet you, sir, and you, ma'am," he said as he nodded to the lady in question.

"I hope you don't mind my intrusion, but I would like to speak to you on a subject that could be of benefit to both of us."

His accent was English, posh English and, the *"benefit to both of us,"* spoken by a person of his obvious standing, usually meant that the benefit only went one way. Michael was cautious in his reply.

"I can't think of anything I have that would be of any possible benefit to you, Mr Doyle."

"Please, call me Gordon and let me explain."

"Now this is where I will leave you both," said Mrs Doyle. She then raised her gloved right hand and touched her husband on the forearm.

"I will see you in the cabin." She looked at him with raised eyebrows; "In about thirty minutes?" Mr Doyle bent his head and kissed her on the cheek. Now don't let him bore you Master Gill, I know what he's like...nice to have met you.

Again, she raised her hand, fluttering her fingers in a little wave as she turned and walked away. Her long, maroon crinoline dress swaying noticeably with the movement of her hips and exaggerated, no doubt, by the motion of the ship.

"Um," Gordon sighed, as he rubbed his chin.

"Now, you're wondering how my wife knew your name?" he looked a little embarrassed as he waited for some reaction from Michael.

"Well," Michael said, his face expressionless, "It did cross my mind".

"The ship's manifest."

"I beg your pardon?" Michael said, bewildered as to the meaning of the word.

"The manifest, the ship's list of people on board."

"So, you have a list of people with my name on it," he shrugged his shoulders. "You were looking for... me?"

"Well, not exactly."

"Not exactly?" Michael couldn't help himself from smiling.

"It isn't your name that interests us, Michael, it's your profession."

"My profession? I'm a stonemason, for heaven's sake."

"And what's this 'us' business?" Michael was beginning to feel a little nervous of this man's interest in him.

"Let me explain," Gordon hesitated, as he could see the beginnings of mistrust on Michael's face.

"Doyle and Simpson are a construction company. We also have interests in land and other commodities. My wife and I have been on a business trip to London and Belfast and are now on our way home.

"At the moment, the construction side of our company is reassessing its personnel," then before Doyle could finish his sentence, the ship dipped into a large swell, causing it to roll. In doing so, most passengers who were standing on deck, including Doyle and Michael, lost their balance. Michael quickly moved his feet to counteract the imbalance but Gordon ended up on his backside. He got up laughing.

"I think we had better find some seats."

"We'll go amidships; it won't roll so much there," Michael said, making the most of his recently acquired seaman's knowledge. They sat on a bench that was fixed to the superstructure.

The ship, still dipping and rolling in the heaving swells, seemed a strange setting for this unlikely conversation. Although Michael was beginning to feel much more at ease in Gordon's company, he was still wary of Gordon's intentions, as he continued to speak of his company's new approach to personnel recruitment. Gordon then went on to mention his personal feelings regarding management and employees, saying that respect on all sides would save a lot of animosity! At this point he changed the subject, much to the relief of Michael, as to him there was and always would be a "them and us".

"Now......," he turned, and looked at Michael, running his fingers through his greying hair, "I've been watching you for a couple of weeks and have come to the conclusion that you are a young man with spirit and ambition, otherwise you wouldn't be on board this ship. I suspect you are of a sober disposition, willing to learn and I wouldn't be surprised if you had a generous nature, one that would be," he paused tilting his head, "sometimes detrimental to your own wellbeing."

Michael, surprised at Gordon's comments regarding his personality, thought for a moment. Then, rubbing the back of his head, he said, "Gordon, you're assuming a hell of a lot, but there is one thing you have forgotten to mention."

"What's that then?" Gordon frowned.

"You haven't asked if I'm a thief and a liar."

"No, I haven't, have I?" he laughed as he slapped his knee. "And are you?" he asked, still laughing.

"Well, I might have thieved a bit when I was a kid... mostly food," Michael added, trying to justify his thieving, "and as for lying...I am a man of my word, Mr Doyle. What about you, are you a man of yours?"

Gordon stopped laughing. There was no expression on Michael's face as he finished speaking. Doyle rose from his seat and stood in front of the young man who had questioned his credibility. As Michael got up, Gordon offered his hand. He pursed his lips then smiled.

"Master Michael Gill, it has been a pleasure meeting you, a young man who reminds me of myself when I was your age." He reached inside his jacket pocket and brought out an envelope. "In here is a letter of introduction... when in New York and if you're looking for work, hand this letter to Jenny in our head office. The address is..." handing Michael another envelope, "...on a letterhead in here. Just before I go, it may interest you to know there is another stonemason aboard this ship. His name is Stanley O'Donnell. Look him up as, like you, he also has a letter of introduction." Gordon turned to go, then stopped.

"Oh, and by the way," he said with a beaming smile, "in answer to your question, *"Am I a man of my word?"* He hesitated, then nodding his head said, "I believe I am, Michael. I believe I am."

"So, this is it?" Stanley asked.

"Looks like it." Michael reached into his trouser pocket as he spoke. He handed Stan a piece of paper.

"Have a look at this; my reading's not that good. It was given to me by a preacher on the ship. He was handing them out to some of the young people. It's... it's about where to look for accommodation...I think."

Stan read the information on the paper, looking at Michael as he handed it back.

"I have a letter here too," he reached into his jacket pocket, "it's from a Mr Donavan, 93 Fulton Street, Lower Manhattan. To my father. "I'll read it," he said.

Mr Donovan's letter to Stan's father had been received by him some months earlier, regarding accommodation for Stan should he decide to emigrate to America. Mr William Donovan was, in fact, a cousin to Stan's father. Mr Donovan stated that since his father had died, his mother having passed away some years previously, he had taken over the family business, a clothes shop that they had acquired some years ago. He went on to say that he had a room to rent that could accommodate two people with ease if he was so inclined to share with a friend or acquaintance. The rest of the letter dealt with family matters that Stan understandably didn't go into. He folded the letter and placed it back in his jacket pocket, "Well, what do you think?"

"It sounds great," Michael said as he ran his fingers through his hair. "He's been expecting you then?"

"I think so," Stan said as he pointed his finger at the mayhem in front of them. The wharf was a hive of activity. All about there was movement. Behind them, a forest of masts and spars, reaching for the sky, moved involuntarily to the swell of the sea. Ropes tying gathered sails, ropes tethering ships to their moorings and ropes just loosely hanging, asking to be tied to something. Ships of all shapes and sizes being loaded and unloaded, ships going to and coming from ports and countries Michael had never heard of.

The street in front of them was bedlam, with people pulling or pushing carts, shire horses pulling drays every which way, the draymen slapping their rumps, egging them on forever forward. Anything that had wheels, man or beast was pulling it. There were stallholders shouting their wares, people jostling for position for a better view of what they were looking at. Pots and pans, clothes, shoes, cleaning fluid, onions and pocketknives; everything. There were wheelers and dealers, con-men and pimps; people seeking people in specialist occupations. The well-to-do meeting other well-to-do's, getting in and out of carriages. There were the Irish runners, ones that could speak Gaelic, promising the poorest migrant's cheap accommodation, accommodation that didn't turn out to be what they were led to believe. The beggars, bums and bankers, the latter touting a home for your money. Then they were told by a passing button and shoelace seller that they, and all passengers on board the *Lady Russell,* were ignorant of the fact that they had landed in the middle of a financial crisis. Michael shrugged his shoulders and said in a manner that suggested he didn't give a shit.

"Christ, I've been in crisis all my bloody life!"

The little man with a crooked nose, wearing clothes that had seen better days, looked blankly at them and said,

"Just don't expect too much." He, too, then shrugged his shoulders, turned and shuffled off up the wharf shouting, "buttons and laces...buttons and laces!"

Stan picked up his large and heavy suitcase. Michael, already with his sailor's kit bag slung over his shoulder, started to walk across the wharf. He didn't have much of anything in it, mainly clothes and a pair of boots, like the ones he was wearing.

"No!" he thought to himself, "I don't have much, but I do have money." Apart from the seven pounds sixteen shillings and threepence he had in his pocket, around his waist, in a cloth pouch that his sister had sewn, he had thirty-two pounds, which was enough to last him several weeks. How many American dollars that would give him he did not know, but he grinned to himself, as he breathed the air of Manhattan.

As they walked, Stan told Michael what he knew of William Donovan. The Donovans as a family had emigrated to America twelve years ago. William's father was a cutter in a small clothing factory in Dublin and hoped to carry on his career in New York but the clothing industry in New York was a far cry from what they had known in Ireland.

"It seems," said Stan, "that the raw material, cotton, is grown here in America, shipped to England or wherever, where it is spun into thread and then sent back as rolls of cloth, or ready-made garments. But the biggest trade was, and probably still is, in the buying and selling of second-hand clothes." He stopped and looked at his father's letter. On the back, drawn in pencil, was a street map.

"Second-hand clothes?" Michael looked bemused.

"It seems so," Stan replied, shifting his suitcase from one hand to the other. "Apparently, they would buy bundles of used clothing, wash it, mend it, alter it, doing whatever it would take to make it presentable for resale."

"And they made a living doing that?"

"My father told me about the hard time they had."

"Didn't we all?" Michael said, thinking he didn't need to be told about the hard times.

"It was the Jews!"

"I'm sorry, I don't understand," said Michael, confused.

"Yes…they were competing against the Jews, who dominated the clothing industry, and it was the Donovans who upset the apple cart," Stan laughed. "No, not really, there were other Irish people doing the same thing. But it was the Jews, hundreds of them coming into the country, just like us. There were German Jews, Polish Jews, and Jews from other parts of Europe.

"Hang on a minute," Michael interrupted, "how do you know all this?

"From letters they wrote home. My father would relate everything that was written, telling us kids that the world doesn't end at the bottom of our street, whatever he meant by that. He didn't go further than the Harp and Whistle himself and that was only at the bottom of our street," said Stan.

As they walked along West Street, the wharf to their right was still busy with the goings-on of a city port, which seemed to stretch for miles. Just ahead of them was

Washington Market on Fulton Street, which ran from the wharf on West Street all the way to Washington Street. As they walked the length of it, Michael wondered at its complicated simplicity, a contradiction in terms, maybe, but that was the way he saw it.

5

For twelve weeks, the training was arduous and draining. Every sinew stretched to the limits, they would march mile after mile with rifle and equipment, each man bearing a total weight of between sixty and seventy pounds. They would reach a designated point then turn around and walk back. Hundreds of men snaked their way along country lanes, only stopping when told to do so. They drank from their water bottles when told to do so; in fact, there wasn't much they did do without being told to do so first. Excitement had turned to near despair. A regime of authority had taken them; it would break them and, when broken, they would be reborn and moulded into fighting units that were unparalleled, digging trenches and shoring up loose soil, crawling along an imaginary no man's land, cutting through barbed wire entanglements, hand to hand combat with rifle and bayonet, throwing live Mills bombs. Every so often, live rounds of .303 calibre bullets would zip through the air over trenches containing troops just to let them know what live bullets sounded like.

"Your individual qualities count for nothing here," shouted Sergeant bastard Billington, pointing through the rain. It was cold, wet and getting dark; thirty men were digging a hole for themselves, a yard square by three feet deep. The rain ran down Bill's neck as he swung his pick to loosen the soil around his feet. He looked up; Sergeant Billington was going up the line of men, cursing each one as he passed them, telling them to hurry up as he wanted to go to bed. Water was running into Bill's hole forming puddles that turned into mud as he moved around, churning it up. He never noticed Billington standing behind him, but what he did notice was his marking rod as it was dropped beside him.

"Another two inches, Jones," Billington roared, "and then you can start filling it in. And when you've done that, you can fuck off; your mate has already started filling his in."

Bill looked to see Jack stripped to the waist and shovelling like mad.

"God help the last man to fill his hole," Billington shouted as he dragged his muddy boots to the next man who was still digging.

Bill's hole was three-quarters full when Jack picked up his shirt, pick and shovel. He was the fifth man to finish filling in the hole he had dug, and as he passed Bill, he muttered something about bastard Billington getting to see his shovel really close up, like in the fucking face. Darkness closed in as, one by one, the men, having accomplished Billington's task of digging a hole and filling it in, made their way to their billets. The logic of the exercise was unclear, but Billington said that they would all thank him one day.

Unsurprisingly, some men didn't have to wait to die at the hands of the enemy; they were killed unintentionally whilst training. Others died in their beds, pneumonia being the biggest culprit. A lot of men were relieved from combat service due to ill health; some were sent home; others were transferred to transport sections and services. Therefore, after three months, the army had allocated a position for all men, the vast majority being ready to fight for their country.

"Well," said Jack as he sat on the edge of his bed drying his hair with a towel. "Our holiday will come to an end next Wednesday." Bill looked up from a book he was reading, "So the rumours are right?"

"It seems so," answered Jack, throwing the towel onto the bed.

"I thought it wouldn't be long," Jim interrupted. "Not after the turnout of troops this afternoon and an inspection by none other than Lieutenant-General E. C. Bethune. There must have been a few thousand of us at Fern Hill today, all looking very smart, even if I say so myself."

"I'll be glad to get out of here," Jack said as he laid fully stretched on his bed with the towel now wrapped around his waist.

"Looking forward to a bit of sailing, are you?" Bill joked, "Never been on a big boat?"

"I've never even seen a big ship," Jim said, smiling.

On a damp Wednesday evening late in April, a large force of men left camp. They marched three abreast, as for the last time they went through the gates of Park Hall.

Jim glanced behind him with mixed feelings of pride, achievement and foreboding. He could hear the battalions band and bugles up ahead as they accompanied the draft to the station. He listened and, until then, had never fully appreciated how the sound of hundreds of soldiers' boots crunching the ground would complement the sound of a marching band. This is it; this is really it, he thought, and then his mind turned to the sense of responsibility he felt for his friends. He had been asked by their mothers to keep an eye out for them and he had said that he would, but in reality, didn't he have to look after himself? He had children and a wife that depended on him and then to be asked to look after two grown men .... or were they?

Through the night, the train, carrying hundreds of men made the journey to Devonport, a distance of 265 miles which, depending on the number of relief stops, would take them between eight to ten hours. After the initial excitement of leaving Park Hall Camp, the men soon settled down and in the dim lighting of the carriages, some men could be seen writing letters, others sleeping and some staring blankly, pondering their future. After a time, the motion of the train would cause some who were poor travellers to access an open window to relieve themselves of their last meal. Bill, sitting beside Ian, asked him if there was a Greek God of War and whether he might be of any assistance to him if called upon. Ian laughed, but nonetheless, told him about Kratos.

"He was the God of personified spirit of strength, might, power and sovereign rule," Ian told him. "He and his three siblings, Nike, Bia and Zelos were the winged enforcers of the God Zeus, angel-like beings who stood in attendance on the heavenly throne." Ian stopped talking and, with a broad smile, looked at Bill. "And if you believe in thinking that Kratos will get you out of trouble in your hour of need, think again," he said, slapping Bill's knee as he spoke.

It was dark when they stopped. Carriage doors were flung open and men spilled out, some dropping their trousers just yards from the railway line. Then there was the inevitable call for newspapers. The men had half an hour to do what they had stopped to do and were told to get on the same carriage that they got off, to prevent overcrowding. The glow from cigarettes could be seen on the track for the full length of the train, men bunched excitedly together anticipating the call to board their carriages and some whose nervous excitement was such that they had to piss two or three times before reboarding.

At 4.30 am, the train pulled into Devonport. They were met by mounted men who escorted the new relief column, marching two abreast along the waterfront toward their appointed ship. There had been trains arriving since early morning, offloading their soldier passengers.

Jack's heart was pounding as he looked around. He quickly adjusted his step with the man in front of him, for marching in unison had become second nature to them all. Was this the outcome of all the training they had done for the last three months, he thought? All that shit they put us through. They may have bent me a little, but they didn't break me. To go through all that so as to end up being the best, well, he conceded, maybe that's how it should be and maybe that's the only way it can be done. There seemed to be something odd about the place, he thought. There seemed to be no sense of urgency about anything. The wharf men seemed to walk slowly, everyone doing things at half pace. Even the seagulls would glide in and land yards away from them, turning their heads to look at the soldiers as they marched past. Then, they would slowly lift their wings to catch the faintest of breeze and be aloft, wheeling about the sky without even flapping their wings. Smoke from the funnels of ships in dock rose lazily in a straight line, seemingly hardly having the energy to rise.

As they marched along the quay, they saw a number of ships of various sizes and uses; there were cargo ships, Royal Navy ships and troopships. Jim looked at them in awe.

"How the hell do these things float?" he said to Jack who was marching in front of him. He noticed Jack shake his head.

"God only knows," Jack said. "As long as they stay afloat, who cares?" High above them, they could see and hear troops that had already gone on board. They were waving and shouting and some of the remarks were of an unsavoury nature. Bill heard one shouting, "The Welsh are here, don't let them get on!"

"How in God's name do they know we are a Welsh regiment?" asked Ian. "The lighting on the docks isn't that good."

"The flash on our backs," Jim said, "they can see our flash."

There were two ship's gangways, both now being used by the men from the 7th. In single file they climbed, and when Bill took his first step onto the gangway, he wondered how long it would be until he would set foot on British soil again. On board, they were given some beef, bread and biscuits, all washed down with a mug of tea. They had eaten well before leaving camp and had taken along with them some sandwiches and an apple to eat on the train.

The upper deck was now teeming with soldiers, everyone excited about the day's events, especially now as they stood on the deck of this floating island. The only ships most had ever seen were on postcards, newspapers and the like, but to be actually standing on one was an adventure in itself.

"If my Mum could see me now," Jack said as he rushed to the ship's outside railing. "Bloody hell. it's a long way down!" he shouted.

The excitement of being on board was evident in the way the young men of the 7th were laughing and shouting to their mates, "Have a look at this" and "Have a look at that." The conclusion for most was that, if they hadn't had joined the army, this experience would have passed them by, and the voyage was still to come. The boys made their way toward the bow of the ship where they caught sight of Skinny Steve. He had just finished talking to one of the crew and, having seen the boys, he dodged his way through a crowd of milling soldiers to join them.

"He's going to tell us all about this bloody ship now," said Jack in humorous despair.

"Now, boys," Steve said standing in front of them, "let me introduce you to this lady of the sea."

"There you are," said Jack, "I told you, go on then, tell us all about the ship, I am all ears."

"Well," said Steve hardly taking a breath, "her name is *Arcadian,* she is nearly eight thousand tons, well seven thousand nine hundred and ninety-nine to be exact, she's five hundred feet and six inches long and the triple-expansion steam engine produces ten thousand indicated horsepower. She has twin screws and was launched in July 1899." Everyone looked at each other in amazement.

"And that's it?" said Jim egging Steve on, "I mean you haven't told us how wide it is".

Steve, deep in thought, smiled, "Fifty-five feet three inches across the beam, with a top speed of eighteen knots and she was built in Barrow-in-Furness". Steve then suddenly stopped; he seemed a little disappointed in himself at not being able to carry on due to the lack of more information regarding the *Arcadian*. He seemed a little lost but then smiled when Ian posed a question

"Why do they call ships *she*?" he asked.

"I really don't know," he answered tilting his head, "but I will find out." With that, he slung his rifle over his shoulder and sauntered off.

Shortly after, the ship's siren sounded and a subtle shake went through her as the engines came to life. The moorings were slipped and slowly the *Arcadian* drifted free from her berth. The high seas awaited the apprehensiveness of the ship's passengers, as much as the passengers awaited the unpredictable high seas. It was broad daylight when the harbour and land faded from view. With three and a half thousand miles, fifteen days and very little to do in front of them, boredom would undoubtedly play its part on the men bound for conflict.

Boredom did indeed play its part on the voyage to Alexandria; on the plus side, the food was good and the weather was becoming less inclement; those who enjoyed reading or writing did a lot of it. Then there were those who did neither, played snakes and ladders, cards and other board games. The keep-fit people would bend their legs, run on the spot and do press-ups, but how long can anyone keep doing that, the lads wondered? Ian and Bill did the reading, Jack did the exercising and Jim just looked at the sea. With over one thousand three hundred men on board, the word confinement took on a different meaning.

To break the monotony of nothing to do, a tug of war competition was organized, as one thing the ship was not short of was rope. Dozens of teams entered, eight men to a team, and the best of three pulls went on to the next round. Jim entered a team with himself, Jack and Bill. Ian declined, saying it really wasn't his thing and that he wasn't as strong as others that they could get. Jim got some lads from Montgomery. The boys won the first round but lost to a team from 'D' Company, Machynlleth, who went on for a few rounds, then lost to a team from Bala who went on to win. Then it was back to having nothing to do. Bill wrote a letter to his mum and one to Megan, conveying the boredom of the trip and how much they were looking forward to landing in sunny Egypt. Now and again a fight would break out, which prompted someone to organize boxing matches, but even this couldn't distract most from the boredom felt.

Eight days had passed since the *Arcadian* left Devonport docks and the only excitement the boys had had was on the third day when the sea decided to jolly things up a bit; waves as high as buildings started crashing over the bow. Orders were given that all personnel were to remain below deck, where the stench of vomit was responsible for some with hardier stomachs becoming sea-sick themselves. Everyone was holding onto something and when the bow of the ship fell into a trough, the stern would clear the water, exposing turning propellers and sending a shudder throughout the ship. Some men, drunk with fear, screamed at the sea, while others laughed at it. Jack thought it was a better ride than being on the water chute at Blackpool. There was one unfortunate incident resulting from the rough sea; a soldier descending a staircase lost his grip on the handrail and fell, striking his temple. He died on the stairwell and was buried at sea the following day. The rest of the voyage was uneventful, but the death of the soldier affected everyone on board ship and a subdued atmosphere persisted for a number of days.

On the west side of the Nile delta, between the Mediterranean Sea and Lake Mariut, is the port of Alexandria. Ian's father had told him that Alexandria was founded by Alexander the Great. He couldn't remember the date of its founding, but it was a long time before the birth of Jesus Christ. He went on to say that it was a seat of learning, having one of the largest libraries in the ancient world.

Alexandria could be seen from many miles out at sea and it was standing room only on deck as the *Arcadian* slowly sailed into port. The sea was calm and the sun gave them some idea as to how hot it was going to get. The humidity was such that their uniform become sodden with sweat and clung to the skin. Even summer uniforms couldn't keep them cool, although most had been wearing their shorts for the last week or so. Below them, on the still water, small felucca fishing boats with their lateen sails were trying to catch the morning breeze. The first to greet them as they sailed into port were the flies, then came the scent of a dozen smells that drifted over the ship. Slowly, the ship edged its way, being pushed by tug-boats into its position against the harbour wall. Then all was still.

The port was teeming with troops, as earlier that morning another ship had unloaded its quota of troops. Below, teams of horses with their drays were moving in two lines, one with their loads ready to be taken off, the other going in the opposite direction empty of the goods they had brought. Bill and the boys, like everyone else, were on deck when he pointed at the ship berthed ahead of them, where many horses were being hoisted in slings and lowered to the wharf below. Bill thought of the thousands of horses that had been requisitioned by the army and a girl he knew, Myfanwy Jehu from Llanfair Caereinion, who had disappeared up onto the moors with her two beloved horses when she got wind of the requisitioning party's impending visit.

When finally ashore, they were marched to a railway station and entrained to Warden Camp some forty miles from Cairo. Many more weeks were spent doing more training before moving on to Wadi Natrum, where they occupied outposts on the Western Desert. From here, Bill wrote to Megan, explaining a little about the place and telling her about a train trip on a narrow-gauge line. It was a branch line to a junction called Khatatatba, which in turn was connected to Wadi Natrum by a line built by the Egyptian Salt and Soda Company.

"We were loaded into small open trucks," he told her. "We saw typical native villages, partly surrounded by cultivated land whose principal crop was beans. The inhabitants were Egyptians and Arabs. Wire entanglements and sand-bagged trenches encircled the whole place. The lads are in good spirits, especially Jack, who loves all the excitement. He told her, too, of the flies and mosquitoes, the heat and sandstorms, the sunsets and cold mornings, but all in all, things were alright.

As Bill wrote, his thoughts turned to Megan herself. She was a pretty girl and, although she was a few years younger than himself, he was glad that she had asked if she could write to him. He thought of the last time he had seen her on the village green, the way she held his arm and the look in her eyes. At the time, his head was full of the future – 'what was in hers?' he wondered. Looking back, was that sadness in her eyes? Or was it that in those eyes he saw fear, and if so, fear of what? Bill looked again at the letter he was writing and carried on, telling her the boys sent their love to everyone, and he signed it – Regards, Bill.

On the 1st of August, troops were sent to Romani. The Turkish army was advancing with large forces across the Sinai Desert towards the Suez Canal and had to be stopped. The 7th were involved in the Battle of Romani, and six days after the event, Bill wrote to his Mother.

Dearest Mother and Father
11th August 1916

Well, at last, we have encountered the enemy. Six days ago, we were involved in the Battle of Romani. We didn't have a lot to do and to be honest, it was the Australian and New Zealand Light Horse Units that took the honours, and I must say those troopers certainly know how to ride horses. Anyway, they and the Imperial Camel Brigade were on the offensive, chasing the German and Ottoman army many miles across the Sinai Peninsula.

The boys and I are well, although Jim has sprained his ankle running after a Turkish soldier who was trying to get back to his own lines. But apart from that, he's fine. We have been told that soon we will be attached to the Desert Column, getting ready to push the Turks back to their own country.

I hope this letter finds you all well and that you are not worrying too much about us. We all send our love and when you see Megan, ask if she has received any of my letters.

Your loving son, Bill.

P.S. We have just been told that we are due for some leave in Cairo.

Bill folded the letter and tucked it into his tunic pocket ready for posting.

Ten days had elapsed between the battle of Romani and having been sent back by train to Kantara, a big camp that was situated beside the Suez Canal. It was a two-hour train journey to Cairo and it would be from this camp that the boys would take their four days leave.

At camp, before leaving for Cairo, there were talks on the expected behaviour of troops when on leave. They were told that when in Cairo, to expect sand and syphilis. The first to be expected, the last to be avoided at all costs. The prostitutes in Cairo were doing a roaring trade and when a cocktail of drink, young men far from home and ladies whose only objective is to serve, for a few shillings, the needs of these young men, the outcome was predictable. Jim looked at Jack, thinking that he would be the front runner knocking on doors before the lady of the house had time to switch on her red lights. As it was, the boys walked the streets of Cairo amazed at the way of life, men sitting outside coffee houses smoking shisha water pipes, wandering through the Khan el Khalili Bazaar, this labyrinth of shops selling everything under the sun; spices, jewellery, textiles, souvenirs, everything. Then suddenly a shop would close and the shopkeeper would place a prayer mat on the ground and start praying. Chants from minarets that dotted the Cairo skyline would echo their call to prayer. "A bit different to Broad Street in Newtown," said Jim as he nearly tripped over a mongoose that was on a lead. A boy of about ten looked indignantly at Jim then, picking up his pet, he walked off, muttering under his breath.

Ian gazed at the tree-lined street they were on. The women were veiled, and, from head to foot, were covered in dark robes, some balancing wicker baskets on their heads, but invariably all were carrying a basket of some description. Children ran around in cotton nightshirts. Some men wore white pantaloon-like trousers with long dark jackets, others wore white shirts that reached to the ground. Sandals were the favoured footwear and Ian noticed that, with every footfall, a little puff of reddish dust would rise from the dusty streets that they walked upon. Above them, shops were shaded by canvas awnings held up with long poles. On the ground, geckos along with cockroaches could be seen scurrying under tables, climbing walls and generally showing little concern as to what, or with whom, they shared their world. Now and then a motor car would pass by

"One day," said Jim, "there will be no horses and carts on the road; the motor car will eventually take their place."

At lunchtime, the smell of food being cooked drifted through the streets. The boys stopped at one vendor and, although it was unclear as to what he was cooking, they thought they would give it a try. All around them the street was buzzing with the native population and troops. The soldiers wandering aimlessly, while the locals jostled with the crowd, determined to reach their destination with haste. Bill and Jack had a meal of bread, lamb and rice layered one on top of the other with vinegar and tomato sauce, while Jim and Ian tucked into a dish of broad beans in sauce with lemon, garlic, potato salad and fish. They sat at a table nearby and talked of their time since leaving home and how, although it had only been five months, to them it seemed a lot longer.

In the afternoon, they again walked the streets of Cairo, taking in the sights and sounds of this strange metropolis. They gazed at splendid hotels frequented by rich and high-ranking military personnel. They went into bars and sampled the local beer and, by late afternoon, they had intentionally made their way to the Ezbekich Quarter of the city where, in the red-light district of Haret El Wazza, the Battles of Wazza had taken place. Thirteen months earlier, soldiers from New Zealand and Australia were blamed for the riots that went on there and, for a while, the place was out of bounds to all members of the armed forces. But for the men here now, some of whom would never realise their dreams and fantasies, that episode, when many of the brothels were burnt and their contents thrown into the streets, was in the past.

Jack, though hesitant and half-drunk, said that his need for a woman and the ache in his loins could not be ignored.

"Well, that's one way of putting it," Jim said, laughing, and Ian, not a drinking man, had changed from being a sound sober soul into a man with primaeval thoughts. He and Jack were goading each other, daring each other to make the first step. Ian, whose speech was almost unintelligible, spoke of the temptation of Eve.

"Jesus, Ian, this *is* the Garden of Eden," said Jack, nearly falling over, "and anyway, your name isn't Adam, is it? Be tempted, and to hell with it!"

At that moment, Jim called Ian over and placed a French letter into his hand.

"Use it," Jim whispered in his ear. With that, Ian sauntered to a doorway where a scantily clad lady hung seductively to the door frame. There was a big cheer as Ian stood in the doorway, then he turned, bowed and went inside. Jack, not to be outdone, followed suit, but not before Jim gave him what he had given Ian with the same advice.

"You think of bloody everything," Jack said, smiling. Then, too much jeering and cheering from the gathered crowd Jack grinned, dipped his head and entered the low doorway. Bill and Jim walked along the crowded street just looking at the goings-on of the youth of what seemed like the world.

"Some will regret this night," said Jim.

And others," answered Bill, "will die not regretting it."

"I suppose so," Jim said, placing his hand on his friend's shoulder.

For three nights the boys slept rough, although not for the first time had they slept in places other than their beds after a night out. But it had never been in surroundings that they now found themselves. More often than not, it would be in hay barns or someone's outhouse. For three nights, Ian would look at the stars and ask God to forgive him for his wayward behaviour, then fall asleep in utter bliss, dreaming of things his father would hang him for.

Jim would think of his wife and children, Bill, Megan and the future. Jack thought of tomorrow; it was always tomorrow, the here and now was his life.

The whole experience was a culture shock to them all and with no worldly knowledge other than that of their own environment, this period of drinking and whoring would long be remembered, especially by Ian whose behaviour was worse or at least as bad as Jack's. On the second night, they visited Haret el Wazza again and it seemed that having a belly full of beer was mandatory before a visit, so they did what had become the normal thing.

During the day, an incident took place in one of the bars some streets away from the whorehouses. The boys were drinking with some soldiers from the Australian 4th Light Horse. The atmosphere was boisterous with the Aussies singing raunchy songs, pouring beer over each other and generally having a good time. Jack, with a digger's hat on his head, was arm-wrestling its owner when, at the bar, right beside Jim, a young Aussie lad fell over.

"Can't take the beer," his mate slurred. No one seemed that bothered, and just let him lie there. Jim was about to help him to his feet when a big Australian told him to leave him where he was.

"Anyway, he needs a rest, and he won't be drinking anymore; we'll look after him." With that, he turned toward his mates and picked up on the song they were singing. Just then, four military police stepped through the open door, stood for a moment and, looking around, spotted the young lad spread-eagled on the floor. The room went quiet and all eyes were on the four men; one of them with stripes on his shoulder took a step forward. "We have reports of a disturbance here."

"That was yesterday!" someone shouted. Everyone laughed.

The man with the stripes on his shoulder was not amused. "That man on the floor," his voice was raised as he pointed his finger at the young lad.

"I am putting him under arrest."

"Whatever for?" Jim asked politely.

"For being drunk and disorderly."

The moment he said that, Jim stepped across the prone figure of the lad.

"He may be drunk," answered Jim, "but he certainly is not disorderly, and if it is your intention to arrest him, then you had better arrest me too." With that, Jack got up from the table he was sitting at and, with the hat of an Australian Light Horseman on his head, he stood by Jim, followed by Bill and Ian.

"Are you looking for trouble?" sneered the man with the stripes.

"I never look for trouble," Jim said smiling. "I didn't come to Egypt looking for trouble. I, like everyone here, was encouraged to come."

"I think you had better leave," said a voice behind Jim. The big Aussie man was now speaking. "Maybe you would like to arrest all of us; there are over forty Light Horsemen here, and if you want disorderly, we'll give you disorderly."

The three men who had come with the man with the stripes were already backing out of the doorway.

"I'll remember you," said the man with the stripes.

"I'm counting on it," Jim answered back.

A big cheer went up as the four military policemen left the building, and everyone went back to what they were doing. Soon after, the boys left, leaving the Aussies still at the bar. Jack came away with a plume of emu feathers given to him from the hat of the digger he had befriended.

On the third day, they caught an early train back to camp. They reported themselves in, their commanding officer having a few words with them at the same time, but nothing really was said. In fact, he asked if they had had a good time, and as they were still officially on leave, he suggested they shower and catch up on some much-needed sleep.

6

In early January, the push across the Sinai began, from Kantara, on the canal, to Palestine. The walk was exhausting; the small villages they passed en route provided some respite, but it proved to be excellent training for the campaigning that was to come. The cholera injections were all part of a medical given before leaving, and at this point, the boys were fit, healthy and had become hardened to the conditions that they were expected to deal with.

All through that month, they made their way north, pushing in front of them the remnants of the Turkish Army. Every so often, there would be more medical checks and men would fall out, suffering from some ailment or other. Sometimes they would stop for a day or so and on these days, there would be more training; training in bayonet fighting, instructions on how to load and ride camels, there would be night operations and sometimes groups would go out in the early hours to reconnoitre the surrounding desert, making their way back at night to join the battalion further up the track.

They made good progress to Romani and beyond and at every step along the way, the railway was being extended using Arab labour and British know-how. The engineers also laid a six-inch water pipe alongside the railway and a wire track was laid which made the marching in soft sand a lot easier and less tiring. At Romani, the mule transport was left behind due to a leak in the water pipe some miles further down, which wouldn't be fixed for some time. So, with the lack of water, the mules couldn't go on.

Day after day, they marched while the daily train running on the new track would bring food and supplies. Men who were due for hospital treatment for sickness, or for wounds suffered during the fighting, were sent back by this train and men rejoining the battalion came up on it.

They marched to Burel Minzer and then onto El Arish, a place that the Turks had abandoned a few weeks earlier. It was during the march between El Arish and Rafa that a section of 'C' Company was called upon to do a reconnaissance march into the desert. Up until this point, the parties that had been out during the march had encountered nothing but the telltale signs of a retreating army.

Jim, Jack and Bill, bored by the same routine day after day, volunteered to go out on one of these trips and asked Ian and five of his friends, David, John, Tom, Ivor and Trevor if they would like to come along. They would be accompanied by a non-commissioned officer. The orders were that they would go out for a distance of two miles, then trek parallel in the direction that the battalion was heading. In the event of sighting the enemy, no contact was to be made - just observe, make note of their position and report back before dark.

The boys were all ready to go, the early morning being unusually cool, when they were notified that the officer that was to take them would not be joining them as he had gone down with stomach pains and diarrhoea. Another officer was found, only to retire suffering from the same ailments after only walking two miles. He had cramp in his stomach, then dropped his trousers saying that he couldn't go on. There was a discussion as to who would take him back to camp, Ian even suggesting that maybe they should all go back. But the officer insisted that he would be all right going back on his own and the boys should go on without him. The decision for the boys to go on was his alone, as he said that the chances of them coming across any retreating bands of Turkish soldiers was, in his view, practically non-existent and the boys, to a man, were keen to carry on.

It was well past midday, maybe two-thirty when they stopped. The first to his knees was Jack, followed by the rest of them. The heat was unbelievable and had been for the last few weeks. Out in the open desert with no shade, the shimmering heat rose from the sand, sucking the life out of anything that walked on it.

Bill looked up to the sun, then at his hands. Beads of sweat seeped from his fingers, and the snow-covered hills and the east wind of Mid Wales came into his thoughts. He could see the snow silently falling and feel the freezing wind in his face, the times he had cursed it, and now he longed for it. He suddenly felt cold and started to shiver, his shivering intensifying as he lay on his back and closed his eyes. On opening his eyes, a blurred figure appeared above him. He felt a hand on his shoulder shaking him, as rain fell on his face.

As they all sat down, it was Ian that noticed something odd about Bill's behaviour; he saw him lie on his back and mumble incoherently as he started to shake. Ian stood up and went over to him, telling the others that there was something wrong with Bill. He knelt by his side, and as he shook his shoulder, he sprinkled water from his flask onto his face.

"The sun has got to him," said Jack as he pulled a rag from his pocket. He handed it to Ian, who poured water on it then proceeded to wipe Bill's face. Within five minutes, Bill was sitting up and wondering what had happened and within ten seemed to be his old self again. He poured a little water over his shirt so that even the warm breeze that blew through it reduced his body temperature. Everyone was so concerned about the welfare of Bill that they hadn't noticed that Jim had wandered off. David spotted him coming down the sand dune towards them. The ridge of sand rose some sixty feet and as Jim got closer, he started waving his arms.

"Bloody hell, don't say the sun has got to him as well," said Ivor as he went to meet him. As they met, they could sense that things weren't as they should have been and when Jim told them that over the ridge and a hundred yards into the hollow there were some Turkish soldiers, they all felt totally drained. Jack, in annoyance, cursed Jim.

"What the hell does he think he's doing, wandering off like that?" Tom replied, "Just as well he bloody did; at least we got sight of them first!"

"How many are they?" asked Bill.

"Between thirty and thirty-five," said Jim looking back toward the ridge.

"Has anyone got any suggestions?" Jim looked around, waiting for any comments.

"What shape are they in?" Ian asked.

"How the fuck should I know? They have eight camels but no heavy stuff; foot soldiers like us."

"We don't even have a camel," quipped David. "Have a little walk in the desert, they said, see what's out there they said, even the chap in charge of us didn't come as he got diarrhoea or something."

"Well, as I see it, we have two choices," said Jim. "We can risk walking out of here and maybe, with a bit of luck, make it to that ridge," he pointed to the nearest high ridge about a mile away to their left.

"And the other choice?" said Ian, looking in the distance at the ridge.

"We take them on," Jim suggested with a shrug.

"Look, while you lot are making up your minds, I think I'll go up and keep watch."

"Good thinking, Bill," said Jack.

"So, we had better make a decision pretty quickly. It would only take one of them to take a walk to the top of this ridge and they would make up our minds for us." As Jack finished speaking, Bill turned and made his way to the ridge.

"I think we could do it; that ridge goes all the way around like a big bowl, and Jonnie Turk is in the bottom of it. If we were to spread ourselves around it, we would be in a good position to make up for our lack of numbers."

"For God's sake, Jim, there are only nine of us! I can't believe you are serious." Tom was shaking his head, "It would be madness, and only you could think of such a bloody stupid idea."

"Firstly," said Jim, his voice calm and unflustered, "it isn't a stupid idea and secondly, I am deadly serious. Just think about it; how would you feel being in the bottom of a goldfish bowl with bullets coming at you from over the top, coming from Christ knows where?"

Jim went on to explain that, after positioning themselves around the ridge, they would fire off five rounds then run twenty yards to their right, fire off another five and keep doing this until the Turks surrendered or they ran out of bullets. He reckoned that, as they all had their full quota of ammunition, their chances of getting away with it were high. On their surrender, Jim, when convinced that their surrender was genuine, would give the order to cease fire. He would then rise above the ridge along with whoever was opposite him, they would both enter the crater and relieve the Turks of their weapons, whereupon the others would join them.

When Bill reached the ridge, he lay on his stomach, With his rifle lying by his side, he cautiously cleared away the sand just enough to see into the base where Jim had seen the Turkish soldiers. A quick count showed that there were thirty-two of them plus eight camels, these being tethered in two groups of four. A canvas sheet had been erected on four poles, with its guy ropes pegged into the sand. He glanced around the ridge and reckoned it to be seven to eight hundred yards in circumference. At its highest point, some thirty paces to his right, the sand fell steeply to a flat base where the soldiers were. The base was oval in shape, probably fifty by thirty yards, with the sand rising at various degrees to the ridge all around. Directly opposite, Bill noticed that the ridge was at its lowest point, around thirty feet, he thought. If under heavy gunfire, it would be at this point that the Turks would make their exit and indeed, by the look of the disturbed sand, this is where they had entered the bowl in the first place.

Looking back, Bill could see that the boys had started their climb towards him and he thought that, whatever their decision, he would go along with it. His opinion of the situation was that they should take them on. Although the odds were four to one in favour of the enemy, the element of surprise, their having the high ground and the fact that there was no cover for the Turks, put the Montgomeryshire boys in one hell of a position.

"We should come out of this without losing a man," he grinned to himself as he approved of his own assessment.

"Well, what do you think?" Jim asked in a hushed voice.

"Definitely worth a try," Bill replied.

"Tom and John have a few reservations about the whole thing, so I told them to have a look for themselves." Then, as Jim and Bill discussed the impending skirmish, the rest of the boys took it in turns to have a look and assess for themselves the likely outcome. Tom and John seemed far more agreeable to the plan after seeing the Turkish soldiers and assured the others that they were fully behind the plan.

"Everyone ready?" Jim said as he looked at his watch. "Bill will stay here, Jack, David, Ian, and myself will go to our right, then we will drop off in that order. Tom, John, Ivor, and Trevor will go to our left, also dropping off in that order; it's important that we know where everyone is."

"I think sixty paces between each man should be enough to cover the area, and if we allow, say, one and a half minutes to cover our sixty paces, with myself being the last in position, plus half a minute to choose your target, Bill will start shooting in, er,........six and a half minutes after we set off."

"Should we fix bayonets? "John enquired.

"No," said Jim shaking his head. "The less they see of us, the better."

Then, as Jim shouldered his rifle, he looked at them all and said, "I know that some of you may think that killing the enemy in this manner, and that is what we are about to do, is, to put it bluntly, not giving them a sporting chance. Well, it may ease your mind if you don't think of them as men." Then he smiled.

"Think of them as rabbits."

Bill flipped the cover of his pocket watch.

"Off you go, boys, and remember to keep your heads down. The shooting starts in six and a half minutes - good luck and make every bullet count."

They all shook hands and, as Bill saw his comrades walk away treading the soft sand beneath their feet, he moved to the ridge and had a quick glance at the enemy.

"Fifty-nine, sixty, this is my spot," said Jack as he stopped.

Jim placed his hand on Jack's shoulder; "See you later," he said and gave him a wink. Then, as Jack made his way to the ridge, he thought about what Jim had said about not giving the enemy a sporting chance and realised that that little speech was intended for Ian. Jack knew that, deep down, Ian was a God-fearing man and to shoot a man in the back would be murder in his eyes. How his conscience would deal with what was expected of him, Jack didn't know, and to be honest, he really didn't care.

Bill looked at his watch; two and a half minutes to go. He had already chosen his target. The Turkish soldiers were pretty much gathered in the centre of the oval, but a group of six were sitting down playing cards and his nearest target, the dealer, had his back to him.

Tom, John and Ivor didn't speak as they made their way to their allotted places, counting off their steps as they went. After Tom's stop, John started counting his sixty paces, and as he counted, Ivor looked into the sky and muttered,

"Did you say something?" John asked.

"Pharaoh's chickens," Ivor muttered again, raising his eyes.

"Pharaoh's chickens?" John said as he looked up.

"The birds, the birds," Ivor said impatiently. "Pharaoh's chickens - Egyptian Vultures."

"Jesus Christ, how am I supposed to know what they are?" John said as he dropped to his knees.

"It isn't so much what they are," replied Ivor "it's what they are doing."

"Flying around in bloody circles," said John as he started to crawl to the ridge.

"And why are they flying around in circles?" Ivor asked.

"I don't know Ivor, you tell me," John found Ivor's conversation irritating, especially now when all hell was about to break loose. Then, as he was about to part the sand to view his quarry and without looking at Ivor, he asked, "And the others, the other birds?" Ivor looked again into the sky.

"Black kites, and they are all waiting."

"Waiting for what?"

"For death," said Ivor as he started to walk his sixty paces, muttering a poem as he went.

> *"The dome of heaven is thy house*
> *Bird of the mighty wing,*
> *The silver stars are as thy boughs*
> *Around thee circling.*
> *Thy perch is on eaves of heaven*
> *Thy white throne all the skies*
> *Thou art like lightning driven*
> *Flashing over paradise!"*

Bill looked at the second hand on his watch, watching the seconds twitch by. He decided that he would count down the last thirty seconds in his head; this would give him enough time to put away his watch and take aim. Twenty seconds to go before that was to happen, he thought.

Jim got to his position and cleared a section of sand from the ridge and, like the rest of the boys, he was looking for his first target, knowing he didn't have much time left to look. But unlike the rest, he was looking for someone special; someone in command.

"I'm looking for the boss man," he said to himself. "Get rid of him and the job's half done." Any second now, he expected Bill's first shot. Then he saw him, the one he perceived to be the one in charge. He was sitting in a fold-up chair, talking to two men standing each side of him. Jim grinned, "Literally a sitting target," he thought.

With his watch tucked safely in his pocket, and his Lee-Enfield nestled snugly in his shoulder, Bill took aim. "Don't rush this first shot," he thought. He had lost count of the seconds he was to count, but now it was of no importance - time was up. The dealer's back was in his sights as he gently squeezed the trigger. A full deck of cards was involuntarily thrown into the air as the dealer slumped forward.

From his flask, Jack poured a little water over his head, running some down his back and wetting his shirt - he was growing impatient. He checked the clip of bullets in his rifle, then took aim at a soldier that was looking into the mouth of a camel. The sound of Bill's first shot didn't faze him, he just pulled the trigger and both man and camel fell to the ground.

Ian knew what Jim was on about when he spoke of killing the enemy in the fashion they were about to; he also knew that his little speech was directed at him. His Christian upbringing was now coming to the fore; he had tried so hard to be like the others. All through his teenage years, he wanted to distance himself from God and put religion a little bit further back in his priorities so as to lead, as he thought, a more normal life. But the constant ear-bashing of the Scriptures by his father all through his life had left its mark.

Joining the army was a way out, and although it created a bad atmosphere between himself and his father, he would not be dissuaded. He remembered well his father's last words as he closed the door to his home: "Thou shall not kill; thou shall not kill." And now, as he raised his rifle and with his father's voice ringing in his ears, he wondered if he could do the unthinkable.

On the sound of Bill's first shot, seven more bullets from seven Lee-Enfields cut devastatingly into the unsuspecting Turkish troops.

Tom's first shot hit the man who sat opposite the dealer in the card school, who lurched to one side, clutching his stomach. Ivor's bullet was aimed at a group of men sitting and standing under the canvas. He didn't take aim at any one man in particular, but there were enough of them in the shade that he reckoned it was bound to hit someone and that someone would just happen to be in the line of fire.

"Just think of them as rabbits," this was in Ivor's mind as he shot a man reading a book. The poor soul didn't even have time to get off his backside before a bullet slammed into his chest.

There was pandemonium on the oval floor. Men were running all over the place, screaming and shouting as they went, until the area looked like a disturbed ant's nest. There was nowhere to run to, nowhere to hide from the rain of bullets that were descending on them

Ian's first bullet never found a target. It buried itself into sand, as did the bullets that followed it. His stomach churned as he recited the sixth commandment over and over again and in doing so, felt purged of any wrongdoing he may have even thought. He felt guilty and elated at the same time; guilty that he had betrayed the need of the group as a whole, but elated that, at last, he had found God and his need for God was all-consuming.

Both David and John, positioned opposite each other, missed with their first shot and David emptied his first clip of five bullets without hitting anyone, until a soldier with a shattered hand was the result from David's sixth bullet. Then they both got up and moved on.

The Turkish soldiers were stunned on hearing the shots of rifle fire coming from the ridge that surrounded them. With the receding echo each shot produced, it must have seemed that an entire regiment of the British army was about to overrun them. Their rifles were placed in stacks like sheaves of corn in the centre of the oval and their only machine gun was in pieces on a canvas sheet, whilst being serviced by two men.

It had been decided that every other man, starting with Jim, would shoot an extra two rounds to maintain continuity of rifle fire. If all eight men finished shooting their first clip at the same time, there would have been a lull in bullets entering the arena during the time they moved to their new positions, and this would have caused suspicion amongst the enemy.

Bill had shot his extra two rounds and had settled into his new position. His rifle sights were trained on a man behind the camel that Jack had shot. Holding his breath, he asked God for a little help with his shooting, then he felt the recoil as a bullet exploded in its chamber, sending death down the barrel and into the heart of a stranger. God answered Bill's call one more time before he moved on.

A bullet zipped into the sand about two yards from where Jack was shooting. It was the second bullet that had come his way. There was no time to look for the man responsible, but he did notice that, during the onslaught, another camel had been purposely shot and lay parallel to the one that he had felled. They lay a yard apart and were being used as cover for the two men with rifles that crouched between them. They were shooting at the ridge but their cover was totally inadequate. Then, as he fired his rifle at one of the men, his subject suddenly crumpled over the front legs of one of the camels.

"Good shot," said David to himself as he pulled back the bolt on his rifle, ejecting the used casing of the bullet responsible for the prone figure that now lay across the legs of the beast that he thought would protect him.

The Turks were shooting back in greater numbers now, but they were in a hopeless situation.

"Why don't they give up and surrender?" thought John, as he saw a man starting to climb the incline directly under Ian's new position.

"He's a sitting duck," he said out loud.

Jim, on Ian's right, and David to his left, both saw the man climbing to the ridge then suddenly he went down, gravity pulling his body down the sand slope a foot or so, then nothing moved, not even the sand. This single event would be prominent in David's mind for the rest of his life, for no other reason than how this man fell. He had seen more spectacular death scenes, but this one would always remind him of his childhood.

As an eight-year-old, stories of the Wild West filled his mind, especially stories of the Indian wars. Crazy Horse, Geronimo and Cochise were names he recognized along with Colonel Custer, Wild Bill Hickok and Buffalo Bill. He always played the part of Sitting Bull in the games of Cowboys and Indians that he and his friends would play. The rule of play was quite simple, in that, if you got shot, you would make a dramatic death scene, lie on the ground and slowly count to twenty, then you would get up and carry on playing until you got shot again. Then, on the 11th of May 1904, the day after his ninth birthday, his uncle took him to see Buffalo Bill's Wild West show in Oswestry, a fifteen-mile trip from his home in Welshpool. There he was to see his heroes, Chief Sitting Bull with his band of Indians and, mounted on a big white stallion, Buffalo Bill himself. Covered wagons would race across the field being chased by Indians with their bows and arrows. He would see the Indians being shot off their horses and their dying scenes were spectacular. But unlike the Turkish soldier, the one on the sandbank, that one just seemed to fall over and not move. There was nothing dramatic about his death scene and over the years, from time to time, David would often wonder whether he had time to count to twenty.

A bullet hit the slope a little short of the ridge just below Tom, who caught a glimpse of the man who had fired the shot. The Turk had dug himself into a hole and was shooting at Tom from the protection that it provided. "If I can raise the angle of my shot just two inches," he thought, "I can give him one of my bullets." So, Tom raised himself two inches.

Bill saw him coming, running and screaming like a banshee above the reports of rifle fire. With his hands aloft, shooting wildly the two revolvers he carried, the Turk started to run up the embankment at an angle that would take him straight to Bill. Bill's bullet hit him side on, it ripped open his stomach and his knees fell onto soft sand followed by his intestines. Lying on his back with head raised, he attempted to stuff his innards back into the place from which they came. Bill looked with disbelief, realizing with horror what he had done. He cursed his mother for having him, and her mother for having her. Then, to his surprise, the Turkish soldiers started to lay down their rifles and raise their arms above their heads; the shooting had stopped as suddenly as it had started.

Jack's last shot was fired at a man who was about to raise his arms in surrender, the bullet passing harmlessly within inches of his upper body. The man, unaware of the closeness of Jack's bullet, stepped into the open leaving a hole in the sand, one that he had franticly dug in front of one of the dead camels.

The Turks were gathering in the centre of the oval, all with their hands in the air. To the men on the ridge, it looked like a gladiatorial scene with both the dead and the living having given their all. And now, now the living were at the mercy of their captors.

Jim rose and stood on the ridge, followed by Bill. There was no sign of elation and caution was their only thought. Jim motioned with his rifle that the gathered prisoners should move to one end of the oval, well away from any arms that could still have been used against them. Then, one by one, the men of the 7th entered the arena. John had only taken a few steps down the embankment when he thought someone was missing. He looked to his left and then to his right. Tom wasn't there; he had a feeling something bad had happened. To secure the prisoners was paramount, so John carried on to the bottom where the Turks, with their hands on their heads, were gathered. There were eleven prisoners.

Like the others, Ivor rose and stood on the ridge. He watched as his comrades started their descent into the arena and, glancing to his right, he saw Bill fix his bayonet before he too started down, but there was no sign of Tom. Tom should have been between himself and Bill and he felt uneasy about his not being there. He started to walk the ridge to Tom's position and sensed that the sand seemed softer on the ridge and it looked like it was moving. Gusts of wind would blast sand up the slope and over the ridge like white horses on an ocean wave. Ivor had taken some twenty paces before he saw Tom and, as he got closer, his heart sank. Tom was lying, face-up, about a yard from the top. He wasn't moving, and as Ivor got to him, he could see straight away that he was dead. A bullet had hit him in the jaw and come out of the back of his head.

Ivor just stood and looked at him. "Poor old Tom," he said, shrugging his shoulders. He was surprised at his lack of emotion; he didn't really feel a thing.

Tom's eyes were wide open, looking into the sky. Ivor followed the dead man's gaze; Pharaoh's chickens were still circling on the warm air currents above them and seemed unconcerned as to who lived or died. It was the dead that interested them, nothing more and nothing less. Ivor stooped and closed Tom's eyes. Even though he was dead, Ivor didn't like the thought of Tom looking at the vultures that were looking at him. Ivor punched Tom lightly on the shoulder, then standing up, he stepped over the ridge.

Below him, the boys had separated the prisoners and placed them into two groups. David and Jack were busy tying them up and the rest, with bayonets and rifles in hand, stood guard. As he approached, everyone stopped what they were doing and looked at him. "I'm sorry," he said, "but Tom will not be joining us," he paused, "on account of him being dead." No one other than David said a word and all he said was, "Oh no, Jesus Christ."

Jack finished tying the hands of the last prisoner and suddenly felt thirsty. "I'll go and see if there is any water about," he said and as he walked to the canvas shaded area, he thought of Tom. He didn't know him that well, in fact, he hardly knew him at all, and now he was dead. Jack found four bottles of water; as for food, he found ample supplies of bread, flour, dried meat and a good amount of olives.

"What do you think?" Bill said as Jim walked over and stood by his side, Bill nodding his head in the direction of Ian. He was kneeling beside the body of a dead Turkish soldier. "He's been going around them all crossing himself and quoting passages from the Bible. It's the first thing he did after coming down from the ridge."

"He's not right in the head," Jack said to himself as he chewed on a piece of dried meat. He had always felt that Ian was out of place in the army. There was something amiss, he thought, as he saw him place a dead man's arms across his lifeless body. Then he started to wonder just how involved Ian had been in the fighting that had just taken place.

Ivor and Trevor were guarding the prisoners as David went among them with a bottle of water; they had also seen Ian going around the dead.

"It's funny he hasn't been up to see Tom," Ivor said.

"He'll get around to it," said Trevor as they watched Ian walk over to the three men that lay amongst the playing cards that they had held some twenty minutes earlier. As they watched, they saw Ian start to pick up the cards, and when he had picked them all up, having had to roll over the three dead bodies to get any cards that they may have fallen onto, he started to look around again.

"He's looking for the bloody box to put them in," said Bill in astonishment, and even as he spoke, Ian bent down, picked up the box and placed the cards into it. Then, with everyone looking, including the prisoners, Ian slipped the box into the shirt pocket of one of the dead. Before leaving them, he picked up what looked like a German Luger pistol and tucked it into his belt.

From the very first shot and the sight of the first victim lurching forward into the realms of the great unknown, Ian had tried to picture it all, but the image and its effect on him was nothing remotely like the image he perceived it to be. He had seen dead people long before coming to Egypt. He had seen them in oak boxes, mostly old people, before the lids went on. His father had wanted him to know about death at an early age. It was all so bloody dignified and natural, he thought, with a service, flowers and singing. It was these people that God had called to his side. It was their time, as his father would say as he threw soil onto the tops of coffins, before the gravediggers began to shovel in the dirt from the hole that they had dug out to accommodate the unfortunate.

Jack was uneasy about the way Ian was acting, with a nagging feeling that there was more to it than his concern for the dead. He looked up to Ian's first position when the shooting started and noticed the body of a Turkish soldier lying spread-eagled halfway up the bank in Ian's direction. Had he kept going a little further, he would have been close enough to shake Ian's hand. He walked to the base of the embankment and climbed to where the body lay, kneeling by his side and immediately noticing that this man had been shot in his lower back. Jack sat for a moment and reached into his shirt pocket, pulling out a packet of cigarettes, "Three left," he thought as he pulled one out and placed it between his lips. He hadn't got a lighter, he'd discovered its loss two days earlier but drew on his cigarette just the same. He thought about Ian and the dead soldier he was sitting by, concluding that, whoever shot him, it certainly couldn't have been Ian.

Jack got to his feet and looked into the arena; Trevor, David and Ivor were guarding the prisoners, Jim was going through the pockets of a dead man who was lying across what looked like a fold-up chair and Bill, on the opposite side to himself, was climbing the gradient to another soldier lying still in the sand. As he started to descend the incline, he drew again on his unlit cigarette and thought of the situation that they now found themselves in, muttering to himself, "and what do we do now?"

The man Jim suspected of being in charge of this raiding party was indeed the only officer in this group. He looked at the crumpled figure lying over the broken chair that he had been sitting on, noticing his epaulette shoulder boards. The embroidered gilt wire edge and gold tape with red centre line told him he had the rank of a junior officer, as he had seen such shoulder boards on prisoners under guard in Alexandria. Jim searched his pockets and looked into what could have been dispatch bags but found nothing. He concluded that this was a band of men whose sole purpose was to disrupt the building of the railway.

Bill was aware of the faintest of breeze that blew against his wet shirt. He had found a water bottle, drunk his fill and then poured some over his head, wetting his shirt in the process. The heat of the day had passed and every hour from now on the temperature would drop. In all the confusion in the last half-hour - he stopped - no he thought, confusion was the wrong word, there was no confusion, they had had a plan and worked to that end.

No, the confusion lay in the aftermath of that end, the death of Tom, the unpredictable behaviour of Ian and the events that would follow in the event of victory. These were things that could not have been foretold, but they were things that would play as major a part in their lives as the part that they had already played. As he walked, he looked up and saw one of the men he had shot, the one that screamed like a banshee running across the embankment. He, like the one Jack had gone to see, lay halfway up the slope, on his back with his head uppermost to the ridge and his hands on his stomach. When Bill got to him, he was surprised to see that he was still alive but his breathing was shallow and slow. 'He's young,' Bill thought, 'no more than eighteen years of age.' He looked at the soldier's stomach; most of his bowel was in the right place but some of his intestines lay in the sand outside his body. His left hand was resting inside the fold of flesh and in his right, he clenched a photograph.

He retrieved the bloodied postcard and gazed at the picture. On the front, he recognized the young man instantly; he was standing with what he thought to be his family, mother, father and three younger siblings. Was this the mother that he cursed for having the young man now dying at his feet? He knelt and turned the card over. On the back was some writing that meant nothing to him. In truth, he didn't want to know what was written and turned the card, again looking at the woman in the photograph. She was sitting next to her husband, with the hand of the young man behind her resting on her shoulder. Bill looked into her face and realised that she

would never again see her son, as a stranger had drifted
into his life, giving her cause to cry and grieve. He placed
the photograph back into the soldier's hand and noticed
that he had stopped breathing. "Amen," Bill said softly, as
he stood and retraced his steps back to his companions,
and on his way, he passed Ian who had just left the three
card players.

Bill stopped and asked him if he thought the dead
that he had just said words over would have appreciated
his religious concern, given that they were of another faith.
Ian's expressionless face and eyes that looked beyond the
abyss replied calmly,

"We are all God's children, Bill, all God's children."

"So, what do we do now?" said David as he placed
some dry biscuits in his shirt pocket.

"We find the railway line, I suppose," replied Trevor,
shaking sand out of his boots.

"And the prisoners - do we take them with us?"

"Do we have a choice?" Ivor interrupted. "Anyway,
we have to bury the dead first."

Jim, standing a few yards away, overheard the
conversation but said nothing. He too had been thinking
about leaving and leaving soon. It was then that Jack came
over, "Can any of you remember shooting that man?" he
said, pointing to the figure that lay below Ian's first position.

Trevor looked up; everyone said, "No."

"And you, Trevor?"

Trevor shook his head for the second time; "No."

"It must have been Ian," Ivor responded, looking at
Ian as he walked toward them.

"That soldier on the bank," Jack asked, pointing to the man in question, "did you shoot him, Ian?"

Ian stopped and looked in the direction Jack was pointing.

"I really can't remember," Ian said slowly, looking at his friends as he spoke.

"But if none of you shot him, it must have been me. I can remember him coming toward me, though, getting closer and closer. Yes, I remember now, I was waiting for a close shot, then I pulled the trigger; yes, that's what happened. Why are you asking, is there a problem? That was the idea, wasn't it, to kill as many as we could?"

Ian was visibly on edge as he spoke; voices were whispering in his head and had been since the shooting started. It was God's will that he was now about.

"Well, there is a problem, Ian," Jack's voice was surprisingly calm.

"Problem?" Ian said sharply. "You have a problem with me shooting the enemy?"

"He was shot in the back, Ian."

"Yes, yes, I remember now," Ian stammered, "as I pulled the trigger, he turned with his back to me."

"Stop fucking lying, Ian, if you had shot him in the back he would have fallen forward."

"And that's what he did, he fell forward," Ian said.

"And if he had fallen forward," Jack answered back, "he would have fallen with his feet pointing toward the ridge."

All heads turned and looked again at the man on the embankment. No one said a word as Ian walked past them, and as voices again entered his head, he started to recite, for the umpteenth time, The Lord's Prayer. Then, as he walked past the sitting prisoners, he pulled the Luger out of his belt and shot two of them in the head, not even interrupting the Lord's Prayer as he calmly walked on.

Shouts and screams erupted as the prisoners scrambled about, not knowing if this was also to be their end. The boys with rifles and bayonets immediately surrounded them, getting the ones that were standing to sit down again.

"Was that necessary?" a voice in Ian's head asked, "It was their time," he said out loud, continuing with the Lord's Prayer, and in between the words 'thy kingdom come and thy will be done', another voice whispered, "Then why didn't you do it before?"

"God has his ways," Ian answered.

"Had I better go to him?" Bill asked in disbelief at Ian's actions.

"No, let him be," said Jack, bewildered as the rest of them as to why Ian did what he did.

Ian stopped at the foot of the gradient, and without looking back, started to climb to the ridge. The two voices in his head were at odds with each other, one asking why he did such a terrible thing, the other approving of it. With one step to go to the top, he turned and looked back, and raising his left hand, gazed at the clear blue sky and cried, "I'm coming, Lord, I'm coming!" Stepping over the ridge, he lifted the Luger and blew his brains out.

Bill was in shock; the lad from Abermule, who wanted to be free of his father, had finally become his victim.

Dropping his rifle, he started running towards his friend. When he reached the gradient, the sand seemed to pull him down but he made it to the top and dragged himself over the ridge. He knelt at Ian's side and watched as the desert sand, like a thirsty dog, drank his lifeblood.

He lay down beside his friend, but it wasn't on this unforgiving land that they lay; no, they lay on green grass in fields that overlooked his home. Bill would spend many happy hours listening, as Ian spoke of things that were not of this world and many things that were. He would recite lines from Shakespeare, explain the Gods of Roman times and Greek mythology, and they would look at the stars and ponder the likelihood of other beings out there somewhere.

Ian, he thought, was not just a friend to him but an educational experience, an experience that had already shaped his mind and that, he decided, was not altogether a bad thing.

It was then that Bill prayed, but not to God. He prayed that the Phoenix would come down and take Ian's soul, to be reborn and live in a better place than the one he had left.

Then, above him came a melodious cry, the like of which he had never heard before. He got up, stood back and looked up. There, with wings on fire, the Phoenix descended and landed on Ian, enfolding him in its wings. And as it arose, Bill saw Ian's soul rise with it, engulfed in flames, and disappear. With a pounding heart, Bill looked at his friend; his body was still there but his soul had gone. He smiled and was content.

7

They turned left onto Washington Street.

"Another ten blocks," said Stan. As they walked, they talked of their trip and of meeting Gordon Doyle. They both agreed that as it was a Thursday, they would go to the company's office the following Monday morning.

"One more block," Stan said as they reached Harrison Street. On the corner of Franklyn Street, they turned right, crossed Greenwich Street and, just before Hudson Street, Stan stopped outside a dress shop. "This is it; 198 Franklyn Street," he said, setting his suitcase on the ground. There were two stone steps to the shop door. In the bay windows were mannequins dressed in fashionable clothing with hats displayed on two stands, one to each window. As Stan opened the door and walked in carrying his suitcase, a brass bell that hung on a spring rang, and was still ringing as Michael closed the door. The room was surprisingly light and airy, its big bay windows making good use of the afternoon sun. Bamboo and papier-mâché mannequins were standing ready to be clothed. The room had a high ceiling, a candle chandelier hung from it and the chain it hung from had a large plaster ornate ceiling rose around it, consisting of roses and cherubs.

There was no-one in the shop, so Stan rang a handbell that was on the counter.

"Coming," a woman's voice could be heard. It came from behind a door at the back of the shop. Moments later, the door burst open as the speaker, laden with an armful of dresses, waddled in.

"And what can I do for you gentlemen?" she asked with a smile, dumping the dresses on a chair. She looked at Stan and Michael. "Now, you both look too young to be buying dresses, unless it's for your mom or girlfriend, but then they usually come in themselves," she said with a smile. The lady was probably in her forties, Michael thought, and quite attractive.

"Is Mr Donovan in?" Stan asked.

"No," answered the lady, "he told me he will be gone for an hour and that was a half-hour ago; can I help in any way?"

"Not really," said Stan and then, introducing himself and Michael, he told her that they had just disembarked from a ship from Ireland and that he had a letter from his father for Mr Donovan.

"Oh," said the lady putting her hand to her mouth, "Mr Donovan is expecting you. He didn't know when you would be arriving, but he was expecting you. Please follow me; your room has been ready for over a week". There was another door to the right of the counter leading to a staircase. "Just follow me; by the way, my name is Nell."

A half-hour later, William Donovan returned and was pleasantly surprised to find that Stan and Michael had arrived. He explained that a tenant had left a week earlier, leaving a room that Michael could rent if he wanted. He was a pleasant man, Michael thought, in his late fifties. Nell had worked for him in the shop since his wife had walked out and not come back. His three children were grown up, his daughters living four blocks away but they called to see their father on a regular basis. His son lived upstate in Albany, having a good job in the lumber industry, but Mr Donovan hadn't seen him in over two years.

"It's sad about his son," said Nell as she poured out two beers, placing them on a small table in Stan's room. Mr Donovan had gone down into the shop, allowing Nell time to settle the boys into their rooms.

"And where do you live?" Michael asked.

"Three blocks away," she said, "over West Broadway on Church Street. You don't know where that is, but we have the weekend coming up - it will give you some time to have a walk around and get your bearings. You will be alright in this area but..." "Nell," Mr Donovan shouted up the stairs, "there is a lady in the shop looking at dresses. Could you come down?"

"But there are places that you shouldn't go; I will tell you about them later". As Nell left the room, Michael looked at Stan. "Places we shouldn't go! That sounds interesting."

As Nell suggested, Friday and the weekend were spent wandering the streets. On the Friday, they walked up Hudson Street to Bank Street, where they changed their Irish banknotes at the Bank of New York.

On the Monday morning, Stan and Michael set off to find the office of Doyle and Simpson. The address was on West Broadway; they soon found it and walked in, presenting their letter of introduction. When they walked out, their short-term employment was secure, with maintenance work four blocks away from where they lived. They were required for the Thursday coming, for two months. They worked with three other men, followed by work on the footings of a new library: all work within two miles of their lodgings.

On several occasions, Gordon Doyle called on-site to see how they were getting on. He always seemed pleased to see them, asking how they were getting on and if they had any questions regarding work, their lodgings or anything else that they would like to know.

'Yes,' Michael thought, 'he was a good man'. He offered them two dollars and forty-five cents a day, and with their board costing two dollars seventy-five cents a week, they were satisfied with the arrangement. They both worked for Doyle and Simpson for three and a half years, before Stan announced that he was going to marry his girlfriend of the last twelve months. After his marriage, where Michael was his best man, Stan and his new bride went away.

Michael was not particularly a drinking man. He enjoyed a drink, but it didn't worry him if he went a fortnight without one, especially in the winter. Now and again, on special occasions, he would get a little merry, like the day Stan went away. He had been drinking with a few of his workmates who were celebrating Stan's marriage. After they left, Michael walked to the end of Franklyn Street where he knew of a cellar bar that played Irish music. Cellar bars were, as the name implies, bars in the cellars of what could only be described as buildings of dubious character that were frequented by seafarers, thieves and their ilk, prostitutes and ladies that didn't do it for a living, but every so often it paid the rent. Most were illiterate, poor and diseased and he wondered what he was doing there. He was propositioned a number of times and, when the fighting started, he left and walked home. The sounds of the night kept him alert, drunks staggering on the cobbled street, couples fornicating in dark alleyways, children in rags begging for money, pigs and rats scurrying in his path seeking out vomit and anything they could eat. These were, as Nell had told him, places that he should not visit. There were other places: Mulberry Street, Baxter Street and all streets around Five Points, where, only three months before he got off the *Lady Russell,* the Bowery Boys and the Dead Rabbit Gang had a riot, resulting in the deaths of eight people and scores of injuries. This was an area of Manhattan that was riddled with poverty and disease. Nell had told him that one in eight children would not live to see their fifth birthday. Dance halls, theatres, street shows, gambling dens and, next door to these places of entertainment... a bordello! Vice, it would seem, was a way of life - it was contagious, like cholera and typhoid.

Three months after Stan had left, Michael had a Saturday off work. He went for a walk, the summer sun casting its rays through leafy trees and creating shadows on the roads as he walked. He found himself on Mulberry Street; he had never been this far along it before, but continued walking, getting more into the slum areas as the tenement blocks passed by. The further he walked, the busier the street was becoming and then, as he approached Mulberry bend, he came upon a small group of people gathered around a man that was laying into a woman lying on the ground.

"Pay your rent, woman!" the man shouted as he swung a leather belt across her back. Without thinking, Michael sidestepped a bystander and grabbed the man by his collar, pushing him away from the woman. The man, surprised at Michael's intrusion, gasped, shouting, "What's it to you? She owes me a night's rent and she ain't got no money."

"How much does she owe?" Michael asked, dipping into his pocket and, without waiting for an answer, shoved a dollar in the man's hand saying, "and that's for another night." The man stumbled, mumbling obscenities, and slouched off. Michael turned and picked up the woman, who dropped the bundle of rags she was holding. On falling to the ground, the bundle unfolded, revealing a newborn baby, blue and very dead. Michael pulled back, dumbfounded and the few bystanders looked, turned and walked away.

"Jesus Christ, what do I do now?" Michael said as the woman went to her knees cowering as she wrapped the infant back into the rags. An elderly woman hurried to Michael's side.

"Jimmy Salter, the health warden," she said, "I'll go and get him - I'll be back in two minutes." True to her word she was back; behind her followed a tall thin man wearing a top hat, looking very much like a person that deals with matters of the dead. He introduced himself; "I bury dead babies. I don't do adults, just newborn," he bent down and placed his arm over the young woman and took the bundle from her. "The child will be given a Christian burial and will be buried in a pauper's grave at St John's Park burial ground. Do you know this woman?" he asked Michael.

"No," he said, "never met her before."

"Where does she live?"

"Over there," the old woman said, pointing to a timber tenement building opposite. "Down the alley, but she has just got thrown out and can stay just one more night." The young woman got up and stood by Michael. He looked at her uncombed hair and blank face; she wore a dirty shawl and her dress was nothing more than a moth-eaten curtain.

"Come with me," he said grabbing her arm. "You will stay in your room tonight and I will come back for you in the morning."

"You won't come back for her," the old woman said. "You won't come back for her," she said again as she followed them down into a stinking damp hovel.

"My baby," the young woman said as she turned and watched the man with the top hat take her baby away.

"It's dead," said Michael callously. "It's dead and you are alive."

Sunlight beamed through the dirty window, casting its light on the woman's face. Michael looked at her as he placed two dollars into her hand. "Get something to eat," he said. Again, he looked at her and, beneath the grime and dark eyes that had sunk into her face, she gave him a look that humbled him and then, holding his arm, she thanked him.

"Will you come for me? Will you take me away from this?" she asked as she looked around to see the squalor she was in. "Thank you again," she whispered in a broken voice. Michael looked at the old lady standing in the doorway.

"Make sure she is here at nine o'clock in the morning. I will come for her, you have my word."

"Bless you, Sir," she said as he pressed fifty cents into her hand. As Michael stepped through the door, he looked over his shoulder and asked her name.

"It's Megan," she said, "Megan."

The incident at Mulberry Bend had a big effect on Michael. As he walked home, he couldn't rid himself of the scenes of squalor and hopelessness that existed not too far from where he himself lived. He saw people walking past him and towards him with kerchiefs soaked with laudanum held to their faces, warding off diseases that were a permanent threat. 'This isn't how it should be,' he thought. He could have abandoned the idea of returning in the morning, but he knew he couldn't; he had made a promise and that promise would stay with him for the rest of his life.

Nell was sitting behind the counter of the shop when Michael came back from his walk down Mulberry Bend. There was no expression on her face as Michael told her of the young lady and the promise he had made. At first, there was no reaction as to the ramifications of his promise.

"Michael", she said, "I believe in you and I trust in your judgement. The cellar," she said, "I think the cellar." Slowly standing, she looked at Michael, "I will do all I can to help, but I want you to make me a promise."

"Whatever it is," he said, "I will do as you say."

"This lady," Nell said firmly, "will be your responsibility. You will look after her and care for her. We don't know anything about her and she may not be the kind of person you may think she is. I will talk to Mr Donovan later. In the meantime, I want you to tidy up the cellar, make room for a cot and get the tin bath off the wall."

Three months later, Michael descended the external stone steps to the cellar of the dress shop and knocked on the door, then entered. In the dim light provided by a narrow window at ceiling height, he saw Megan sitting upright in the cot that Nell had made up for her.

Thoughts of a romantic nature had never entered Michael's head, and for the first few weeks, he saw to it that Megan had the best of care. Nell had taken her to the New York Infirmary a few days after moving in and was relieved to find that she was suffering from nothing more than malnutrition and exhaustion, nothing a few weeks of a healthy diet and rest wouldn't cure.

"Are you ready?" he said as he stood in the doorway.

"Ready," she answered back.

The light from the window lit her smiling face. "This isn't the same girl," he said to himself. "This isn't the wretch I brought home." But it was the wretch he had brought home. She had put on weight; her sunken face was full and taut and her long hair had a sheen to it that he hadn't noticed before. She stood up.

"Do you like my new dress?" she said turning around. "It was one of Mr Donovan's' daughter's dresses," and as she looked at Michael she started to cry. "None of you have asked anything of me and you've given me everything; how can I ever begin to repay you?"

"Megan, please don't think like that; we ask nothing of you. If you're the person I think you are, your gratitude will be our reward."

"So, where are you taking me today, kind sir?"

"Central Park; it's a lovely sunny Sunday and the walk will do you good."

Megan had already told him about her past. She and her husband Danny had got married two days before they set sail for New York. Having arrived, they moved into Mulberry Street. They were only there six months when Danny died of dysentery; she was seven months pregnant at the time. She had enough money to last until she had the baby, after which she had no idea what would happen to her. She had the baby in the room where Michael had left her with the old lady. She, the old lady, Megan told him, was the only one present when she gave birth. The baby lived two days then died in her arms. She had no money left and held her dead baby for a day before the landlord came for his rent. That was when, she told him, that God had sent him. Michael told her that God didn't send him, he just happened to come along. But Megan had told him that she would always believe that God had sent him.

On the twelfth of April, 1861, Civil War had broken out and Fort Sumter was its first casualty. It happened one week after Megan had moved into the cellar of 198 Frankwell Street. Although Michael had no interest in the goings-on of politics, he did, however, disagree with the practice of slavery and the treatment of such people. But it was not his problem; it was not his fight and he had other things more pressing. When they got to Central Park, they sat on a wooden bench. Michael had not let go of her hand since they left home. He took a deep breath; the stench of Mulberry Bend and its adjoining streets was not evident here. Here, he could smell flowers and the scent of Megan. He felt at peace, just as he did when he stood on the bow of the *Lady Russell* as she dipped and rose with the ocean's swell. Over the last month, his feelings for Megan had changed, from her needing him to him needing her. He had fallen in love with her, spending every moment he could in her company, and he had a feeling that she felt the same for him. The months that followed opened a new world for him. Megan moved into his room and everyone was happy about it; she helped out in the shop and became close to Nell; they would chat away like old friends. She still had moments of sadness thinking of her baby, but when these moments came, Michael would comfort her the best he could. They had been together for ten months when they decided to get married. He went to a jeweller's shop and bought a gold wedding ring. A week later, Megan didn't feel well, becoming feverish with chills and a cough. Michael thought she had merely caught a cold, but she got worse. On the third night of her illness, Michael opened the little box that held the wedding ring he had bought and as he held her hand, he slipped it onto her finger; she looked at it and cried.

"Will it ever happen?" she asked sadly.

Michael had had two days off work but had to go in the following day. "I will work till dinner time," he told her as he put on his working clothes. At dinner time, Nell met him at the foot of the stairs; she was sobbing her heart out. Michael brushed past her, rushed up the stairs and into their bedroom. Megan was dead.

At the age of twenty-two, Megan was buried in the same graveyard as her baby. Michael shook hands with the few people that were there. Mr Donovan closed the shop for the day. Mr Doyle told him to take as much time from work as he needed, but it seemed all to be a dream; nothing was real. Nell had cleared everything of Megan's out of his room; it was as though she hadn't existed. He told her he didn't want anything to remind him of Megan since he had all he needed in his head.

Michael worked for another four weeks, then joined the Irish Brigade and went to fight in a war that had nothing to do with him.

8

On Jack's birthday, the 4th of March, an advance party of C company came under fire as they were leaving the outskirts of the small town of Khan Yunis, some sixteen miles from Gaza. A dozen or so Turkish troops could be seen scrambling over a rocky outcrop that rose above the last dwellings on the outskirts of the town. The boys had been aware of these marauding forces ever since their encounter with them in the desert, and to come across them again sharpened their senses and put an extra beat in their hearts.

The onset of rifle fire sent the few local people in the vicinity scurrying for cover. Jack and Bill ran for the safety of some large boulders that formed the boundary of an apricot orchard, as bullets slammed into the earth some yards behind them, causing puffs of dust to rise. The men from Jack and Bill's platoon returned fire, shooting from the cover of adobe homes at the base of the small hill. Most of the Turks made it over the brow and were safe, but there were three soldiers pinned down with volleys of fire from the platoon, one of whom laid in a hollow behind a rock twenty yards above Jack and Bill, the other two another ten to fifteen yards above him.

"I can't get a shot at him," Jack said, jostling for a position that would give him a clear target. "These bloody men coming out of the desert just to take potshots at us are a pain in the arse. I wish they would piss off and follow the rest of their army and go back home."

"I'm not worried about his bullets," Bill shouted, "but if he were to throw a grenade, we would be in trouble."

Six yards to their left, another boulder stood with another behind it leaving a gap of some three feet between them. Bill nudged Jack with his elbow and nodded in the direction of the boulders. Jack dashed toward the boulders followed by Bill. There was no rifle fire from the man on the hill as they made it to the safety of the boulders and, although they could not see the man on the hill, Jack still emptied a full clip of bullets in his direction.

Bill looked toward the adobe homes from where his platoon were shooting and noticed a figure appear from the corner of the nearest building. A woman carrying a baby stepped into the open and started running across the orchard toward a building opposite, only yards from Bill and Jack's position. As she passed them, she disappeared in a cloud of dust, an explosion throwing her against the mud-brick building. Her body was slumped at an angle with her back against the wall; she was naked from the waist up with her black robes hung in shreds around her legs. Her right arm and shoulder had all but gone and her baby.... Bill looked for her baby but couldn't see it. The woman's head was drooped forward, with her loose black hair hanging down covering her face. Bill stared in disbelief as he saw a crimson streak of blood run from her neck down the left side of her right breast and into her navel. He looked at her and noticed the drip, drip, drip of breast milk leave her body. It also ran to her navel and from there, a pink flow of the fluids of life itself ran over her stomach and disappeared between her legs. Bill looked on in despair; nothing on this earth could have prepared him to see such a scene that he had just witnessed. Sorrow seeped into his heart, followed by rage.

"This isn't how it's supposed to be," he screamed, but his screams were only in his head and not heard by Jack who just looked up and saw a dead woman. Bill wasn't even sure if Jack cared.

"Don't think about the rights and wrongs of the things that we are here to do," Jack had said on more than one occasion.

Ian had confronted him once about his attitude, asking him if his soul was devoid of compassion. To this, Jack typically answered back,

"We find ourselves in a situation where compassion can be dangerous, and I would do anything to save your life, Ian, but not your soul. It may not be the answer you were looking for, but it is the only one you are going to get."

Bill closed his eyes and counted to ten, a small lapse of time to take deep breaths and clear his head. He wasn't aware of when the shooting had stopped, wasn't aware that Jack had left his side. He just sat with his back against the boulder, his mind willing him to take control, telling him that the stupid woman would still be alive if she had stayed where she was. Whatever possessed her to run into the open like that, he had no idea. Bill stood up. Jack was coming down the hill stepping carefully over loose rock that slid beneath his feet, then he stopped by one of the few acacia trees that grew on the small hill. To his right, two Turkish soldiers with their hands in the air were being accompanied by their captors.

"And the other one?" Bill said

"He's dead," said Jack. "Stuck his head a little too far above the parapet, so our boys got him."

Then, as they walked to the end of the orchard, Bill reached up and picked a peach from an overhanging branch.

"They're not ripe yet," Jack said as Bill took a bite.

"I know that," he said.

"And?"

"And what?"

"What do they taste like?"

"Bitter," said Bill as he screwed up his face.

Jack laughed, then Bill stopped walking.

"By the way, Jack, have I wished you a Happy Birthday?"

Jack turned and smiled, "No, you haven't."

"Well, in that case, Happy Birthday!" and he handed him the peach.

Anxiety filled Jim's mind as he gazed upon the lines of men making their way north. Hundreds and hundreds of them, as far as he could see, were on the march. The build-up of troops to execute an attack on Gaza had taken many months. The brigades, mainly from Commonwealth countries, had been arriving in Egypt ever since the onset of war sixteen months ago. He was sitting on a sandhill as he watched soldiers of the Indian Army pass by; these troops were easily recognizable by their turbans. He had been told that they were mainly responsible for forcing the Turkish army from the area of the Suez Canal.

He took a deep breath and thought of dear Violet and his children. It had been over twelve months since he had seen them and, in that time, he had received three letters from her and, at three private moments, he had given them to Bill to read to him. It was at these moments that he felt the most vulnerable and inadequate, inadequate in that he was unable to read the words that she had written. Maybe Violet wanted to say things that she couldn't, he thought, knowing that another man would be reading them. Troops of the Australian Light Horse were now passing, followed by a mounted regiment from New Zealand. How splendid they looked, he thought, with their slouched hats and bandoliers slung over their shoulders. He had replied to Violet's three letters with three of his own, asking Bill to write them for him. He found it difficult to express his love and how he missed his children, and of the loneliness he felt some nights. Jim was not one for words, especially ones that would reach Violet through another person and, knowing Violet, she would tell in a minute if the words she read were truly Jim's.

From his vantage point, Jim saw a unit of the Imperial Camel Brigade cut across the Anzac line heading for the desert. "The most uncomfortable ride you will ever have," he said to himself. The Sinai was now pretty much clear of Turkish troops and those still in the desert were surrendering to the British forces.

Jim stood up and slung his rifle over his shoulder. They were a hundred and fifty-odd miles from the canal and sixteen from Gaza. There had been several skirmishes along the way that they had encountered, these contacts with the Turkish forces coming at different times and different locations. Everyone was reminded that their identity tags could end up in a little canvas bag, with the company Chaplin saying a few words that would get you into the kingdom of God.

With that in mind, Jim walked down the hill to join his friends.

As Jim approached, Bill was reading a leaflet handed to him by a soldier who was giving them out. It was important to the boys of the 7th, as it was to all participants of the forthcoming Battle of Gaza, that the geography of the town and its surrounding landscape be known. Bill read that Gaza stood at the junction of the roads to Beersheba and Jaffa, on a plateau about two miles inland from the sea, its importance being simply strategic. He continued reading that it was screened in the south-east by a line of features known as Samson's Ridge, Green Hill and Ali Munter. These hills were being held by a strong force of Turkish and German troops. Bill finished reading then handed the note on to a group of men passing by. Jack thought to himself that the information that Bill had just read out would prove of little importance to him, as he would be following orders anyway and that the hills and valleys of Gaza were already known to the men that would be giving them.

It was well after midnight on the morning of the 26th of March that the 7th moved, along with the 158th

Brigade, by night march towards the dry riverbed, Wadi Gaza. During the march, a heavy fog came in from the sea, making it even more difficult for the men to walk the unforgiving route that they had to travel. They crossed the Wadi Gaza and marched a further four and a half miles to their objective, Mansura Ridge. At this time, at about 8.30 am, the fog had lifted and the enemy on Ali Munter was clearly visible at around 5,500 yards. For the next three hours, the men rested and, during this time, the plan of operations was explained and in due course, orders were issued.

During the late morning, the attack began. Jim, with Bill by his side, along with the rest of the 7th, moved forward. The brigade was supported on the right by the 159th and on the left by the 160th brigade. In front of them nearly 2,000 yards of open ground and, under heavy rifle and machine-gun fire, the men charged forward with many men falling under the onslaught. And amongst the sound of shells, bombs and bullets, amongst the smell of cordite that sent steel into the soft flesh of mankind, were the screams of the dying. They had heard it before and had seen its aftermath. Jim had thought of the fear that every man, friend or foe, felt before engaging the enemy and in between, when fear had given way to a madness that was not of their making, was a time to run, run and run, some more toward the chequered flag that would end their adventure, and to the winner a bullet, a bullet that screamed allegiance to the man who sent it.

Jack, blind to everything around him, charged forward. He could hear the sound of shell fire; a battery of guns 1,000 yards to his rear had opened fire on a thick cactus hedge where the Turks were entrenched. With his bayonet glinting in the sun, he made it to the cactus hedge slashing and shooting his way through. He then found himself looking into an enemy trench. Some Turkish soldiers had started to run before their trenches were breached, making for some good shooting for those who had time to stop and take aim. But others would stay and fight it out. Bill got to the hedge; he was twelve steps to Jack's left, going through a section that was blasted away and shooting a soldier as he did so. Even as he pulled the trigger, another was raising his hands but it was too late, Bill's bayonet was already on its way.

All along the line, fierce fighting was taking place, the Herefords having great trouble getting through the hedge and losing a lot of men in their frantic efforts. The attacks on Samson's Ridge and Green Hill were proving costly to the British forces, which made the advance on Ali Munter difficult. But by half-past three in the afternoon, the Fusiliers were on the hill and two hours later, Samson's Ridge and Green Hill were taken. Jack and Bill on Ali Munter spent some time looking for Jim and were getting anxious as to his whereabouts when Bill spotted him coming up the hill with other men of the 7th.

"Look who I bumped into," said Skinny Steve upon reaching them. "I saw him go down at some distance from me and when I got to the hedge, I had a quick look round and saw some movement, so I thought at least he wasn't dead. After the fighting, I rallied some of our boys to go and look for him and found him stuck in a hole!" But for now, the sheer joy of standing on Ali Munter alive and in one piece was enough.

Jim explained what had happened, saying that as he ran toward the cactus hedge, his foot went into a hole causing him to fall over; he tried to get up but his foot was stuck. "I thought I was done for! With so many bullets flying around, I lay back down again and started piling as many stones as I could reach in front of me, even taking the stones I was lying on. Then I wriggled as much as I could to lower myself into the ground, even if it was only by an inch or two. I dug a hole with my hands and stuck my head into it, waiting till the fun was over."

"And the Montgomery boys?" asked Jack.

"As you heard, Steve saw me go down - he thought I was shot and when he looked back, I was already stacking stones. Anyway, they came back for me."

"And your foot?" asked Bill.

"Nothing wrong with it," said Jim, laughing. "It was my boot that got stuck and I wasn't going to sit up and take it off, was I?"

As the sun was setting, the Australian Light Horse joined the 7th on Ali Munter and, to the boys' surprise, the lads that they had met in Cairo were amongst them. "And where is the little shit that caused all the trouble?" Jim asked the big man who had threatened the military police with a disturbance that they would never forget. The big man slapped Jim on the shoulder as he called out for the source of the trouble in Cairo. In less than a minute, a young lad leading a black horse came forward, looking sheepishly at Jim and offering his hand in friendship at the same time.

"This is the man that stood over you when you were drunk and disorderly," said the big Aussie, to which the young lad answered back, "I may have been drunk, but I wasn't disorderly!"

Everyone laughed as the lad repeated the words Jim had spoken at the time of the incident. Jack had sought and found the man that had given him the emu feather plume from his hat. They embraced like old friends and talked with the excitement of children. Bill also embraced men that he had recognized; it was a surreal experience he thought, to be on a hill in the company of men they had never expected to ever see again. Then, when one of them asked the whereabouts of their friend, the other lad that was with them on that day, Bill realised, and maybe for the first time, that Ian was one man that he really would never see again. When he told them he was gone, they expressed their sorrow and one of them placed his hand gently on Bill's shoulder and told him that they too had lost some of theirs.

Bill looked up to see Jim walk over to stroke the neck of the young trooper's horse.

"What's her name?" Jim asked as he ran his hand over the dusty hide of the black mare.

"Midnight," said its proud owner.

"And yours?"

"Peter, Peter Boland." Peter came from the Hunter Valley in New South Wales. He told Jim that he rode Midnight from his home to Sydney where, along with hundreds more horses and riders, they embarked on a ship at Circular Quay, sailing away to find themselves eventually in Gallipoli.

"You were in Gallipoli?" asked Jim.

"Yes, it was a fucking disaster from the start."

"And you ended up here?"

"A bit like you."

Jim tilted his head.

"In what way?"

"Well," Peter answered, "we are both a long way from home, in a place we don't want to be and we don't know if we will see our loved ones again." Midnight snorted.

"Never mind," Jim said, "you have Midnight here to see you through."

It was dusk when the boys said their last farewells to their friends of the Light Horse and when Jim saw Peter Boland sit astride his mare, he was saddened to think that the chances of Midnight ever galloping over the Australian outback again were slim, if ever she would.

Later that evening, orders were received that all troops on Ali Munter, Green Hill and Samson's Ridge were to withdraw. It was decided that if Gaza itself wasn't taken at dusk, and it wasn't, the whole operation was to be abandoned.

Two weeks later, a second attack on Gaza took place and, although there was fierce fighting and some objectives were successful, the ground taken could not be held. So, for the second time, British Forces had no choice but to withdraw, taking with them some two thousand enemy casualties and prisoners.

It would be another seven months, five days after the taking of Beersheba, that Gaza finally fell.

On the next day, the 6th of November, twenty miles east of Gaza, the 7th took up position for an attack on Khuweifeh Hill. Again, the boys stood side by side and again they wished each other luck, with Jack telling Jim to mind where he was putting his feet. The battalion moved forward and, in under an hour, the boys were standing on the flat-topped hill after rushing the Turkish front line under a barrage of artillery fire. A large number of Turks were bayoneted in the attack and, to the surprise of the boys, their own losses were light in comparison.

The 7th weren't on the hill for long before the enemy launched a strong counter-attack and, by sheer weight of numbers, succeeded in pushing them off the crest. But they were greeted by a short artillery bombardment and the 7th, seeing an opportunity to retake the hill, took it at the point of the bayonet. As Jack, screaming like a stuck pig, was pushing man after man off the end of his blade, Bill sidestepped one Turk only to be met by another, screaming in Turkish, lunging at him with a bayonet of his own. He missed Bill by inches before falling over with the momentum of his charge, with both men being taken care of by Jim following three steps behind his friend.

Five separate counter-attacks were launched by the enemy during the next twenty-four hours and twice the Turks regained the summit, only to be driven off with heavy losses by the 7th.

The fall of Beersheba and Khuweilfeh became a turning point in the Palestine campaign and the way to Jerusalem was now open through the Judah hills. It was hard going, soldiers and pack animals struggling through rain and snow, caked in mud and living on half rations whilst boys of the 7th, along with the 5th and the 6th RWF, kept the vital supply road from Beersheba to Hebron open as the 24th and 25th RWF pushed northeast to Jerusalem.

Jerusalem fell on the 9th of December and, later in the month, the 7th stood by in the defence of it as Turkish forces tried to retake the holy city and the surrounding area. A further advance was due to take place immediately, but the Turks attacked first and for some time there was a great deal of uncertainty as to the British positions on the adjoining hills. The following day, the 7th attacked and captured an adjoining hill, Ras Arkub es Suffa, which dominated the Jericho road, and no time was lost in fully securing these positions as they intended to stay there for some time.

On the 27th, the battalion was ordered to retake White Hill which had been captured by the Turks; the 7th went into the attack with the bayonet clearing everything before them. In less than an hour, the Turks counter-attacked, inflicting many casualties, but the positions were held.

At dawn the following day, along with others of their company, the boys were on fatigue duty clearing the battle area of abandoned arms and collecting the dead. Picking up dead bodies was not a job for the squeamish, but it was a job that had to be done. It wasn't the first time the boys had been given this task; Jim remembered well taking with him a canvas bag onto the battlefield at Romani to collect body parts of the Unknown Soldier.

Jim stopped and looked at the carnage in front of him, picking up the right leg of one unfortunate and placing it into the bag. A few feet away was another leg, this one from the knee down, it was also part of a right leg. This he also placed into his bag; two legs from different people. Sometimes a bag contained no head, especially if a shell had exploded amongst advancing troops. One by one, he would take the bags back to a collection point. He dropped the bag at the feet of a chaplain who was moving between all the other bags of body parts, making crosses in the air. He looked at Jim and asked,

"Is this one only known unto God?" Jim stared into his eyes.

"I don't think even God would know who this one is," he replied, then he stooped and flicked at a moving dark mass on an empty bag and, picking it up, walked back to the battleground.

Clouds of flies would be brushed away from the bloated forms of the dead, their faces and exposed flesh having started to turn various shades of colour, with the smell of decaying bodies akin to the smell of a rotting sheep carcass that had been left in a field for days.

"This one is alive," said Jack, as one soldier exhaled and groaned as he was being moved, although realizing immediately, and for the second time, that what he had heard was the noise of gases escaping from the swollen stomach of the deceased. Having laid him on the stretcher, Bill covered his face with a small sheet, then placing themselves at either end, he and his companion lifted him and carried him down an incline to the collecting point, placing him down in a line of other stretchers. Jack looked up and noticed the chaplain walk slowly down the row of stretchers, then they left him to his pointless gesturing and mumbling incantations.

Jim was returning with his last bag of body parts when he noticed a motionless body lying in a hollow, face down and the flies, forever present, were crawling into his ears. Then, for a moment, a warm breeze swirled past him and into the hollow, lifting the black flash that denoted the soldier's regiment. He lay with his hands by his side, his rifle two feet away, its bayonet pointing in the direction from where the bullet came that ended his life. Jim went into the hollow and knelt by the soldier's side; he reached over his body, and grabbing his shoulder, turned him over. The shock of seeing Skinny Steve was overwhelming; he shrank back, unable to comprehend the devastation he was feeling. He looked into Steve's staring eyes, eyes that were now crawling with flies; he sat down beside him and, cradling his head in his arms, started to rock back and forth with tears falling on the ashen face of the young man that was a friend to everyone. As he rocked, visions of home came to mind and as he spoke of those visions he looked into the sky.

"Winter nights and rainy days, from rolling pastures to the tops of green hills and the slow turning wheels of flour mills,"

Jim smiled through his tears thinking to himself.

"Jim, you're a poet. I think I'll write Steve a poem one day," and an inner voice said, "but you can't write Jim."

"No, I can't, can I?" Jim said loudly as he closed Steve's eyes. It was then that he made a vow; "I swear to

God that one day I will speak to his mother." Jim had often sworn at God, but not too often did he swear to him.

"I will lie to her and tell her I was with him at the end. I will lie to her and tell her of his last words, tell |Mother I'm sorry." Jim stood up, took a deep breath and picked up his bag. He turned slowly, whispering, "I'll send the Montgomery boys to pick you up, Steve; they will look after you."

The death of Steve was a severe blow to a lot of men in his company and as men kept dying in battle after battle, holes were dug for men to be lowered into. Christian rites and words from the good book were spoken, together with the lamenting sound of a lone bugle, whose haunting notes would sweep over the lowered heads of those that were there. 'Was this the stuff of nightmares?' thought Bill, as he looked at Jim standing motionless, staring at a row of hastily made wooden crosses. Services like this were being held in battle areas all over Egypt. All were memorable in their execution, but the irony, it could be said, was that sad moments like this could also be beautiful ones.

All through January and February, the battalion continued to hold a strong outpost line to the east of Jerusalem, as troops gathered and spread up the Jordan valley. The chaotic mass of arid hills falling from the highlands into the valley was impassable.

The country in the line of advance was wild and picturesque, sparsely dotted with ruins and villages with fig trees, olive groves and vineyards all painting the hillsides with different shades of green. But, apart from

these cultivated pockets, it was a succession of scarred
hills, separated by deep and sometimes precipitous valleys.

"Here we go again," Jack said, as news came through
that an attack on various hills in the surrounding area
would be taking place within the next few days.

Chipp Hill, one of the highest hills in Judea and an
enemy strongpoint of great importance, was one. It was
one of a number of hills that had been under surveillance
for weeks. This hill would be one of the first to be stormed
and the storming, in the first instance, would be done
by the Herefords, followed by the 5th and 6th RWF. The
7th would be the last to go in.

Tell Asur was another hill; in fact, it was the highest
point of all and northwest of it, on the forward slope of a
hill, was Selward, the first objective of the 231st Brigade,
to be taken by the Shropshire Light Infantry.

"Guess where we were at this time two years ago?"
asked Bill as he stood up and stamped his feet, making
sure they fitted snugly in his boots.

"At Park Hall Camp," replied Jack after a moment's
thought.

"Good God," said Jim, "sometimes it seems like
yesterday and other times it's like we've been here forever.
Christ," he added, "I'm getting fucking tired of all this."

He stood up and grabbed his rifle which was lying on
the ground, then moved off in the direction of his fellow
soldiers.

Jack looked at Bill.

"He hasn't been the same since he found Skinny
Steve, has he?"

"No," said Bill, "and I don't think he's the only man affected by Steve's death."

No more was said about Steve; he seemed to have passed into that category of memorable moments that is etched into people's minds; the birth of a child, an achievement so richly deserved, the passing of a loved one, and to these men, their contribution in the making of history.

9

There was an east wind blowing as Michael wrapped an old trench coat about himself. The logs he gathered from the shed were from the stack he had built up over the summer months. It surprised him to see that there was still plenty left. The pains in his stomach had eased since he had seen the doctor. He had given him something, he didn't know what, but he had heard the word "opiates" in one sentence and "liquorice troches" in another. Anyway, whatever he was taking, it was doing him good. Michael knew that whatever he had was going to kill him. Some days he would feel good and some days he would feel bad, but the bad days were getting worse.

Today was Friday. He had been up since daybreak, doing odd jobs about the house, after which he began cleaning and dusting, putting back things that were not in their rightful place. In doing so, he noticed that things hadn't been moved about as much as they used to be. But then, he wasn't as active as he used to be. He had been doing this religiously on a Friday for the last three years, ever since he had asked Megan Davies from the blacksmith's shop if she could help him to improve his handwriting and spelling. Not that it was altogether the truth, although he did enjoy writing poetry and a second opinion on his work was welcome. Michael felt a need for company and it didn't really matter from where it came. And today, he thought it ridiculous that he should still be doing this, cleaning his house in anticipation of Megan's visit, especially as he was so ill. But in truth, she came because she enjoyed his company. In the beginning, she did indeed help him with his work; not with the writing and spelling so much, but by being a critic of the poetry he wrote. She protested, saying that she knew absolutely nothing about poetry. Also, that she had no right, or sufficient knowledge of the subject, to criticise or praise his work. Michael persisted; he knew she was well-read and assured her that she was an ideal person to form an opinion.

Over the years, Michael had become proficient in his ability to master the English language. He had various teachers along the way; from the sailor on the *Lady Russell* to his workmates; his Megan, the street urchin that would polish his boots, and the one hundred and one teachers he had had since. There was still the hint of his Irish accent, smothered in there amongst all the other voices and dialects that he had encountered through the years. Now there was a colour in his voice, a colour that made it warm and comforting. For the last few months, he had rarely put pen to paper, however, Megan still came. At half-past two every Friday afternoon on the dot, she would gently tap on the door and walk in, come rain or shine, in summer or winter. Michael would put the kettle on.

A clean cup, a jug of milk and some honey on the table. Megan would tell him all the local news, the goings-on at the Rectory and there wouldn't be many weeks when the boys weren't mentioned. If she had a letter, she would tell him all that was relevant, in particular, she would mention the wellbeing of Bill.

Up until a few weeks ago, at five o'clock, she would help him on with his coat, place his hat on his head and take his arm. Together they would walk down the hill road and into the village, passing the old church and its graveyard as they went. Outside the pub they would part; Michael would go in for his customary three pints of bitter and Megan would walk the forty yards to her home. Two hours later, Michael would walk home, have a slice of bread and butter with two chunks of cheese, then go to bed. It seemed unlikely that the ritual would happen very often again. His mastery over the printed word and the ability to read and write it was such that Megan laughingly accused him of getting her there under false pretences. But he intrigued her and it was she that would become his confidante.

Michael thought for a long time about who he could talk to. Someone who would understand, someone who would not judge him, his logic, his actions, or his reasons for doing what he had done. Someone who would just listen and try to understand. He realised that he didn't know anyone well enough to say what he wanted to say. It was over the last eighteen months that he had started to tell Megan about his past; little bits here, little bits there. Although she was young, he was heartened by her enthusiasm for wanting to know. Megan was absorbed by his tales; she would sit for ages listening to his stories like a novel she couldn't put down. He told her that every life has a beginning and an end, and to get to the end you have to go through the middle.

She told him that she had read about things. Things not of her world. "Stuff", as she put it, stuff that she would never see, and stuff she would never do. She reasoned that to read about stuff, you could almost be there, and listening to people talk about stuff that they had seen and done, well, that was about all she could do. He told her about his childhood in Ireland, his days on the *Lady Russell*, Manhattan, the deprivation and disease he had encountered. She hugged him when he told her about 'his' Megan. She held her tears until she got home; Mr Donovan, the war, his going back to Ireland, his years with a tortured mind. She realised that there were things that he didn't tell her. She sensed that he wanted to but he didn't; maybe it was best she didn't know everything. Only two weeks ago, he had said that in war you do some terrible things... things you will take to your grave. As he spoke of these things, Megan thought of Bill.

Michael looked at her.

"Don't think the boys will come back the same as when they left." It frightened her when he said those words. He could see it; he held her arm, a gesture that for him had more meaning than any passage in the bible. She looked down, her eyes filling with tears.

"Do you want me to lie to you? Will you be able to handle the stuff that is coming your way? If you can't, walk away." He softened his grip. "But you know, Megan, I think you are made of stronger stuff." His voice was soft and caring. "You are not a quitter." He let go of her arm.

Tears were rolling down her cheeks, coming together on her chin, and dripping onto the arm Michael had just held. Then, reaching for Michael, she whispered, "Will you be there for me, Michael…, will you tell me everything is going to be all right?"

"Ah, Megan," he reached and brushed her hair with deserving tenderness, her hair falling through his fingers like chiffon over glass.

"If only I could; I will be gone, Megan. It's you that will find the answers, but believe me when I say that you will be fine. Like me, Megan Davies, your life has a beginning and it will have an end, and …."

"And," Megan interrupted, "to get to the end, you have to go through the middle." She looked up and, through her tears, she smiled.

10

The attacks on the Judean Hills were successful but, as with all victories, there was a cost and the costs weren't just in lives lost or the life-changing injuries that came with success. To see the broken bodies of men strewn across this harsh foreign landscape affected the living in ways that they never would have imagined. Jack had seen this first-hand when they went in to attack Chipp Hill. With bullets and shrapnel flying all around, he dived into a shell hole for cover and discovered a young lad cowering and shaking, with his hands covering his head. Safe from oncoming bullets, Jack crawled over to him thinking he was hit.

"Are you all right?" he shouted across the din that was all around them. The lad didn't take any notice of Jack as he lay curled up. He was shaking and shouting, saying that he couldn't take any more and he wanted to go home. There was fear in his eyes as he asked Jack if his mother was coming to get him. Jack shook him and told him that he would be fine if he stayed with him, but Jack could see this lad was in a bad way and there was no way he was going anywhere. Jack held him in his arms trying to calm him, then he gently took away the lad's hand from his ear and told him that he would come back for him and bring his mother. On hearing the word Mother, the lad for a moment stopped shaking and, looking at Jack, asked, "I can go home, then?"

In circumstances other than this, Jack would have called him a coward and not fit to be called a soldier. He would have been the first to condemn a man for refusing to fight, but this man wasn't right in the head; this man wanted help, not ridicule. Jack left him as he found him, squirming and shaking like a frightened rabbit.

'I can't afford to think about him,' were his thoughts as he ventured from the shell hole and started to run with renewed vigour toward the enemy.

It was much later; the sun was going down when Jack went back for the man in the shell hole and was surprised to find that he was sleeping. The thought of this man sleeping in the middle of a battle, while all around him men were fighting for their lives, was more than he could take.

"Wake up, you bastard," Jack shouted as he shook him roughly by the shoulder. The man woke up immediately, then sitting up, he smiled at Jack then looked around.

"Is Mother not with you?" There was a vacant look in his eyes and, as Jack's anger subsided, he said the first thing that came into his mind.

"She missed the train," Jack paused, then said gently, "Do you know where you are, lad?"

"I'm in Egypt," he said, still smiling.

"And what are you doing here?" The man seemed bewildered as to Jack's question.

"I don't know," he said as he remained sitting but continued to slowly look around before his gaze settled and he focused on Jack.

"Could you tell me what I am doing here?"

"Well," Jack said as he gently placed a hand on the young man's shoulder, "You were fighting a war."

"Did we win?" the lad replied excitedly.

"Yes," said Jack, helping the lad to his feet. "But now I think for you the war is over. Now, pick up your rifle and come with me." The lad looked at the rifle lying on the ground close to where he had been sleeping.

"Is that mine?" he asked. "Is it a real one?"

"Yes, it is." Jack paused; "On second thoughts, I think I will carry it," he said as he bent down and picked it up, throwing it over his shoulder to join that of his own. Jack helped the young lad out of the shell hole and, as they made their way to some tents that had been erected to accommodate wounded personnel, he told Jack that he lived on Crescent Street in Newtown and had been in the army for a long time. Sometimes his answers to Jack's questions were what would have been expected, giving away nothing that would cause anyone to think there was anything wrong with his mental state. But then he would go off at a tangent, telling Jack that his mother would box his ears if he was late for tea, also telling him that she would be picking him up after visiting his granny. Jack left him in the care of two stretcher-bearers, after giving them an account of what he had observed about the young man from Crescent Street. One of the stretcher-bearers wrote some notes in a pocketbook, Jack giving his name and the information as to his relatives that they asked for. Jack didn't get the lad's name but as he left, the lad asked for his.

"I'm Jack," Jack said. The lad then held out his hand and, as Jack shook it, the lad smiled.

"Thank you, Jack, for looking after me; come and visit me sometime."

Jack smiled back.

"I will certainly do that," said Jack as he turned and walked away. Jack had killed men that day and had seen dead men from his own Battalion but none of this was on his mind as he walked away from the stretcher-bearers and the young man he had left in their charge. No, his mind was on a mother whose son would be forever late for tea and one day he may well go home, but to another mother who will still have lost her son to the war.

Later in the month, the battalion advanced up the Jordan Valley and, on Good Friday, March 29th, they crossed the River Jordan by way of the Gharaniyeh Bridge. For days, the intense heat and dust storms made it impossible to do much. All through April and right into September, the 7th were holding the line covering the Nablus road and the Jordan valley. Then came the rain; dry river and creek beds started to run with water and, for a short while, this caused great inconvenience to the 53rd Division, as they were at that time deployed in the making good and improving roads and tracks that would be used for mule and camel trains, transporting munitions, food and water. Work was also carried out strengthening defence outposts, in the now unlikely event of Turkish units coming back and having another go. At this time the 52nd and the 54th Divisions were being withdrawn for services elsewhere.

Then came news that Major T. E. Lawrence and his forces of the Arab revolt were on their way to Deraa. There was some rejoicing in camp as the news spread and, for the first time in a long while, there was talk of the war coming to an end soon.

"Don't count on it," said Jim, as he joined a group of men discussing the exploits of Major Lawrence.

"Remember Aqaba? Lawrence just walked into that place and the word then was that the war would soon be over - that was twelve months ago."

"I know that," said a man standing by Bill, "but the Turks are running out of somewhere to go."

"And look where we are," said someone eager to have his say, "we have fought the buggers all the way from the Suez, and Damascus is still a hundred miles away".

"Well, as I see it," Jack interrupted, "Major Lawrence and his Arab mercenaries are out there," he raised his hand and pointed to the horizon. "He's in the Syrian desert blowing up trains and bridges, in general causing mayhem and, if he comes in from the interior and takes Daraa, all he has to do is turn right and sixty or so miles in front of him is Damascus. We already know columns of mounted troops are pushing up the Palestine coast, sweeping up what scant Turkish resistance they encounter and taking thousands of prisoners in the process. My guess is that Lawrence will be the first to enter Damascus and when that happens, as it surely will, this war will be at an end."

No one spoke for a moment then a voice casually asked, "And what do we do then?"

"Then," Bill said, "then we go home. But before that happens, there is a little matter of some mopping up to do."

On the night of the 18th of September, the 7th, along with the Cape Corps and the Indian 21st Punjab's, attacked several enemy strongpoints. At the village of Mughier, just east of Ramalla, was based the headquarters of a Turkish Battalion. Only a few hours into the attack, the commanding officer surrendered and hundreds of his men were taken prisoner.

That same day, on his way to Deraa, T E Lawrence blew up his seventy-ninth bridge as Turkish troops, by their thousands, were retreating from all directions and heading for Damascus. There was wholesale slaughter as the Arabs gave no quarter to their fleeing enemy.

On the 21st, the British cavalry had already begun turning inland from their charge up the coast, leaving enemy units in Palestine in imminent danger of being encircled.

Deraa was taken on the 28th, having been abandoned by up to six thousand Turkish and German troops the day before. Major Lawrence rode to the outposts of the British Fourth Division and guided them into Deraa, where they stayed overnight, leaving early the following morning for Damascus. Lawrence stayed on in Deraa to meet with King Faisal to discuss plans for establishing a provisional government when Damascus was taken.

On an evening out in Cairo in July 1917, Lawrence and his party left the Windsor Hotel to visit a club just off Opera Square. As he entered in his flowing Arab robes, he asked the gathering crowd whose Rolls Royce was parked outside the building. A lady approached and introduced herself as Aileen Bellew, saying that the car belonged to her. Likewise, Lawrence introduced himself to her, then announced that he was commandeering the car in the name of His Majesty's forces. The lady reluctantly agreed (not that she had much choice in the matter), telling him that the car's name was *Blue Mist.* Lawrence then, with an air of self-importance, stepped outside and drove the car away, saying "in the desert, a Rolls Royce is above rubies."

Then, on the morning of the 30th of September, 1918, after Damascus had been taken, Lawrence and his driver left Deraa in the Rolls Royce that Lawrence had commandeered from outside the club in Cairo fourteen months earlier, to travel the sixty-two-mile journey to Damascus. They drove through a landscape littered with the corpses of men and animals, some of whom had perished in the Turks' desperate flight. To the Arabs and local people who had been under the boot of the Ottoman Empire for decades, revenge was sweet. By evening, they had reached a ridge overlooking Damascus. The ridge was crowded with Arab and Expeditionary forces units poised to advance into the city at first light.

On the 1st of October, the war in Palestine was over.

As for Major T.E. Lawrence, he entered Damascus in his Rolls Royce and, on the steps of the City Hall, he greeted Henry Chauvel, the Australian Commander of the Egyptian Expeditionary Force Desert Mounted Corps, whose forces had entered Damascus at much the same time as Major Lawrence's forces.

The taking of Mughier and the surrounding hills by the 53rd Brigade on the 18th of September was practically the end of the fighting in the Jordan Valley area. When news came of the occupation of Damascus, the boys of the 7th, like all combatants, were relieved that at least no more lives would be lost due to the continuation of the conflict. But the end of the war didn't mean the end of military service; the sound of reveille was still heard in the morning; inspections, parades, medicals and the transporting of goods and services didn't suddenly stop. What did stop was the preparation for battle, the sound of bombs, rifle fire and the screams of men.

There would now be the withdrawal of military hardware, the deployment of troops to secure the holding of thousands of enemy prisoners and, in the coming months, the evacuation of the Egyptian forces' troops back to their homelands. Later, sadly, came the systematic slaughter of hundreds and hundreds of military horses that, due to the cost of feeding and transporting them home, had become a commodity that could now be dispensed with.

11

"And how long have you been coming to the village, Miss Mavis?" Megan asked as she arranged some gypsophila and tulips in a vase and placed them on a dresser in Mavis' bedroom. It was mid-morning on a Saturday and Miss Mavis was in residence. She came bouncing into the bedroom still dressed in her crepe-de-chine pink cami-knickers and waving her arms like the prima ballerina she had seen the week before at the Gaiety Theatre, London. She ignored Megan's question as she glided as best as she could over the Axminster carpet that lay on her bedroom floor. Her age and generous figure became a disadvantage to her as she attempted a pirouette followed by an allegro in one movement. Then, attempting to stand on one leg, let alone on the toes of one foot, it all became too much and she collapsed onto her bed. Megan couldn't stop laughing as Mavis lay there condemning the years that had made it impossible for her to become a ballerina.

"I'm sorry, Megan," she said as she gasped for air, "but it was such an exciting evening. The Russian ballerina Anna Pavlova was just amazing; she was floating on the air like one of those seeds, the ones you blow off a dandelion. Anyway, I must get dressed, and what shall I put on today?" she said as she went up to Megan and gave her a hug.

"Anything you take out of that wardrobe," Megan said pointing to a walnut mirrored wardrobe, "makes you look a million dollars."

"You are such a sweet girl, Megan, and say the nicest things. You were saying something as I came through the door," Mavis said throwing open the wardrobe doors. "I'm sorry I didn't answer you; I was on such a high," she giggled.

"It was nothing, really," Megan answered, "I just wanted to know how long you have been coming to the village."

"Ah," Mavis sighed as she laid an orange pleated dress on the bed, "I first came when I was twenty-five years of age. Of course, my brother wasn't here at the time, he came many years later. I came with an old girlfriend of mine. My God, Megan," Mavis stood rigid, "I'm sixty-six now, so how long ago was that?"

"Forty-one years ago," Megan said. Her next choice of dress was a plain turquoise one and as she laid that one on the bed, she sighed.

"Forty-one years ago," she whispered, not quite believing it. "It was my girlfriend's father; he was vicar here at the time and she asked if I would care to visit for a few days. God, Megan," she said again as she picked some fluff off the orange dress, "it was like going out to the colonies."

Megan couldn't refrain from holding her hand to her mouth as a stunted laugh erupted.

"It's true," Mavis said as she carried on. "We were met at Montgomery station after what seemed like a trip through the Badlands of Siberia, except, of course, there was no snow. We were told in London that Wales was tribal and that under no circumstances were we, as young ladies, to venture into fields or leave the safety of the roads. We were told that local men would have no compunction in molesting us or taking our virginity," she stopped and looked at Megan who was now sitting on the bed but still held her hand over her mouth; "that is," she said slowly, "if there was any virginity to be taken!" Mavis thought for a moment; should she really be talking like this in front of a young girl…?

"I remember," she said without stopping, "that we even picked up a traveller, a bearded man, halfway between Montgomery Station and the village. He frightened the life out of us. I may have been twenty-five, Megan, and thought I knew everything, but in reality, I knew nothing." "It's a funny thing," Mavis continued, sounding more serious, "but I've never forgotten that man."

"Why?" said Megan still laughing behind her hand. "Did he molest you?"

"Oh, no," Mavis replied, "on the contrary, he was a gentleman; he didn't smell, was polite and knowledgeable. He seemed to know London a lot better than I did, and when he alighted from our carriage, he took my hand and kissed it."

"Were you not offended at him taking such a liberty?" Megan asked.

"No," said Mavis; she hesitated, "it just seemed to be the right thing to do, and as our pony stepped forward and the wheels of our carriage started to move, I looked into his face and the last thing I remember of him was the twinkle in his eye." For a moment, Mavis sat with the orange dress on her lap and said nothing; she just stared at her reflection in the wardrobe mirror then got up.

"He taught me a lot, did that man," she spoke as if there was no-one in the room and Megan sensed a loneliness in Mavis's life but dared not pursue the subject.

"I'll wear the orange one," she said as she hurriedly went into the bathroom. When she came out, she was back to being the same bubbly Mavis that Megan had got to know so well.

"And it was another twenty years before I visited this village again," said Mavis as she sat down at the dressing table. "That was when my brother became the vicar here."

Megan removed the vase of flowers then stood behind Mavis and took the hairbrush that she offered.

"And even then, I only visited once a year and not every year at that. It has only been in the last six years or so that I have visited on a more regular basis, and the reason?" she asked herself out loud. "Maybe I don't live the life I once did and maybe the life I once lived doesn't hold the same interest as it once did; either way, I got to like visiting every few months or so, and I like seeing you, Megan." All the time Mavis was speaking, Megan was brushing her hair and there was always a hairpin in Mavis's hand ready for Megan to take whenever she needed one.

"And Bill, Megan, how are Bill and the boys?"

"The boys are well," Megan replied, "but they won't be home for a long time yet. The war may be over, Miss Mavis, but it could be another six months before they walk the roads of Montgomeryshire again."

"And Michael, how is he?" Mavis asked.

"He's fine," said Megan as she placed a champagne feather fascinator that was fixed to a champagne velvet headband on her head.

"Should I have it placed to one side," asked Mavis, "or just in the centre?"

"Just to one side," said Megan as she slid the headband to the right.

"I am not sure about this flapper look," said Mavis. "For one thing, I am too old, and for another, I am the wrong shape. It's all very well for you young people; the world is changing and I welcome it, it's just that it's changing a little too late for me. I'm not saying for one moment that I haven't had a jolly good time, I have, but when you've been in the kind of company that I have kept, things can," she stopped and looked at Megan in the mirror, "well let's say, get a little out of hand. Bugger! Megan, I haven't talked about my decadent life for years and I am enjoying telling you."

"Well! and?" Megan asked, encouraging Mavis to carry on.

"For instance, the suffragettes."

"The suffragettes!" Megan gasped, dropping the hairbrush at the same time,

"You were part of the suffragette movement?"

"I certainly was."

"Did you know Emily Pankhurst?" Megan was excited now as she was a supporter of the suffragette movement herself.

Even as a ten-year-old, the age when she had lost her mother, Megan had already gained from her not only the need for a good education but a sense of equality. There was never a moment that she could remember when her mother ever admitted that women were subservient to men, even to the point of fixing posters that read, "VOTES FOR WOMEN" on the walls of the blacksmith's shop in Llandinam. Even on leaving their old home, Megan took with her copies of the Suffragette Weekly that her mother had paid a penny for and which were now in a cardboard box under the stairs in her home in Llandyssil.

"Knew her? I marched alongside her and Violet Bland, Jessie Kenney, Millicent Brown and a lot more! I held banners, was arrested and spent a day in the cells, was spat at, pushed and shoved about. Jesus, Megan, I was at Epsom races the day Emily Wilding Davison ran in front of the King's horse and was killed. It happened not twenty yards from me. Mind you, the day wasn't all bad I was taken there by a gentleman friend and he gave me ten shillings to have a bet, so I put it on an outsider at one hundred to one. It's strange, don't you think, Megan, that on the same race as poor Emily was killed, I won fifty pounds when my horse, Aboyeur, crossed the finishing line in front of all the others?" Mavis took a deep breath, "Emily didn't actually die on the racetrack; she was taken to Epsom College Hospital but passed over four days later."

Megan had stopped working on Mavis's hair but still stood behind her, her mouth wide open. She wondered, who exactly was this lady sitting down in front of her? There were so many questions she wanted to ask.

"And the man," Megan blurted out, "the man at the races?"

"Oh, him? He was just an acquaintance," Mavis stopped talking. "What is the date today, Megan?" she asked.

"It's the first of June."

"Do you realise, Megan, that in four days' time, that incident at Epsom Racecourse will have occurred exactly six years ago? My God, Megan, I was an old lady even then!"

"Miss Mavis," Megan said with some resonance in her voice, "you may be a lot of things but being old is not one of them. Old ladies do not talk openly about their life experiences, especially to young people like me. You may be old in the sense that you think may be true, but fifteen minutes ago you were attempting to do a Swan Lake in the middle of your bedroom. Now, pray, how many sixty-six-year-old ladies do that? They may think of doing it, even dream it, but to attempt it? No, Miss Mavis, you are not old, not in the sense that I mean, and it gives me pleasure to think of you as I do."

Mavis, still sitting in the chair in front of the mirror, was silent, then she stood up.

"Young lady, sit in this chair as I would like to brush your hair."

"I can't do that, Miss Mavis," Megan blurted out, "it's not my place to…."

"Megan," Mavis said softly as she held Megan's hand, "sit, and as for it not being your place, I will decide that."

Megan sat down and, as Mavis untied the dark blue ribbon that held together Megan's hair, she closed her eyes and felt the brush run the length of her back to the end of her shining tresses. Then a feeling of melancholy swept over her, as she felt caring hands on her head and the faint sound of a lullaby drifted into the room. She was a little girl again. The soothing melodic sound of Sou Gan, the Welsh lullaby filled her senses as her mother ran the brush, time and time again, through her hair. Sometimes she would fall asleep as the hands of love would clean her grubby face and wipe away her tears. In the mirror, Mavis could see the tears run down Megan's cheeks, but she didn't stop humming the tune that her mother hummed to her, and she didn't stop brushing Megan's hair. She could see that Megan was in a place that she could not enter and she wanted her to stay there for as long as she needed to. Megan opened her eyes and looked at Mavis.

"I'm sorry," Megan said, wiping away a tear with the back of her hand. They both looked at their reflection in the dressing table mirror.

"Megan," Mavis paused, "were you just thinking of your mother?"

"Yes," said Megan nodding her head.

"And I was thinking of mine," said Mavis.

"And that lullaby, Sou Gan, how do you know it?" asked Megan.

"Is that what it's called?" smiled Mavis. "It's a tune my mother would hum to me when I was a little girl.

Don't ask me where she got it from as I don't know, but it has stayed with me all my life. Your mother sang it to you in Welsh, Megan?"

"Yes, she did; what made you ask?"

"Because now and then, when I was humming it, you would accompany me, singing words that I didn't understand."

"Did I really?" said Megan, sounding surprised.

"Yes, you did, and maybe one day you will teach me to sing that lullaby as it was meant to be sung."

"Well, before I do that Miss Mavis," Megan smiled, "I would have to learn it all over again."

"Now we have half an hour before I make my appearance in the dining room and this, may I add, is to satisfy my brother's wishes, not mine. You may well know more of the guests than I do, Megan, and I swear he only uses me as some kind of catalyst to humour and to jell the unsuspecting guests like some Barnum and Bailey circus master."

"Men," Megan suddenly said, "tell me about some of the men in your life?"

"Megan," Mavis said slowly, "I said we have half an hour, not all day." They both burst out laughing. "I was very prim and proper in my late teens and early twenties and indeed, I am still prim and proper today. But that isn't to say I've not rogered a few men and flattened a lot of grass in my time. But you know, Megan, I've never found true love and, with hindsight, I don't know if I was looking for it," she hesitated; "having too good a time, I suppose."

"And now?" Megan enquired.

"Well," said Mavis, "I still enjoy the company of men, but most of them are married and those that aren't shouldn't be. I still enjoy a gin or two and as for champagne, I can take it or leave it. I've had trysts with more unsuitable lovers than I care to mention, and proposals of marriage that I've lost count of. But I have also met some wonderful people and some honourable men. And by honourable, I don't mean by virtue of them not wanting them to bed me. Then I look at you; you haven't even set foot on the road to ruin, let alone wanting to get off it. And before you say a word, I got off that road a long time ago. It's having the balls to want to get on it in the first place, and then having the wisdom of not letting it get too late to get off".

Mavis reached under the bed and brought out a pair of two-inch-heeled nude T strap shoes.

"How will these do?" she asked.

"They will do just fine," Megan answered. "You say... you say you have never been in love, but you must have liked some of the men you have been with?"

"Liked! Liked some of them?" Mavis rolled her eyes and smiled. "I liked them all, Megan," and still smiling, "I liked them all. I may not have liked them in the morning, though, and I'm not sure who would have instigated proceedings the night before. Maybe I would see them again, maybe I wouldn't, but most were like ships in the night - that sort of thing. But you are right; some I liked a lot and some of them are still my friends today."

Megan was on one knee, fastening Mavis's shoes when there was a knock on the door.

"We will be down in ten minutes," Mavis called out, without waiting to be told that her presence was wanted. "I've had a very privileged life, Megan, I know I have. I come from a wealthy family; my great-great-grandfather was in the tobacco business and somewhere down the line someone gambled a lot of it away, but I still have enough to live the lifestyle I've always lived, and for better or for worse, I've always been content with who I am. No regrets, Megan, no regrets. Now that we are both ready, you will accompany me down the stairs and see me into the dining room." Megan closed the bedroom door behind her then followed Mavis. At the top of the stairs, she stopped and turned. "Megan," she said as she reached for her hand, "it may be none of my business, but this gentleman friend of yours?"

"Gentleman friend?" said Megan, looking confused, "I don't have a gentleman friend."

"Yes, you do," said Mavis, "Michael, Michael Gill."

"He's not my gentleman friend," said Megan with a little laugh.

"I didn't mean it that way," said Mavis, giving Megan a little nudge with her elbow. "But he is a gentleman and he is your friend."

"Well, yes, but I don't think our relationship should be termed in that way."

"I agree, so how would you describe your relationship with Michael?"

"Well," said Megan, "I hadn't really thought about it, but I would say he is like a grandfather to me, or how I would perceive a grandfather to be."

"It is as I expected," Mavis sighed, "which is a beautiful thing. And Michael, who incidentally I would like to meet, has no family?"

"No, he has no family and I am sorry if I have not told you more about him. Maybe I should have, but he is a somewhat private person, and like you, I regard our conversations as confidential and under no circumstances would I betray that trust."

"Megan Davies, I don't believe you! Just where on earth did you come from and at what schools were you educated?"

"You know very well where I came from, Miss Mavis," Megan said as she held Mavis' arm on descending the stairs. "But I must confess if I haven't told you before that my mother was an intelligent lady and, as well as teaching at Llandinam school, she also taught my brother and myself. She taught us up until the day she died. Now, Miss Mavis, I shall open the door and close it behind you, then I shall go and help out in the kitchen."

"Will you be serving drinks?" Mavis enquired.

"I don't think so, Miss Mavis, but whoever it is I'll make sure your 'Gin Ricky' is on the salver."

"Thank you, Megan - you're an angel."

"Not yet," said Megan as she opened the door to the dining room.

Everything went well, as it always did at the Rectory charity party. Local dignitaries, army captains and their subordinates and a number of wealthy guests who were staying at the Rectory, along with the Matron and an administrator of Montgomery County Infirmary were also present.

On this occasion, the intention was to raise money for the purchase of wheelchairs for the hospital. Men were still arriving home from the war. For some, it was too late and they died during their stay convalescing, but for others, a wheelchair would be their saving grace. Mavis had been to many such charities in London where she had encountered the rich and famous, the haves and the wish-they-hads, then aiming her eloquent charm and saucy innuendos at selected individuals, money would be forthcoming without the aid of a gun. The rich would still be rich and the famous a little more so if they got their names in the gossip magazines. The haves would have a little less and the wish-they-hads had already excused themselves and disappeared to the water closet.

Megan entered the dining room with a tray of cucumber sandwiches and was immediately besieged by guests with little plates in their hands. People were hovering around the dining room table on which was spread food that was gleaned from far and wide; a big bowl of Caesar salad stood in the centre; around it were salvers of cold fillets of trout with horseradish sauce, cold pork and beef, hors d'oeuvres, canapés, slabs of cheese, tomatoes, jelly trifle, chocolate-covered fudge, angel cakes, ham sandwiches and the only hot food on the table - two terrines of hot potatoes. Megan stood by the French windows that opened to the lawns outside. The sun was shining and a faint breeze disturbed the curtains she was standing by.

She sensed an air of excitement in the people who were gathered; she didn't doubt that the ending of the war had a lot to do with it, and the realization that many more young men would not die at the hands of other young men. A lot of people would sing and dance and would hug everyone that would hug them back. Then there were those who would go into the bedroom of a loved one and weep.

A tall good-looking gentleman in army uniform approached Megan and placed two empty sherry glasses on her tray, thanked her, then picked up two full ones off the dining room table. As she looked at him, her mind strayed to Bill, when the unmistakable voice of Enrico Caruso singing Santa Lucia could be heard. Megan looked for the source of the sound that everyone was listening to. In the right-hand corner of the room, the Reverend Jenkins was holding the cover of Enrico's recording. Reverend Jenkins usually kept his phonograph in the sitting room, but on occasions like this, it was brought into the dining room as he wanted to let people experience the voice of this master of the opera.

Where was he, Megan thought. Probably still in Egypt, but doing what? They can't sit in the sun all day. Megan was about to return to the kitchen when Mavis came through the French windows, her arm threaded through the arm of a man with a lot of medals on his chest.

"Captain Matthew Saunders Wilson, I would like you to meet…." immediately the officer looked around to see who Mavis was introducing him to now. "This," she said, stopping in front of Megan, "is my personal assistant and confidante, Miss Megan Davies." The captain looked disappointed when he realised that Mavis was introducing him to a housemaid.

"Pleased to meet you, Miss Davies," he said as he bowed his head.

"Likewise, I'm sure," Megan replied as she did a little curtsey.

'Difficult enough,' thought Mavis, 'while holding a tray of glasses.' As they turned, Megan overheard Miss Mavis say, "Captain Wilson, we must never assume that some people who are there to serve us have nothing more to give. Some of your men gave their lives and Megan's knowledge of opera is such as to put us both to shame."

As they walked away, Mavis turned and gave Megan a wink. Megan disposed of her tray of empty glasses and, on her return, Dame Nellie Melba and Enrico Caruso were singing a duet. It was, as the Rev Jenkins informed Megan a few days earlier, an aria from Puccini's La Bohème.

Guests were mingling and placing money into wine buckets, encouraged to do so by, amongst others, the Matron of Newtown Hospital who had made a speech telling of the sacrifices our soldiers had made. It was an emotive speech, making everyone aware of the need to help these men.

Mavis got to her feet and, leading by example, placing in a bucket what clearly could be seen as a twenty-pound note. Megan felt there was a genuine feeling of gratitude as she walked outside and onto the lawn. She noticed that, after making their donations, some people started to leave, while others were content to stay sitting and talking, enjoying the afternoon sunshine.

Megan saw her brother and Rose sitting at one of the tables; David stood as Megan approached. Placing her tray on the table, Megan smiled. "It's nice that both of you could call," she said. "I was beginning to wonder if I'd see you."

"Bill's mother called," said Rose, "and offered to look after the children for an hour or so and we took advantage of her offer, so here we are."

"Have you had anything to eat? There is still food on the table," said Megan. "Go and help yourselves and have a glass of wine, as you know it has all been donated."

"Wine?" asked David.

"Yes," said Megan, saying that some of the wine was homemade and given by local people. David and Rose helped Megan fill her tray with more empty glasses, then followed her across the lawn and into the dining room.

Caruso and Dame Nelly Melba had finished their aria and the record had been placed back in its cover, their singing having been replaced by someone playing the piano. Megan looked up and saw Miss Mavis heading in her direction, weaving past people but never losing eye contact.

"Megan," Mavis said on reaching her, "I was wondering if I might ask a favour of you. You remember this morning us talking about your friend, Mr. Michael Gill? Well. I was wondering if you wouldn't mind introducing me to him one day, maybe one day next week."

"Of course, I wouldn't mind," said Megan as she lifted another full tray. "I think it's a lovely idea." David, standing close by, said hello to Mavis and told Megan that he would see her later.

"I go up on Tuesday after I leave here, so if you would care to come with me, I will introduce you to him. Oh, and by the way, Miss Mavis," Megan said smiling, "you know that I know absolutely nothing about opera." Mavis, with eyes wide open, looked at Megan and chuckled.

"Well," she said, "Capitan Mathew Saunders Wilson doesn't know that, does he? He's a nice man but has delusions of grandeur and I don't care much for men who perceive themselves to be something they are not."

She turned to go, then turning back, she said, "Could you come and see me before you go home? Now I must mingle," she added as she turned and waved at someone who had caught her eye.

Delusions of grandeur, Megan thought to herself, was something Miss Mavis did not have; indeed, Miss Mavis was grandeur itself. Megan smiled as she headed for the kitchen.

Later, Megan knocked and entered the drawing room. She stood for a moment.

"Yes, Megan?" said Reverend Jenkins on seeing her.

"Miss Mavis requested that I see her before leaving."

Mavis, seated with her back to Megan, rose to her feet on hearing her voice. "If you will all excuse me for a moment," she said, placing her drink on a side table as she walked toward Megan. On reaching her, she whispered, "Come with me, I have a little something for you." In her bedroom, Mavis opened the top drawer of her bedside table and brought out a little black box. She handed it to Megan.

"Open it," she said softly. Megan did as Mavis asked, and inside was a small bottle of perfume.

"That," Mavis said excitedly, "is a French perfume. A lady friend of mine bought me a bottle from the Caron

Perfume House, 10 rue de la Paix, Paris. It's a new perfume called Tabac Blond Caron. Megan, this may not even be on the streets of London yet, so I thought I would give you some especially for you to wear when you give Bill a hug when he returns home." Megan looked at the bottle, her eyes filling up.

"Miss Mavis, you are so kind."

"Open it, Megan, and have a smell." Megan took the glass stopper off the bottle and bent her head.

"It's like something I have never smelt before - I can smell vanilla, carnation, cedar, and there is a leathery scent to it."

"Megan," Mavis exclaimed, "this will be the scent of the twenties!" Now you get yourself home and thank you for all your help; it has been a very successful day. No doubt I will see you tomorrow."

"You will, Miss Mavis, you will - and thank you."

When Mavis had closed the door behind Megan, her brother, who had seen them both leave the main guest room together and on hearing the outside door being closed, approached his sister.

"Mavis", he said frowning, "I hope you don't mind, umm... I need to talk to you." Mavis tilted her head, knowing that something was coming, "Don't you think that your relationship with Megan is," he hesitated. "Well, don't you think you're getting a little too familiar with each other? I mean, we mustn't lose sight of the fact that she is a maid in this household and not a guest." She looked him square in the eye and said;

"Brother dear, my relationship with Megan is my business. You know how well we get on, and to me, she is much more than a maid, she is my friend. You know her history as well as I do. She is honest, trustworthy, never shies away from tasks she has been given and her hunger for wanting to better herself without being bullish is exemplary. Good God, Daniel, I can't believe that you have even questioned my relationship with Megan; and that's another thing, my use of what some people may say inappropriate, or should I say, language unbecoming for a lady, never mind a vicar's sister." Mavis glanced away, "I know sometimes I let you down in that department and I'm sorry, really sorry, but I am who I am and I'm afraid you will have to put up with my shortcomings like you always have." She looked up and smiled. "To me, you are my brother, not a man of the cloth who preaches the word of God on Sundays. You are a good man, Daniel and I understand your concern for Megan, and maybe your concern for me comes into it. Could it be, you think that by spending too much time in my company, she will end up like me"? Mavis gave a little laugh.

"Well, you can rest assured, Megan will never end up like me. She's too smart and I would never let her. Now, we will have no more of this kind of talk, I have said my piece." Mavis slipped her arm through her brothers and patted his hand.

"Let's rejoin our guests." Daniel walked with his sister, not daring to say a word. She was right, he thought, she was what she was and maybe he should be thankful for it.

12

The following morning, Rose hurriedly called at the Rectory to inform Mavis that Megan was unwell and was in bed with what she suspected to be the flu. Rose had quarantined Megan, not even allowing the children upstairs. Mavis then told Rose that the Reverend Jenkins had also gone down with flu-like symptoms; she had also confined him to his bedroom, insisting he receive no visitors. Thankfully, the virus that was causing concern was not the one that was widespread throughout the country, causing the deaths of so many people during the last year.

Two days later, Megan was sitting in the parlour when Mavis walked in. Rose offered her a seat and asked if she would like a cup of tea.

"Thank you, Rose," said Mavis, "that would be lovely.

And how are you feeling, Megan?" Mavis asked as she sat down.

"A lot better, thank you. All being well, I'll be back at the Rectory tomorrow."

"How is the Reverend Jenkins?" asked Rose, as she placed a cup of tea on the table in front of her.

"First things first," answered Mavis, "Daniel is not expecting you tomorrow, Megan, as everything has been taken care of. And secondly, he is up and letting everyone know it. Thank goodness I am leaving tomorrow, as he has driven everyone to distraction. I mean, he gets a new recording and plays it over and over; there is only so much of Caruso and Dame Nelly Melba one can stand. He was playing it as I left the Rectory to come and see you."

Megan and Mavis talked for half an hour, Megan apologizing for not taking Mavis up to meet Michael and saying that she should call and see him herself.

"You don't need me to introduce you to him," she said.

"I wouldn't dream of it," Mavis said. "Anyway, it wouldn't be the right thing for me to do to knock on someone's door and introduce myself. There will be another time, Megan. Now, I will leave you in peace, as I have some packing to do and I'm afraid I won't be seeing you for some time, as I have a friend in Switzerland who has invited me to stay for a while. I will tell you all about it when I see you next."

From Megan's door, Mavis didn't go to the Rectory to pack. She walked on up through the village, passing some allotments on the left and the Upper House on the right. She stopped and looked at the inn and thought that in all the years she had been coming to the village she had never stepped inside the building. "Must call in next time I'm here," she said to herself. Fifty or so yards further on, there was a branch in the road. It turned right, and if she were to walk up the steep incline, it would take her to the village graveyard; another hundred yards further on the right was Michael Gill's stone cottage. As she stood looking at the road, temptation and curiosity nearly got the better of her, but then she thought of Megan, turned and walked the walk she had intended doing. Mavis had been walking no more than five minutes when she stopped to pick some wildflowers from the hedgerow. 'I'll put these in my bedroom,' she thought. As she looked up, she saw a man walking towards her. He had a walking stick and what looked like a rabbit over his shoulder. As he got closer, she noticed he was not a young man and, not surprisingly, walked with a slight stoop. He was clean-shaven and wore the customary cloth cap. As they met, he smiled.

"Been picking wildflowers?" he asked, looking at the small posy that Mavis held.

"Yes," Mavis said then, smiling. She looked and nodded at the rabbit; "and you have got yourself some meadow beef"!

"Meadow beef!" replied the man with a chuckle, a little surprised at her remark. "Caught two with some wires I put down yesterday."

It was then that Mavis noticed another rabbit hanging down his back, both rabbits being tied by their back feet and slung over his shoulder.

"You are not from these parts," he said.

"No", I'm from London. I visit every so often; my brother is the vicar here."

"The vicar Reverend Daniel Jenkins, here in Llandyssil?" the man said, still smiling, "so, he is your brother?"

"Yes, he is, and my name is…"

"Don't tell me," the man said with some excitement in his voice.

"You're Miss Mavis, aren't you?"

"Yes, I am, and you are?"

"I'm Michael Gill."

"I thought you might be," Mavis said. "Delighted to meet you."

Mavis offered her hand and, as Michael shook it, he remarked;

"It's nice to finally meet you. Megan has told me so much about you."

"Yes, it is, isn't it? Megan has told me about you too."

"Now," Michael said. "You must come with me; we can't talk here on the road. I believe you are going back to London tomorrow? and unless you have other things planned."

"Yes, I will be returning to London tomorrow, Michael, and as I have an hour or so, I would like to see your home."

"It's not as grand as homes you are accustomed to, Miss Mavis, but it's my home."

Mavis stopped and faced Michael.

"Now, Mr Gill, there is one thing I would like to make clear before we carry on and that is, to Megan, on account of her position at the Rectory, I am Miss Mavis. It is a name we have both got accustomed to over the last four years, but there is absolutely no reason for you to address me as such."

"And pray, how do people at the Rectory address you?" Mavis looked at the rabbits that hung on Michael's shoulder.

"Miss Mavis," she said quietly, "except for my brother and he calls me a lot of things".

"So," said Michael, "being that you are known as Miss Mavis at the Rectory, and everyone in the village refers to you as Miss Mavis, including people who you have never even met, I would be pleased if you didn't make an exception of me by insisting I call you anything other than Miss Mavis. In any case, Miss Mavis suits you."

"Alright, Mr. Gill, I will, with reluctance, concede to your request; and how would you like me to address you?"

"You, Miss Mavis, can call me Michael. It's my name and I've had it a long time. Now, let's climb this hill and sit you down."

Surprisingly, Mavis had no difficulty climbing the steep hill to Michael's home and, as they walked, they chatted away like old friends that hadn't seen each other for a long time. Outside Michael's home, they turned and looked across the valley.

"You didn't come to the charity party?" Mavis said, still gazing at the view.

"No," Michael answered. "I'm afraid I'm not one for crowds of people. It isn't that I don't like them, I like them a lot but, unlike you Miss Mavis, I'm more of a one to one person and, heaven forbid, the world should be full of people like me. You, on the other hand, are like," he paused, "like a heartbeat." Mavis turned her head and looked at Michael, who himself was still looking at the hills and valleys that lay before them, "always there taking charge, like a captain of a ship, steering people towards being the best they can be."

Michael then turned and, with a big smile, looked Mavis in the eyes. She, in turn, did the same and saw a twinkle that she had seen before.

"My God," she said as she grabbed his arm, "it's you, isn't it?"

"Yes, it is," Michael said.

"My God, you're the man we gave a lift to all those years ago, the man with the beard, the man who kissed my hand. My God, Michael, I have to sit down, this is all too much!" There was excitement and joy, touched with a little anguish, in her voice, as Michael reached for her arm and guided her through his door.

Sitting her down on his chair, he went outside and took the rabbits that were still slung over his shoulder, hanging them on a nail that was driven into a mortar joint in the wall outside his door. When he went inside, he found Mavis with her hands to her face, laughing and crying all at the same time. He placed his hand on her shoulder as he dragged over another chair, asking if he could sit next to her.

"For Christ's sake, Michael, it's your bloody chair!" she said laughing.

"Well," he answered, "I didn't want to appear too familiar."

"Too familiar!" Mavis exclaimed, still laughing, "it didn't seem to bother you thirty-eight years ago when you kissed my hand."

"It seemed the right thing to do at the time," Michael said, timidly. They both burst out laughing.

"And when did you know it was me?" she asked.

"The moment you told me you were from London; plus, on the right side of your neck just below your earlobe you have a little mole. I saw it when you brushed your hair back, just before I kissed your hand."

"You remember that?" Mavis said in a surprised voice.

"Yes, surprisingly enough, I do."

For the next hour, in short, sharp, breathless flurries, they told each other their life stories, only omitting those details that decorum decreed could wait until later.

"Now, Miss Mavis," Michael said as he rose from his chair, "would you like a drink?"

"Michael," Mavis answered, "you wouldn't have a little something to calm me down, would you? At the moment, I feel like a little girl who has opened other children's Christmas presents."

"I think I have just the drink for you," he said as he opened his bedroom door. Mavis looked around; she noticed how bare it was. The room was clean and tidy; even the slate hearth was free of ash. Everything was in its place except for a large silver candelabra that stood on a dresser alongside the bedroom door. But there was something missing, thought Mavis. Pictures on the wall, a shotgun leaning in a corner, boxes of cartridges on the windowsill, a cloth cap hanging from a nail in the oak lintel above the fireplace. The only thing of a feminine nature in the room was a tatted-edged tablecloth on the kitchen table behind her. Maybe it was that the room lacked the feel of a woman's presence, although what it did have was a feeling of being lived in; it was "cosy", Mavis said out loud, as Michael came through the door carrying a bottle. Behind him, walking slowly and unsteadily on his feet, was Shy, who went up to Mavis and laid his head on her knee.

"This is Shy," said Michael as he placed two sherry glasses on the table.

"Yes, I know," Mavis replied, stroking his head, "we've met before. At the Rectory when Megan has brought him along and a couple of times in the village, once outside the shop, probably waiting for you."

"Probably," said Michael.

"Shy; it's an unusual name for a dog, isn't it?" Mavis queried.

"He and the ones before him were named in memory of a man I once knew who fought in Shiloh during the American Civil War," Michael explained as he walked from the table and handed Mavis a glass of...

"Damson gin!" said Mavis.

"Now," said Michael, "is that a question or a statement?"

"A statement," said Mavis smiling.

"So, you already know what it is?"

"Yes."

"And how do you know what it is?" asked Michael a little bewildered.

"Because it says so on the bottle." Michael turned and saw the bottle on the table, the label Michael had placed on it clearly visible from where Mavis was sitting.

"My God, Michael, that's some good stuff," Mavis said as she took a sip.

"It's last year's; made myself a few bottles," he said as he held his sherry glass and sat down again next to Mavis.

"Megan," Mavis said suddenly, "you know she thinks of you with great affection?"

"And I do her," said Michael in a more serious tone. "Surely after all the time that I have known her, you are not about to question my relationship with her."

"Michael...Michael," Mavis whispered, placing her hand on his arm, "Megan has known you for much the same length of time as she has known me and, like you, I have seen her grow from an insecure yet determined fifteen-year-old into the sophisticated young lady she is today. She has told me a little about you and no doubt she has told you a little about me. When I first met her, she reminded me of myself. I liked her from the moment I met her and I was determined to mould her into the woman she was destined to be. Mould is probably the wrong word, but I know that she will be the woman she wants to be. As for you, Michael Gill, it is no wonder she has turned out to be what she is. In you, she has found strength and many things that I could not give her and although, until today, we didn't know each other, I am secretly rather proud of you." Mavis looked up to see Michael sitting in silence as she spoke of Megan.

"I...." he was about to speak when Mavis interrupted.

"Did you know that she regards you as being like a grandfather to her?" Michael smiled.

"That's nice," he said, "and you, Miss Mavis, have been like a grandmother to her. She tells me of the little things you bring her, which means you think of her even when you are in London."

"Yes, I do," said Mavis. "I can't help it."

"So, where do we go from here?" he said, taking the few steps towards the kitchen table, bringing back the bottle. "Another one?" he asked as he filled up his glass.

"I will", she said as she handed him her empty glass.

"We just carry on like we have done," she said as he handed her back her glass. Mavis then stood and faced Michael.

"I think," she said, "we should make a toast."

"To what?" Michael asked.

"To the future of all three of us." Michael smiled as they touched glasses.

"Down in one."

"Down in one."

Then, just before they drank their toast, Mavis exclaimed, "I never thought myself as being a grandmother, but I like it," she said as she raised her glass, "I like it."

"And now, Michael, I must be off or Daniel will be wondering where I am." Michael walked to the door then turned to face Mavis.

"Thank you, Mavis, I have really enjoyed your company and I hope you will call again."

"Michael," Mavis said reaching for his arm, "would you do me a big favour? It is something I have never asked a man to do before and I promise I will never ask you again."

Michael answered with a surprised look on his face.

"Miss Mavis, if I can, I will."

"Will you give me a cwtch? Megan has told me that a cwtch is something special and, at this moment, I need something special."

"And at this moment it seems the right thing to do," said Michael with a smile. That sentence meant everything to Mavis; he wrapped his arms around her, and hers around him. Then, with her head on his shoulder, a feeling of content swept over her. She had a sense of being held, for no reason other than being held, with no commitment on her part to give, as he took her breath away. When they parted, Mavis said quietly, "My God, Megan was right."

Michael walked her to the road, then she said, "Michael, you know that promise I just made, would you mind terribly if I were to break it?"

"Not at all, Miss Mavis, not at all," he said and then, for the second time, he kissed her hand.

Mavis didn't look back, she couldn't look back for fear of him standing where she had left him, watching her walk, what seemed like the loneliest and longest road in her life.

"My God," she said, words stuttering from her mouth, "did that really happen? Was it him? Was that really him?" Once she realised she was out of his sight and Michael could no longer see her, she stopped. She looked at her hands; they were trembling, her breathing was as erratic as her heartbeat and her mind was somewhere it had never been before. "For God's sake," she said, stamping her feet. "Mavis Jenkins, you are a sixty-six-year-old woman and things like this don't happen to a woman of your age." Then her thoughts began to tumble over themselves.

"What things don't happen, Mavis? You bloody well know what things; you're not in love with him, are you

Mavis? Don't talk so bloody stupid and anyway, I won't let it happen," she muttered to herself as, with some determination, she stepped forward.

"Thank God, I am leaving tomorrow," she said as she passed the pub and, "I am not going to call at Megan's, I am not going to call at Megan's."

Megan answered the door as Mavis was turning away, already cursing herself for her weakness in calling. She wanted to carry on but her feet found themselves outside Megan's home and her hand knocking on her door.

"I'm sorry," Mavis blurted, "I didn't want to call but I had to."

"Mavis," Megan exclaimed, "whatever is the matter? Has something happened?"

"You could say that," Mavis said, her voice shaking. "I have to tell someone and you are the only one I can talk to… you are the only one who will understand."

"For goodness sake come in and sit down. We can talk in the sitting room. Rose has taken the children for a walk and David is in the blacksmith's shop." When Mavis was seated, Megan asked if she would like something to drink.

"Another damson gin!" Mavis cried.

"Another?" said Megan raising her eyebrows.

"I think you had better sit down, as after I tell you what's happened, you may want a damson gin yourself. You know me better than anyone," Mavis said, looking down, wringing her hands, "you know me better than I know myself."

She raised her head and looked at Megan, "How the hell did you get to be so mature at such a young age?"

"I think you had a lot to do with that, Miss Mavis. You, David, Rose and of course, Michael. Why, is there a problem? And where, might I ask, have you been since you left here over two hours ago?"

"No, there is no problem; I just went for a walk."

"And?" said Megan.

"And I met someone," said Mavis, calmly.

"Can I ask who?"

Mavis told Megan everything, even telling her about Megan's thoughts on Michael being like a grandfather to her and his suggestion that Mavis, much like himself, treated Megan as a granddaughter. Megan sat through it all and didn't say a word, except when Mavis told her that she asked him if he could give her a cwtch before she went.

"A cwtch!" said Megan smiling, "that was a fatal move."

"And don't I know it," said Mavis slowly, closing her eyes at the same time.

"I walked from his home in goddamn pieces," she giggled. Megan got up from her seat.

"You know that drink you said we both may need? Well, I just so happen to have a bottle of damson gin myself, one that Michael gave me. Fancy one?"

"Are you kidding? But only if you are having one," Mavis said, sounding a little apologetic. Megan went and opened a drawer in the Welsh dresser opposite.

"I'm afraid we don't have any sherry glasses," she said, "you will have to drink it out of a small tumbler."

"Megan, at the moment, I would drink it out of a small bucket."

Megan poured the drinks and handed one to Mavis.

"So, what are you going to do about it?" Megan said as she sat down.

"I don't know," Mavis answered with a groan. "I will go back to London tomorrow and think, think long and hard. The truth is I have never felt like *this* before."

"Never?" Megan interrupted.

"Never; if I had I would have told you so."

"You said," Megan queried, "that you have never felt like *this* before - just what exactly is... *this?*"

"Now don't you put me in a corner, Megan Davies, you know what I am talking about!"

"No, I don't, how should I know what *this* is? I am nineteen years old, Miss Mavis, how should I know?" Megan grinned at Mavis before taking another sip of her drink.

"Tell me, Megan, are you in love with Bill?"

"That is different," Megan answered back.

"Is it, is it really?"

"Yes, yes, it is. I may have been writing to him for four years, but I was fifteen when I last saw him."

"You last saw him four years ago. I haven't seen Michael for thirty-eight years, what's the difference?"

"Thirty-four years," said Megan laughing.

"Very good answer," said Mavis, almost laughing herself. "But you still haven't answered my question."

"Yes," she said, "yes I think I am in love with Bill, but I won't know until I see him."

"No, of course you won't."

"Is this what it's all about, Miss Mavis, you think that you could be in love with Michael?"

"I don't know," said Mavis with a slight shake in her voice, "I really don't know. Now, I really must go," Mavis said, as she placed her tumbler in Megan's hand. "You don't know how much better I feel. I walked in here in pieces and I am walking out, still in pieces, but not so many of them." As they walked to the door, Mavis stopped; "Can I ask you for some advice?" she said softly.

"Ask *me*... for advice?"

"I would like your advice if you have any."

Megan thought for a moment, "Don't wait too long."

"Too long," Mavis repeated.

"Don't let this moment slip through your fingers. Next time you see him you give him... a cwtch."

Megan closed the door and, with a heavy heart, she leaned against it, tears starting to run down her face. "How much time will she have with him?" she thought in despair, for Michael is a sick man.

Four weeks later, Megan was surprised to learn that Mavis was due back at the Rectory. On her arrival, the services of Megan were again required and as she carried her cases up the stairs and into her room, Mavis started to tell Megan all about her travels. After being settled in, she told Megan of her thoughts about leaving London and coming to live permanently in Llandyssil. Megan's response was one of caution, reminding Mavis that living in Llandyssil was a far cry from the excitement of living in London. To this, Mavis replied that she had already had all the excitement that she needed in her life, stating at the same time that she intended to pursue a friendship with Michael, who had been constantly on her mind while she was away.

13

On the 29th of October, the 7th Battalion marched to Latron and then on to Ramia, a town twenty-three miles from Jerusalem. From there, they boarded a train to Kantara on the Suez. There were mixed emotions on the train journey back to Kantara. Jim sat by a window looking at the passing scenery that he and his fellow soldiers had walked. Now and again, he would recognise a hill or a section of barren landscape that he would like to forget. They would pass gangs of Turkish prisoners working on the line and every so often, the train would pull off the main track to let another pass, going in the opposite direction. He looked over to see Jack slumped in his seat sleeping, and Bill was busy writing but soon gave up as the motion of the train made his handwriting illegible even to himself. He noticed other men, who were doing much the same things.

Bill reached into the breast pocket of his tunic, pulling out a packet of cigarettes and a trench lighter. He casually looked at the packet. On the front was a picture of a British soldier carrying war souvenirs, and underneath were the words, "Some souvenirs, but - I'll give them all for a Helmars. Makers of the highest-grade Turkish and Egyptian cigarettes in the world." He took out a cigarette and was about to light it when the train stopped. He looked out of the window and saw some wooden structures and men scurrying back and forth, some carrying picks and shovels, others, he presumed, filling up the water tanks of the train.   Again, he looked at the buildings and then the surrounding landscape, realising with some remorse that this was the place that they arrived at, after coming out of the desert, all that time ago. He thought of Ian, Tom, Ivor and Trevor, Trevor having perished in the First Battle of Gaza and Ivor falling sick soon after.

It took seven hours to travel the 230 miles, pulling into Kantara late in the evening. Two days later, the Turkish armistice came into force, ending hostilities. It would be another sixteen months before the boys set sail from Alexandria and, during the tedious period of waiting for demobilization, the boys had seen thousands of men leave. Each time a ship sailed, they wished it was them going home but it wasn't to be.

Football became an interest to them, as the Battalion team advanced to the finals of the Egyptian Expeditionary Force's cup. The game was played off in Cairo where the team, under the captaincy of George Latham, beat the Royal Irish Fusiliers 3 – 0. There was a lot of rejoicing as the winner's cup was presented on the pitch by Lady Allenby, wife of Field Marshall Edmund Allenby, Commander of the Expeditionary Force in Egypt.

Bill wrote numerous letters to his mother and Megan, explaining their situation of not knowing how long they would have to remain in Egypt. Letters he received back, especially from Megan, he would read many times, particularly the one when Megan had heard of the war's end. In it, she spoke of her joy that he was still alive and well, and it didn't matter how long she would have to wait until she would see him again, but wait she would. She never mentioned anything about Jack or Jim and, whether it was intentional or an oversight, he didn't know, but her longing to see him was evident in her writing. She closed her letter with the words "Come home soon, all my love, Megan". All her letters after that ended with those words, "love, Megan". During this time, Bill had begun to teach Jim the fundamentals of reading and writing. He had already learnt how to write his name and his ability in learning to read surprised Bill. His writing and spelling were another matter, however toward the end of their stay in Egypt, he managed to write a letter to Violet.

Jack was still full of army life; he seemed to like it, especially now the war was over, and he wasn't as keen to go home as Bill and Jim were.

"What have I got to go home to?" he would say. "Jim has a wife and children, Bill a lovely lady waiting for him and if I want a lady, all I have to do is go to Cairo," as he did when they went there to watch the final of the football match.

Then, in early February 1919, while on guard duty, the lads were relieved of their posts and were moved to the transit camp in Port Said. Six days later, on the 21st what was left of the 7th proceeded to Alexandria. The following day, these men, all fifty-one of them, embarked for the UK on His Majesty's troopship, *Cear*.

The journey home was, in some respects, a sombre one. Their trip to Egypt, unlike their journey home, was then a journey into the unknown, full of nervous excitement and adventure like no other. Now, after three years and ten months of being away, this trip home may well be a trip of nervous excitement, but it was nervous excitement of a different kind. The adventure was over and their thoughts now were of holding loved ones in their arms once again.

Everything seemed to happen so quickly; one minute they were on a ship and the next they were on a train going home. There were many men of various regiments saying their goodbyes as they left the train and then, before the train's doors slammed shut, their shouts of delight could be heard as they stood once again on familiar ground. At Welshpool, more men got off, these being men of the 7th, men that the boys had got to know well. Hands were shaken and farewells were said. Then, on the last leg of their journey, the lads learnt that a homecoming reception awaited the Newtown boys, with the Silver Band, local dignitaries and, no doubt crowds of people to cheer them as they stepped down from the train. Most were excited about the prospect, but there were two who didn't want to be part of it and decided they would get off the train at Abermule, the station before Newtown, and walk home. At Montgomery station, seven men got off the train: Bill, Jack, Jim and four others; they stood and watched the train disappear up the track in front of them.

As the Montgomery boys walked away, Jack turned and muttered, "I think I'll go to Montgomery with these boys. They're going to the Checkers for a drink, so I'll tag along." Jim and Bill walked in silence for a while.

"What are you thinking?" Bill asked, not looking up from the road.

"I don't know," Jim answered. "My stomach is in knots and I don't know how I will meet Violet and the children." Bill stopped.

"Jim," he said, "would you mind if I leave you? These hills await my footsteps." He smiled; "I have a need to walk the fields before I go home."

"Not at all," Jim said, smiling, "I have a need to be alone myself." With that, Bill climbed over a gate then turned and with a half-smile said,

"I'll be seeing you Jim; it hasn't exactly been fun has it?"

"No," replied Jim, the smile not leaving his face, "no, it hasn't."

With that, Bill quickened his pace, as to walk through a lush green meadow was something he had yearned to do for such a long time.

14

In New York City on the 25th April 1865, Michael Barry Gill found himself marching in the funeral procession of Abraham Lincoln. The President of the United States of America had been shot and killed eleven days before, at Ford's Theatre in Washington. Posters of the wanted man accused of his murder were to be seen everywhere - in shop windows, tied around lamp posts, even people on street corners were handing out sheets of paper on which the image of America's most wanted man was printed. There was a bounty of 100,000 dollars for the capture of a man named as John Wilkes Booth and his accomplices.

Marching in the funeral procession was the last military act Michael did as a soldier. At sunset, he returned to his barracks, only to find the Irish Brigade didn't want him anymore and he didn't want them. He handed in his rifle and walked away. The war for Michael was over. Carrying his belongings, he walked to Manhattan and found lodgings not far from where he used to live. For two weeks, he indulged himself in his own company, and in those two weeks a lot of things came about. A day after the funeral procession, John Wilkes Booth had been found, shot and killed. Michael called around to see his last employer, Gordon Doyle, and his wife Margaret. They welcomed him like a long-lost son, overjoyed that he had come through the war alive and well. He was offered his job back and told that he could start whenever he liked. As they talked, Mrs Doyle excused herself and left the room, only to return carrying a small cardboard box.

"Your box, Michael," she said, "the one you left for safekeeping."

"Ah, my box. I had almost forgotten about it - thank you for looking after it."

"Not at all," said Margaret through a beaming smile, "it's so nice to be able to give it back to you." They talked some more and as Michael was about to leave, Gordon asked him if he was alright for money.

"That's very kind of you," Michael answered, "but really, I have enough to last me until my next week's wages."

They laughed at Michael's answer, suggesting that he would be back at work when he was ready. As the door closed behind him, Michael, with the cardboard box tucked under his arm, thought of the people he had just left. His heart was lifted by their generosity and thoughtfulness, but he knew that one day he would say goodbye to them, never to return.

Two weeks to the day after handing in his rifle, the American Civil War was over. And it was two days after, that a past employee of Doyle and Simpson resumed work again.

It was three years before the pangs of home started to seep into Michael's mind. Although he loved his work and the friends he had made, even with a growing feeling of being a part of somewhere, it didn't stop his yearning to see home. His social life was steady but sometimes lonely, and when he felt lonely, his Megan would enter his mind and the thoughts of how life could have been, had she lived, didn't sit kindly with him. His need for a woman, however distasteful to some, was satisfied in the company of the ladies of lower Manhattan. But it was never enough; he wanted more, and with no plans for the future, he decided to return to Ireland, even if it was for only a short while.

In a matter of weeks, he was striding the gangplanks of a steamer, having acquired a one-way ticket to the country of his birth. Saying goodbye to his friends was hard and saying goodbye to the Doyles was harder still. They had asked him to call on the morning of his leaving, which he did. Mrs Doyle had made him a packed lunch that she had placed inside a small bag along with three books. As she hugged him, she said that she didn't think they would ever see him again and wished him a safe journey. Gordon handed him an envelope and asked him not to open it until he was aboard.

Halfway through the journey, Michael celebrated his 30th birthday; he had been away for eleven years.

Michael's trip back to Ireland reminded him of his journey going the other way, the contrast being that he was a different person now. Now he understood the insecurities he had experienced as a young man, although at the time there was no one more ready for the adventure that he was then to undertake. Even so, he had now experienced life and death in all its forms. He had learned to navigate the pitfalls of poverty and the joys of what an affluent lifestyle could bring. But he, like everyone else, recognised that the dominant factor in realising your dreams and aspirations was nothing more than having the financial means to do so and, in that, nothing had changed.

He looked at the sea; it was the same sea but with different waves. The waves now crashing into the bow of the ship were like the challenges to his life, ones that had tested. and always would test. the man that he had become.

Michael had read the books Mrs Doyle had given him and, interestingly, in one of them was a loose page of printed paper containing some writing of what he presumed to be an American poet.

'*I Taste a Liquor Never Brewed*'

Michael read the composition a number of times and as he did, his thoughts returned to the parks and gardens of Manhattan, the ones he would walk after Megan's death, and again at the end of the war. Some lines were poignant to his thinking at this time. A sense of peace and tranquility began to fill a void that he didn't know was empty, as he spoke out loud, reading one of the verses.

'*When landlords turn the drunken bee,*
Out of the foxglove's door,
When butterflies renounce their drams,
I shall but drink some more'

He wondered if Mrs Doyle had placed the paper inside the book intentionally for him to read. If she did, he smiled, then she knew Michael's mind as much as he knew it himself. He then opened the envelope that Gordon had given him; inside was money and a letter. The money was an extra two weeks' wages and the letter was one thanking him for his service to the company over the last few years. It also contained an address in London, should he ever get there. He placed the money in his trouser pocket and the letter amongst the pages of one of Mrs Doyle's books.

Michael entered the port of Fenit on a grey and dismal day, not unlike the one he had left eleven years earlier and was met by his sister and her family. There was a lot of rejoicing that night with singing, drinking and dancing, something he had missed over the years. For the next eighteen months, Michael stayed and worked in Ireland, but the yearning to travel some more got the better of him. He caught a boat to Liverpool with the intention of working his way around England. Eventually, after three years of doing just that, he arrived in London.

London, at the latter end of 1874, was as busy as any time in its history. New buildings were going up all over the city and Michael took part in its development. He took lodgings just off Regent Street. His first job was on Regent Street itself, building a store called Liberty's. For the next seven years, his work never moved from Regent Street, working for the builder whose address Gordon Doyle had given him in his letter, the one he had opened on board ship on his return to Ireland.

Michael was forty years of age when he boarded a train out of London. His destination: Birmingham, and from there he travelled to Shrewsbury. He had never been to Wales, so he got on another train and headed for Aberystwyth but, for no other reason than curiosity, he got off at Montgomery station and started walking towards a little village he didn't know existed. As he walked, he was offered a ride in a horse-drawn carriage, the occupants of which were two young ladies whom he presumed to be in their mid-twenties. They never gave their names and he never gave his, but they had London accents, so they indulged themselves talking about London. The carriage stopped in a little village, and as he alighted, he held the white-gloved hand of the lady who had sat next to him and kissed it. He thanked them and waved them goodbye. Michael looked around; he was standing on the village green of Llandyssil and there he stayed, never to travel far again.

15

Bill had slept in his own bed for four nights before the nightmares began, four blissful nights of unconsciousness. The transition from army life to normality was unnerving. It was in the mornings that he felt it most; it was quiet, there was no shouting, no bugles being played, no sound of activity that hundreds of men would make in their eagerness or reluctance to start another day of soldiering. Instead, he would awake to his mother's voice asking if he was indeed awake. She would place a hot cup of tea on his bedside table before commenting on what sort of a morning it was, then asking if he had slept well.

In the four days that he had been home, she had not once asked about the fighting he had witnessed and, for that, he was grateful. She, like Megan, had followed the exploits of the 7th Battalion in the local paper and, throughout the war, had seen photographs and read about the deaths of local men, or boys, as she preferred to call them.

He knew she carried the pain of their mothers; even here in a house lost amongst the normality of civilization was a woman that the war had also touched. It saddened him knowing that things would never be the same again.

But not to be downhearted, he would, after a hearty breakfast of bacon, eggs, a slice of bread with dripping and two mugs of tea, don his cap, put a scarf around his neck and reach for his old overcoat that had hung on the back door for nearly four years. Once outside, he would walk towards the fields and woods that had been, and always would be, an important part of his life. 'The weather is quite mild for this time of year,' he thought. Although he had noticed it to be frosty in the mornings, by mid-morning, the sun would have come out and bathed the countryside in sunshine, melting the ice crystals that had covered the land during the night. With well-greased boots, thick corduroy trousers and an overcoat, he was well prepared for any cold winds that might come his way.

In the first three days, he had walked miles, north, south, east and west, crossing streams and brooks, climbing hills and descending valleys. He purposely kept away from villages and towns and if he came across any farm worker, he would acknowledge his presence and walk on. He found solace in his own company and the company of the birds and animals that he would meet. He would talk to them as if they were old friends; not that he expected them to talk back, but it gave him an inner peace to be amongst familiar surroundings and, probably for the first time, see things with eyes that had, in the past, missed so much. From the shire horses that would shy away on his approach and whose numbers were vastly reduced due to the war, to the red squirrels that looked inquisitively at him from behind tree branches. On the odd occasion, he would come upon a fox who would slouch away, showing no urgency or panic in its bid to distance itself from him. In the sky, buzzards would glide on outstretched wings, effortlessly soaring over open fields, looking for food that wasn't as forthcoming as in the long and bountiful days of summer.

He loved this life and thought he knew all that there was to know about country living. He had good teachers: his father, who had taught him how to tickle trout in the brooks and streams, his Uncle Mark who showed him at the age of six how to set snares to catch rabbits, this being food that didn't need money to acquire. He could name every bird that flew and every creature that walked and, until he had joined the army, this way of life was all he had known. Indeed, to a greater or lesser degree, every living person that he had known from childhood was accustomed to the ways of country life. Hard work and simple pleasures were common to them all, their place in society preordained and they would all serve the masters of their existence. It was expected of them and, knowing nothing else, they complied.

16

It was on the fifth day, while walking the railway line from Abermule to Kerry, that Bill came upon a blackbird with a broken wing. It fluttered and scrambled over the railway track, dragging its useless wing, making its way down a short incline, finding it difficult to negotiate the grass and undergrowth. Finally, it managed to crouch under the branch of a fallen tree, lying parallel to the track. Bill reached between and under a branch. Brambles had grown thick over the fallen tree, giving protection to the life that had sought sanctuary, a life it wouldn't give up without resistance. With scratched fingers, he retrieved the bird from its hiding place and there, in his cupped hands, was a very frightened and painfully injured bird. He could feel the vibration of its heart beating against the palms of his hands as he held it. Stroking its head with his finger, its jet-black feathers felt like velvet beneath his skin; it looked at him with fear in its eyes, a look he had seen many times before. His first instinct was to end its misery, but he couldn't bring himself to do that, so he placed it back under the branch and left it in the care of the brambles and briars. Nature would take its course, he thought, as it would be dead by morning anyway.

He was in open fields when Kerry station came into view. He had followed the railway line through a wooded dingle, its track twisting in line with the valley and, below the track, was a small river. The constant sound of its running water was in contrast to some of the quieter walks he had been on.

Turning away from Kerry station, he climbed a gate that ran alongside the railway line. It started to rain as he made his way towards a hay barn that was situated in the far corner of the field he was in. Reaching into his shoulder bag, he took out the small canvas sheet he carried, put it over his head and ran the last hundred yards to the barn. The rain was now quite heavy and it looked as if it was going to get worse.

Once inside, he removed the sheet and his overcoat, giving each one a shake and a rubdown with dry hay. The sound of the rain falling on the corrugated roof was such that he couldn't see himself moving from there for at least an hour. Making himself comfortable, he watched the rain fall.

His thoughts turned to the blackbird that he had left behind and concluded that the right thing to have done was to have knocked it on the head rather than to prolong its suffering by leaving it. He was annoyed with himself for letting his compassion interfere with the reality of his dilemma.

When Bill awoke, the rain had stopped and daylight was fading. He looked at his watch, it was ten past four.

He had been asleep for over two hours. With haste, he gathered his things and left the warmth and comfort of the barn. The musky smell of last summer's hay harvest accompanied him all the way home.

That night, after tea and during some light-hearted conversation with his parents, his mother informed him that Ian's father, the Reverend Daniel Brown, would be holding a special service in memory of Ian this coming Sunday and asked if he would be going. She already knew Bill's opinion of the vicar and wasn't surprised when he said he wouldn't be going. He could see the hurt in her eyes and felt the anguish in her voice as she tried to persuade him to go. He was tempted to deny himself and go along with her wishes, but his resolve was such that it would be wrong of him to go. How could he sit and listen to his friend's father rant on about the will of God, turning the other cheek and that bit about forgiving your enemies. He had heard it all before and thought that, if God is responsible for all the good in this world and the devil for all the evil, it seemed to him that God was on a winner whatever happened.

He rose from his chair and, placing his hand on his mother's shoulder, kissed her forehead and bid them both "goodnight." Glancing at his father, he thought how frail he looked sitting in a chair that was as old as himself and whose armrests were threadbare and worn. Leaning forward, his father reached for the poker and then shifted the burning logs that were in the fireplace. Reclining in his chair, he drew on his pipe, the smoke rising to further stain the ceiling that had become discoloured over the years.

Bill's mother was sitting opposite him in her chair, knitting an object which was, at this stage of its growth, unclear. The ball of rough home-spun yarn, probably made from the wool off the back end of a sheep, fell off her lap and onto the floor, rolling across the flagstones and under the Welsh dresser that stood opposite the fireplace. Retrieving it, Bill said goodnight, climbing the narrow stairs with the light from his candle casting moving shadows of himself on its walls. They followed him to the landing and into his bedroom. The shadows with undefined lines moved like a ghost drifting across the ceiling,

"Don't forget, I want a hand with Dick Morgan's pig in the morning," his father's voice, barely audible, drifted up the stairs into his room.

"Dick Morgan's pig," Bill repeated to himself, "Christ, haven't I seen enough blood?"

He undressed and put on the nightshirt that had been neatly folded and placed at the foot of the bed. He pulled back the covers and lay on the feather mattress that had been in his dreams many times whilst he was away. It wrapped itself around him like mist around a mountain top. It made him feel warm and secure. Childhood memories entered his mind and, just as quickly, they disappeared. He lay on his back and looked at the ceiling and upon its uneven and somewhat cracked surface, another shadow was now moving back and fore. The dark shadow seemed to fill the room; it danced from side to side, up and down and around in circles. He turned his head and saw a moth hovering above the flickering flame of the candle. "Goodnight, moth," he said as he blew out the subject of its interest.

Sleep did not come to Bill Jones that night, or subsequent nights thereafter. For when evenings came and darkness stealthily crept over the horizon, he dreaded what it would bring. New visions of old faces would smother him. His fears became twofold: firstly, the fear of sleep and secondly, the fear of his dreams, as to achieve the first would guarantee the second.

Bill turned on his side and, closing his eyes, thought of Megan Davies. But Megan wasn't in his thoughts for long. For somewhere along the way, she became the blackbird with the broken wing and, no matter how he tried, he couldn't rid his mind of this confounded creature. His fantasies of Megan were continually being interrupted by this bird and each time it returned, it became larger and Megan grew smaller, until Megan was no more but the blackbird stayed. In his dream, the blackbird was as big as an eagle. He asked it to leave and not to bother him anymore but the bird's ghostly eyes just stared. Then, turning, Bill ran, he ran down country lanes and over blue fields and when he stopped, the blackbird was still there behind him. He swam green oceans and climbed yellow mountains, upon which, each summit presented his tormentor. He then found himself back in the desert, running between cherry blossoms and above him always the blackbird, its presence never leaving him. Dick Morgan's pig ran by his side, blood pouring from a knife wound to its throat. It looked up at him and in an excited childlike voice shouted, "This is fun, isn't it?" In front of them, many Turkish soldiers lay spread-eagled in the sand, their faces turned to the sun, each one with a bayonet embedded in his chest as they sang, "For he's a jolly good fellow." He could see clearly, a partly dismembered woman in a shredded white shroud slumped up against a date palm with pink milk dripping from her breast. Then, from under the shadow of the blackbird, the pig ran ahead of him and out of sight.

Bill awoke with fear in his heart and an emptiness in his soul. He lit a candle and dressed as quickly as he could. He had to get out of the house; he had to see the stars and breathe the cold night air.

It was half-past three when he closed the back door. He had left the warmth and comfort of his bed and, like a man with the plague, he slipped into the night unseen and unheard.

The night was clear and frosty, the light from the moon creating a haunting silhouette of the hills and trees that surrounded him. The only sound he could hear was that of the metal studs of his boots as they made contact with the road as he walked. Quickening his pace, he walked into Llandyssil.

The village was stark and empty, the cloak of darkness having consumed all life until sunrise. He walked through the village passing a row of brick cottages on his left and to his right was Varley's shop and the village blacksmith where Megan lived. He glanced up at a bedroom window and wondered if it was her room. Bill imagined her tucked up and sound asleep, dreaming dreams of a different nature to his. He wondered if there was joy and laughter in her dream time; did she run through open meadows chasing butterflies, in a land where the rain refused to fall and the sun refused to set, a land whose doors shut out all pain and suffering?

A dog barked and he hurried on, a little ashamed that he should be imposing his thoughts on the private world of a young lady as she slept. He turned up the collar of his overcoat as he passed more cottages, then came upon the village school, its playground empty of children. Bill stopped walking and cast his mind back to another time, a time when he had played in the playground with such carefree abandon. He closed his eyes and could hear the chattering and laughter as they played their childish games. He moved on and, turning right, he stood in front of the church; it loomed high above him, its dark shape, like a prehistoric monster, stood motionless and cold, offering no comfort for the likes of him. As he gazed upon this monument to man's weakness, he wondered how many men had died in the name of this merciful God and how many other righteous religions condoned mankind's continuous belief that their Gods were on their side. He walked with anger building within him. He crossed the Rectory field and another field beyond that, from which he climbed over a gate and onto a road. Ahead of him, at a hundred paces, stood the Presbyterian chapel standing alongside a crossroads.

Upon reaching it, the chapel, not as grand as the church, looked less threatening. Frost upon the wrought iron fence around its perimeter glistened in the moonlight. Its gate, leading to the porch of the building, was half-open and, in its isolation and loneliness, he felt at one with this house of God. It seemed to beckon him without wanting his soul. Could this building absorb his turmoiled mind without asking anything in return? He placed his hands on the gate and swung it back and forth, its metal hinges creaking with the motion, disturbing the quietness of the night. He closed the gate and walked away, taking the hill road to Montgomery.

17

Bill's parents had gone to bed at their usual time of half-past nine, but Jessie couldn't sleep. Her concern for her only son was making her ill. How much longer must this go on, she wondered? It had been almost two weeks and this walking the hills at night was something she found difficult to cope with. She had tried to speak to him some days before, but he dismissed her worries saying that he found it hard to settle. Albert, sleeping soundly by her side, was unaware of the extent of Jessie's worries. He expected a change to his son's character and found Bill's explanations of his inability to sleep acceptable. He considered that it didn't warrant any advice from him, so he left it at that. In any case, what could he say? From stories he had been told and accounts of the conflict he had read, he had tried to imagine what it must have been like, but realised that, in the world of imagination, where there are no boundaries of thought, nothing but the experience could qualify him to speak on such matters. He was, of course, very proud of Bill and, although he would never admit to it, had often said a prayer for him. Jessie, as he was always telling people, said enough prayers for both of them.

She cautiously slipped out of bed and felt for her housecoat that lay on the floor. A rumble of thunder made her glance towards the bedroom window just as a flash of light filled the room. Again, in darkness, she felt her way to the door that opened onto the landing and stairs. Inside the living room, the glowing embers from the fireplace gave enough light for her to see the way to her chair.

As she sat down, the grandfather clock struck one o'clock. Its chimes seemed a lot louder than in the light of day. Even its predictable tick-tock appeared to bounce off the walls and fill the room.

She looked at the timepiece, its brass pendulum swinging back and forth, counting off the seconds of darkness. She picked up her knitting and carried on from where she had left off only some few hours before. As the thunder and lightning gave their all, outside was not the place to be, she thought, for neither man nor beast. She wound the Aran wool around her fingers ready to take the number six needles, but the smooth wooden shafts felt clumsy in her hands and the cable stitch required more attention than she was prepared to give it. After two rows, she placed the tiresome bundle back on the sideboard and, as she turned, she picked up a small picture frame and carried it back to her chair. A feeling of foreboding came over her as she gazed into the fire; its dying embers with its warmth almost gone, would be replaced by the cold night air that, having waited patiently outside, was now taking advantage of the cracks and gaps in windows and doors. Clutching the picture frame in one hand, she placed fresh kindling onto the dying fire with the other. She shivered and pulled more tightly the ragged cord that held the near-useless garment around her body. Above her roof, the rain fell and the thunder rolled on. She prayed for it to stop, even if it were for only a few hours, just until Bill got home. Night after night she would lie awake, waiting for his return, waiting for the sound of the back-door latch being lifted and the door scraping the flagstones as it was opened. Night after night she would ask God to ease his troubled mind. With her index finger, she drew circles on the thin glass of the picture frame.

Beneath the glass, the image of her son smiled back at her. The photograph had been taken in Cairo and, apart from a kiss, it was the first thing he gave her on his return. Holding it to her breast she started to rock, a tear rolling down her cheek, followed by another and another, all following the same lines on her ageing face. Her quiet sobbing disturbed nothing: there were no arms to comfort her, no words of assurance reached her ears. She felt God had delivered her son only to take him away again. There were many times when she was envious of mothers who had large families. She thought that if a woman with six children was to lose one, at least there would be five left and, although it may be un-Christian to think such things, it was nonetheless a fact that one from six leaves five and one from one leaves nothing. It was this calculation that left her cold and fearful.

She brushed away the tears and consciously thought of the good things in her life. Her family was fortunate to enjoy good health; even when sickness came to the village, it seemed to pass them by and when, from time to time, sickness did come amongst them, she would mix preventative potions, potions that had been handed down to her from previous generations. Just how her remedies repelled fever and illness she didn't know; she even doubted the effectiveness of many but she made them up just the same.

Financially they paid their way without too much trouble. Albert had permanent work as a farm labourer and, to bring in a little extra money, he pleached hedges and killed pigs. Jessie also worked at the same farm for three hours a day helping Mrs. Mary Thomas, the farmer's wife, with the housework and washing. Mary had seven children, so Jessie's time there was well spent. The Thomas's, as well as being their employers, were also their landlords. They had originally come from another part of the county many years previously and, apart from the farm, they owned two cottages and a malt house. Arthur Thomas came from a family of maltsters and, for years, had produced malt, selling it to public houses and farmers within a radius of fourteen miles.

Albert had often helped Arthur turn the barley and pump water at the malt house and, when Arthur bought the farm with its thirty acres, he asked Albert if he would like to work for him full-time. He pointed out that as he already spent half the week doing jobs for him, he might as well work the other half. Albert was assured that he could relax in the knowledge that his employment was secure, possibly until he could work no more. Jessie thought about her life since her son walked out of the door to join his friends in going off to the war.

She missed him terribly; it broke her heart to see the boys so full of optimism and excitement. She saw them walk away seemingly with not a care in the world. Three hours after they had gone, she was on her knees in Llandyssil church praying to God to keep the boys safe. There was little joy in Jessie's house, but what joy there was came from an unexpected quarter.

Four months after Bill went away, she was sitting alone in her usual church pew awaiting the start of the Sunday morning service. The congregation, a mix of village people and the inhabitants of the surrounding district, were quietly acknowledging the appearance of their fellow worshippers. Jessie had sat alone for the past three months, ever since her church companion, Nell Roberts, had died of a stroke. Since then, no one had asked for her company and she had not approached anyone for theirs. People still spoke to her as they had always done and she continued to play her part in village life, but she was aware that there was something missing - why did she feel so alone?

"Mrs Jones," Jessie opened her eyes from silent prayer.

"Mrs Jones, may I sit next to you?"

"Certainly," said Jessie, "Megan, isn't it?"

"Yes," Megan whispered, "I have been meaning to speak to you for some time."

"It's your Bill's address I'm after. I spoke to him the day he went away and I promised to write to him. I thought it would be nice for him to think that he and the boys were not forgotten and that they were all in our thoughts."

Jessie looked at the young woman seated next to her; she smelt of rose petals. Her white blouse was spotless;

frills of white cotton ran up the front and formed a ruffled collar and a cameo brooch with a horse's head covered the topmost mother of pearl button. Her hair was tied in a bow of white ribbon, the tails of which fell halfway down her back. It complemented the thick black hair that fell with them. She wore a plain black skirt that cleared the floor by precisely two inches. In those first few seconds, Jessie was aware of her presence, not her physical presence although endearing as it was, it was something else. There was a vibrancy about her. She sensed an urgency of youth, an urgency that would not be deterred. Of course, she was no stranger to Jessie, she would see her most Sundays as she would most of the congregation. Normally, Megan would sit with her brother and sister-in-law in the same pew as Dennis and Eileen Potter.

"I hope you don't mind. Mrs Jones," Megan's voice faltered.

"I am so sorry, Megan, I was miles away. Of course, I wouldn't mind if you write to him. It's a lovely thought, Megan, thank you. I don't have his address on me, but if you have time after the service you could come home with me and I will give it to you."

Megan glanced at Jessie; had she been a little forward in her manner? She didn't think so, but then she knew she had a tendency to speak her mind and her approach may have been seen as being a little too familiar. Megan knew she had to learn to be more tactful. After the service, she accompanied Jessie and was somewhat surprised how at ease she felt in her company. Megan picked primroses and bluebells from the ditches and hedgerows. The spring sunshine, having left the cold and dreary winter behind, was awakening the countryside like nothing else could.

Megan even felt the urge to skip and sing her way to Jessie's house, but suppressed this childish instinct and was content at a leisurely pace to walk the quarter-mile with her new companion. With her hand full of wildflowers, Megan entered, for the first time, Jessie and Albert Jones' cottage. She immediately asked Jessie for a vase so as to arrange the flowers she had gathered. As Jessie watched this fifteen-year-old busying herself, she realised just how long it had been since her home had witnessed such a youthful zest for life. For two and a half hours they talked and laughed and, although in her Sunday clothes, Megan helped Jessie with her cleaning and dusting, stopping every so often for a cup of tea. They spoke on many subjects, each giving their opinion when asked, but it was Megan who did most of the asking. She loved talking to older people, as she told Jessie, "I won't learn by my mistakes, I'll learn by other people's."

Jessie didn't mind being classed as old, knowing that in Megan's eyes she was old and, for most of the time, she felt old, even older than her fifty-nine years. Today was different, she thought; today it took a fifteen-year-old to make her feel like she was twenty-five again and she liked it!

There was one subject that wasn't spoken of and that was the war, Jessie, because she thought Megan was too young to understand, and Megan because she understood the anguish that Jessie must have been going through. Only when Megan was leaving did Jessie hand her an address that, she said, may or may not reach Bill. She stood in the doorway as she watched Megan walk the lupin-lined path to the road, her skirt brushing their colourful array of petals and disturbing their stillness. Jessie likened them to a gathering of people at a carnival, watching with interest the display of colour that the passing parade would give.

"Megan," she said, and the girl turned on hearing Jessie's voice.

"Yes, Mrs Jones?"

"I'll see you next Sunday and thank you for your company."

"The pleasure's been mine, Mrs Jones; see you Sunday."

At the end of the path, Megan walked through the open gate and onto the road. Jessie could see Megan's head bobbing up and down beyond the hedge as she skipped and sang her way home.

Once inside, Jessie went to the kitchen; she stood by the sink and turned on the tap, the cold water falling onto the rose-patterned cups and saucers that she was about to wash. She hesitated, then turned off the tap and listened; apart from the ticking of the clock, there was silence. She missed Megan already.

18

Megan hurriedly climbed the stairs to her room. For the last two days since her return from London, all she could think about was Jessie's invitation to dinner the following Saturday. Well, the following Saturday was now here. As she entered and closed the door to her bedroom, she stood for a moment and looked at the four walls that in recent months had embraced her private world. Her whispered dreams and sighs of a wanted love were heard by these curtains of lime and stone but they would never betray her. In the early years, they were witness to her sobs of despair and, as time went by, the loving memories replaced the anger and heartache she felt on losing her father. Then, when laughter came into her room, sadness excused itself and left, never to return.

She looked at her bed; white cotton sheets were folded neatly over a patchwork bedspread. At each side of her bed stood a bedside cabinet, on the one an oil lamp and a novel by Jane Austen. Megan had read all six of her books and now, for the third time, Pride and Prejudice was responsible for the burning of oil in Megan's lamp. It lay open, its well-fingered pages a testimony to its literary quality and, although its author had died over one hundred years earlier and by all accounts had a loving and fulfilling life, Megan began to wonder if, in truth, she was a lonely lady. On the other table, in a turquoise glass vase, stood eight paper flowers. They were of no particular variety, just flowers. Megan was drawn to their vibrant colours and also the link between them and a future love.

Some months earlier, three gypsy caravans had passed through the village. Their annual arrival was, as always, a colourful event. Like Megan's flowers, colour seemed to be an integral part of gypsy life. Their caravans were painted like rainbows and the horses that pulled them wore ribbons of silk. One horse, a grey mare, was brought to the smithy requiring a set of shoes and Megan, always the opportunist, told David to charge for three shoes, the fourth one would be paid with a dozen pegs and the fortunes told of both Rose and herself. There was some light-hearted bargaining but, in the end, Megan had her way. Her fortune was told and, for the third successive year, Megan's need for a suitor was foretold by the tea leaves that lay in the bottom of a china cup, but this time she was assured it would come to pass. The old gypsy lady held her hand as she told of the happiness and contented life that was owed to Megan. It was as if a debt had to be paid by life itself. Then, as Megan was about to leave, she was handed the flowers that now stood in the vase of Megan's bedroom.

"Keep them close," she said, "for they will bring you luck."

Megan sat on her bed and wondered how many young women had been told by the gypsy that love would soon come into their lives. She smiled as she thought of the hundreds of thousands of men that had returned home from the war and guessed that the old lady's chances of being right in her predictions were better now than they had ever been.

She rose and went to her wardrobe. On opening its mirrored doors, she took from within all the clothes that would be suitable for her dinner invitation. She laid them out on her bed; four dresses, four skirts and four blouses. She looked from one to another then back again. Clothes were Megan's only weakness and, with a little help from Mrs. G and Rose, she would recreate the fashion dresses that she had seen in shop windows. She would make sketches and note the materials used.

Sometimes her creations would cause heads to turn and occasionally people would make unkind comments. It wasn't the clothes that prompted their disapproval, but the person who wore them, for people of Megan's standing did not wear clothes that elevated their position in society. Time spent at the Rectory had given Megan an insight into the ways of the upper classes. Visitors would come and go and she was secretly impressed by their worldly knowledge and impeccable manners. Some of the more regular visitors would seek her out for conversation and, in their so doing, Megan had gained self-confidence and had acquired the ability, without pretence, to adapt comfortably to their differing social class, although not all visitors were pleasant people. There were those who were bigoted and pretentious, opinionated people whose ability to be rude knew no bounds. This kind of behaviour, although disappointing to Megan, was not uncommon.

"Such people live in our own midst," she told Mrs. G, "only they use different words to convey the same meaning." Such a person was Trevor Thomas, whose reputation as a poacher was widely known. Once on the village green and in the company of his friends, Megan overheard him say that she, Megan Davies, should spend more time with her own kind and less with the likes of them from the Rectory. His comments were, she suspected, intended to be overheard and she confronted him there and then. With an air of grace and control, Megan walked up to the group.

"Trevor Thomas, is it true that you can skin a fox faster than anyone you know?" Trevor's jaw dropped, totally confused on being caught off guard by Megan's question. He hesitated.

"Is it true that you can skin a fox faster than anyone you know"? Megan repeated. Immediately, because of his hesitation, she felt already in control of the conversation. Trevor looked at his friends; Jimmy Smith stood open-mouthed and Brian Cadwallader, at eighteen and the youngest of the three, looked sheepishly at Megan.

"What's it to you?" Trevor said curtly, hoping to gain some ground with a question of his own.

"Well, either you are the fastest, or you're not. And if you're not, would you mind telling me who is?"

Trevor was again on the defensive; he was annoyed that Megan had the nerve to confront him in the first place, but to question his supremacy in the way he skinned a fox was, to him, blasphemous. However, like all good poachers, he held his nerve and spoke defending his reputation.

"If there's a skinner faster than me, I have never met him." Trevor, still confused as to Megan's reason for asking, could not contain his curiosity and asked Megan what possible need did she have to know.

"My need is quite simple," she replied. "Some weeks ago, in a shop window in Shrewsbury, I saw a fox fur hat and the only way I could possess one would be to make my own. By the way, I have already dismissed your unkind remarks about me and furthermore, I am proud of who I am and what I am. You may be very good at what you do, Trevor Thomas, but your character reference would impress no-one! Now, are you going to teach me how to skin a fox or not?"

Inside, Megan was loving every minute of this encounter. She was making him look a fool but, to his credit, he seized the opportunity that Megan had presented him and bowed out of what could have been an embarrassing situation, agreeing to show her how to remove a fox skin from its rightful owner.

Early the following Saturday, he called at the blacksmiths and presented Megan with a parcel. Inside she discovered two fox pelts already treated and tanned. Megan made her hat and, on a day suitable to both, she duly skinned her fox.

Megan had, on other occasions and by other people, been invited to dinner but never once had she laid her clothes out on her bed, never once had she pondered on the suitability of her dress and now, in the back of her mind, it was Bill she wanted to impress. She wanted to be desirable without being vulgar, irresistible yet appearing unattainable.

She touched the sleeve of a white cotton blouse: too Sunday-ish, she thought. She turned and looked at her reflection in the wardrobe mirrors; her hands reached behind her back and undid the bow of her pinafore. She began to feel uneasy as she continued to undress. Bill was in her mind. He was in the room watching her; he watched as she folded the last of her clothes, he saw her stand in front of the mirror and, as she gazed at her image, she saw herself through his eyes. From her stocking-less feet up, she studied herself, turning from side to side. There wasn't anything in particular she didn't like about her figure. She had a slim strong body. Again, she thought of Bill seeing her this way; butterflies were in her stomach and a warm glow came to her face.

She was under no illusion that he would not desire her, nor would any other man if it came to that. But it was Bill whom she had chosen and, although she didn't really know him, and had only so much as touched him once, it was Bill that would hold her.

Still looking at herself, she sat down again on the bed. A blue-grey dress crumpled beneath her; it had four pleats to its front and each one ran from the waist to the hem. It was Megan's favourite, but the particular attention she had paid to its ironing accounted for nothing. She closed her eyes and let her mind wander. She had allowed herself fantasies of men before but this was something else.

She imagined going on long walks with him by her side, holding hands as they wandered down leafy lanes, strolling through woods and summer meadows. Then the thought of him kissing her. She closed her eyes, she longed to be held in strong arms and to hold in return, to experience the feeling of warm breath on damp skin, sincere lips that would kiss and linger.

She was surprised as to the detail of her thoughts and, for a young woman whose lips had never sought a mans, she asked herself whether it was healthy to have such an imagination. Was lust only a prerogative of men? She decided that her imagination came from an enquiring mind and there was little she could do, or even wanted to do, to change anything that was God-given. The question of lust was a little different and fornication was, understandably, a subject not discussed by ladies; well, not the ladies that Megan knew. Young women her own age would hedge around the subject, none daring to enlighten others with their own experiences. There were hints and innuendos and a lot of wishful thinking spoken, some of which Megan suspected to be the truth. Her own experiences with men were limited, from the uninvited attention and shameful suggestions of some young men from the village, to stolen kisses under the mistletoe at Christmas from the same.

Her only romantic encounter had happened in the last week of July, twelve months earlier. A Captain Clive Robinson, the son of an acquaintance of the Rectory household, was on leave and, before re-joining his regiment in France, had accepted an invitation to stay for a few days.

As it turned out, he stayed for a week. He was tall and slim, he had wavy blonde hair and blue eyes and, sporting a two-inch scar on the lower part of his right cheek, he was, Megan decided, not that good-looking. After a few days, she reappraised his looks. It wasn't a disfiguring scar to his cheek, it neither improved nor enhanced his looks, but it turned a plain face into an interesting one. So much so that, as the days went by, she sensed there was a mutual feeling of interest.

Captain Robinson was, by his own admission, smitten the first time he laid eyes on Megan, but was apprehensive of his feelings for this beautiful vivacious young woman, for, at twenty-six, he felt old, too old to think she would ever entertain any feelings for him. Megan became more aware of Captain Robinson. He would make excuses to visit the kitchen whilst she was there and, as she went about the house doing her duties, he would enter the room she was in on the pretext of looking for a book, or to ask Megan if she had seen other objects he had misplaced. He seemed shy and unassuming, his gentlemanly manner hiding well any dominant side that he may have had and, when alone in Megan's company, he became nervous and unsure. His nervousness made Megan feel uncomfortable. It wasn't a threatening unease that she felt, but she wished he could feel more at ease in her company. Polite talk was all very well, thought Megan, but she felt sure he wanted to converse on a more personal level and time was running out.

"Mind the step, Megan," Captain Robinson held out his hand as she placed her foot on the bottom step of the small horse-drawn carriage. She reached up, the captain's gloved hand firmly holding hers and not letting go until she was seated by his side. "Thank you," she said softly. She was immediately aware of the closeness of his body as he sat beside her. He took hold of the reins and urged the horse forward with a command that surprised her. His voice and actions were assertive and unfaltering.

Earlier that morning, Reverend Jenkins had burst into the kitchen and asked Mrs. G, through a mouthful of toast, if Megan could be excused kitchen duties as his sister Mavis would be visiting and would be arriving at Montgomery station on the 11.30 am train. He wanted Megan to accompany Captain Robinson who, he explained, had never met Mavis. And Mavis, he suspected, would be most annoyed to be greeted at the station by a total stranger, irrespective of rank or title. Mrs. G hated him doing this, but it was not uncommon for him to announce impending visitors at the last minute, like today - a Friday of all days.

Miss Mavis was a visitor whose company Megan greatly enjoyed. She was a fun person, visiting her brother and staying at the Rectory five or six times a year. On their first meeting, Miss Mavis had insisted that Megan was to be her personal maid. Her visits would usually last for seven days, but Mrs. G didn't much care for Miss Mavis's visits because it meant that Megan's time was taken up with pandering to Mavis's every need. Megan was fully aware of her own position in the Rectory household but, because of Miss Mavis's jovial nature, she found it difficult to maintain the sense of decorum that she expected of herself.

Unlike other lady visitors to the Rectory, Mavis's visits were like a fresh breeze. Everyone knew when she was in residence; her laughter could be heard cutting through the somewhat sombre atmosphere that seemed to be forever in the building.

Mavis knew of Megan's love of making her own clothes and she also knew that to make clothes one needed material, so every now and again she would bring with her a small suitcase full of her old clothes and give them to Megan to do with as she wished.

For the first half a mile, they rode in silence. Megan closed her eyes as she drank in the summer sunshine. It's comforting warmth, the repetitive rhythm of cantering hooves and the physical contact of her body against that of her companion slowly, but unmistakably, brought about a feeling of intimacy within her. She had for some time imagined this feeling but had never before experienced it.

"Megan." She opened her eyes with a start and sat upright, slightly moving further away from Captain Robinson. He pulled on the reins and the horse slowed to a walking pace.

"Megan, may I ask you a personal question?" then, without waiting for an answer he carried on. "As you know, I will be leaving at lunchtime tomorrow and, as time is its own master and pays no heed to the wishes of any of us to prolong a period of that we wish to prolong, I am bound to ask if you have anyone in your life?" He turned and smiled. "I mean, is there a man in your life?" Megan looked at him and smiled back. She hesitated, then, understanding perfectly well his motives behind such a question, realised she could have ended there and then any notions of a romantic nature he may have had, by saying that there was indeed someone in her life.

"No, Captain Robinson, there is no man in my life." Then she added with a chuckle, "Why do you ask?" Still smiling, he shook his head.

"Megan Davies, I do believe you are laughing at me and please call me Clive." He turned his head and again looked at the narrow road, its twists and turns being negotiated by a horse that, over the years, had become accustomed to the fact that its reward for every hard pull up a hill was an easy pull down one.

"We are not at the Rectory now, Megan. Out here we can be who we really are. The need to impress or indulge the wishes of others does not apply here and, at this very moment, we are the servants of no man." He paused, thinking if what he had just said needed any correction. Then he raised his voice.

"But come tomorrow...ah, tomorrow." He lifted a clenched fist above his head, then, with a little anger, a little mockery and a lot of truth he shouted, "Tomorrow I shall again take up my sword and march good men to their own Armageddon." Megan, taken somewhat at the change of his voice, took a sideways glance. The contented smile that had lit his face had gone. Blankly staring at the shimmering road was another Captain Clive Robinson, one that dreaded his return to France.

Three weeks later, Reverend Jenkins entered the kitchen and announced that Captain Robinson was dead. Details of his death were somewhat vague, but apparently, he had got caught up in barbed wire while advancing towards the German lines. For two days, the wired coils held his bullet-ridden body, two days before their barbed thorns were persuaded to let him go.

Megan recalled it was Captain Robinson's second encounter with barbed wire. The first became known when Mavis, never one to show a lack of interest in other people's misfortunes, immediately upon being introduced to Captain Robinson, enquired as to how he came by the scar on his face. This sixty-something lady, whose blunt and sometimes tactless approach was in contrast to her generosity and an endearing concern for others, stood and looked at the Captain, her posture demanding an answer. Captain Robinson, a little bemused at the forwardness of his appointed charge, looked at Megan then back at Mavis.

"Actually, I was helping some men lay wire for our defences when a coil sprang forward and a barb caught my cheek. It happens sometimes," he said with a shrug of his shoulders.

"Ah well," Mavis replied with a smile, "with all the lines on my face and that one on yours, one could assume that barbed wire has treated you kindlier than time has done for me. Now come on, young man," she patted his back, "take me home and, by the way, I hope you have been nice to our Megan."

On learning of his death, Megan cried. Although she had known him but a week, she knew him well enough to cry for, and in hindsight, he was worthy of her tears.

Still sitting unclothed on her bed, she leaned back and thought of the last time she had seen Captain

Robinson. She had been polishing the stairs that Saturday morning. For a moment, she couldn't remember his first name. "Clive", she said out loud, then realised it wasn't that often his first name was ever used; it had always been Captain Robinson, everyone called him that. She could see him standing on the landing of the stairs. She could even remember which step she was polishing at the time; it was the third. She looked up; he was ever so smart. He beckoned to her and, as she rose up from her knees and climbed the remaining steps to see him, she knew he was going to kiss her goodbye.

She gripped the polishing cloth tightly as he held her hand. Then he eased her fingers and, gently pulling on the cloth, said, "May I?" She let the cloth slip through her fingers. "May I take this with me? I would like something to remember you."

"It's a polishing cloth," she said nervously.

"I know it is." Megan was aware of a peaceful resignation in his voice.

"Just think of all the soldiers that take to war mementoes of their loved ones. Many will take what others take, but none will have what I have." Then he looked into her eyes. "Which makes you rather special." She felt his hands on her waist, his lips on her lips, then he was gone. Megan sat on the stairs. Her mind had no place to go except to recall the last few minutes over and over again. It was their last meeting; she had spoken just four words and goodbye wasn't one of them. She thought of her polishing cloth buried with him in some quagmire in France. She had never doubted that he loved her, never doubted that in his pocket was a rag that to him meant so much, a memento that like countless others would stay forever with their keepers. It brought the war a little closer to Megan, to associate her polishing cloth with death moved her deeply and it was at this time that she began, in a different light, to think of Private Bill Jones.

She stood up and went to her chest of drawers and out of its top drawer she removed clean underwear and placed them on the bed. In an hour, she would be sitting at the same table with, dare she think it, the man she had grown to love. She knew she was being presumptuous in her choice of thoughts, even naive in thinking that her love would be returned in kind. Maybe she was in love with the thought of being in love. It was true that, due to his mother, she had learned all that there was to know about him, his likes, his dislikes, his passive and yet determined nature, and of his interest in Greek mythology. Uncharacteristic as it was in a country lad, she found it rather amusing.

She went back to her chest of drawers and from the same top drawer she took out a bundle of letters. There were twelve; she didn't untie the blue ribbon that bound them. The contents of Bill's letters she had read many times and many times she had tried to read beyond the words that he had penned. Like Bill's mother, she would cross-reference the dates of his letters with newspaper reports of the conflict, acquiring a better understanding and becoming more knowledgeable about the activities of the 7th Battalion.

She thought of one letter in particular and, although all his letters were very formal, this letter, dated the 15th of May

1917, was markedly different, for in it he mentioned that John Woods of Llandyssil had been killed on the 26th of March.

At half-past eleven on that morning, the 7th Royal Welsh Fusiliers, along with the 158th Brigade, began an attack on a Turkish-held hill called Ali Munter, on the outskirts of Gaza. For nearly two thousand yards, the advance was made across open ground, in full view of the enemy, and under heavy rifle and machine-gun fire. It was Jack that had seen Woodsy go down, machine gun bullets racked across his chest, just five minutes into the attack. Many men of the 7th died in that First Battle of Gaza and, although the Fusiliers stood on the hill at Allimunter at 3.30 and were still there when the 10th Australian Light Horse joined them at sunset, all was not well. As Gaza itself had not been taken, they were all ordered to withdraw.

While reading of the death of John Woods, Megan became aware of Bill's tiring pain as he spoke of his wanting to see leafy woods and green fields, and of his need to see his family and friends, and to sleep. Megan had memorized the last line of this particular letter. She held the bundle to her chest and closed her eyes, her mind repeating his words, "Keep warm and sleep well, Love Bill". This was the first time that he had shown any personal interest in Megan's well-being, especially at the end of a letter, for all his other letters ended with the words, "Regards Bill". In her first reading of this letter, she remembered how she was struck by a sense of truth that, hardly noticeable, seeped from its pages. This letter was a revelation, as it told more about him that he would dare reveal; there was compassion and warmth. There was humanity and there was love. At first, Megan misunderstood the last two words; "Love Bill" didn't mean that he was in love with her, it was only after she had read the letter a few times did she understand that in the context it was written, "Love Bill" was the only way he could have ended it.

She rose to her feet and held the letters to her lips, she kissed them softly before replacing the lavender-scented words from a soldier back in her lavender-scented drawer.

She dressed slowly, occasionally looking at herself in the mirror as she did so. She was almost ready when Rose's voice was calling her from the bottom of the stairs reminding Megan of the time. "Coming now!" she called back. She nervously took off her gloves then she put them back on only to take them off again. 'I'll carry them,' she thought, as she opened the bedroom door and descended the stairs.

Rose was seated in the living room darning socks and looked up when Megan entered the room. She smiled as Megan twirled around and around, asking at the same time for Rose's approval. Rose looked at her sister-in-law; she wanted so much for Megan's dream to come true. How could Bill Jones not love her, she thought? On her last turn, Megan stood facing Rose, then she stooped and kissed her on the forehead.

"Whatever was that for?" Rose said with surprise.

"For being my best friend and for putting up with a jealous and thoughtless little girl. When you came into my life, I had visions of your taking my brother away from me and, for the first couple of years, I was unkind and resentful of your love for him, for in my mind, no one had a right to his life but me. I've wanted to say something for some time but there has never been a moment when I have felt comfortable talking about it. And why I am apologizing for my behaviour now, I don't know!"

Rose reached for Megan's hands, tears welling in her eyes; she knew well what Megan was talking about. She remembered how intrusive she must have seemed when David first introduced herself to Megan, but her patience had its rewards, for, as the years went by and the children came along, when birthday cakes and Christmas dinners were placed on the table, Megan began to realise that she had a family again. And like chaff in the wind, the friction that had existed between them was blown away, being replaced by a bond and a closeness that Megan could never have imagined. Even five minutes earlier as Rose darned her husband's socks, she was fearful that Megan would one day want to leave their home and she was truly saddened at the thought.

"You don't have to say another word, Megan. I understood then and I understand now. Now, be off with you and enjoy the afternoon." Still holding Rose's hand, Megan again kissed her forehead then turned and walked to the door, picking up an umbrella on the way out.

"Oh, and another thing," Megan glanced back at Rose, with a mischievous look in her eyes as she spoke. "The ironing, could you finish it off for me? On the top of the basket is David's Sunday shirt; I think it's time I gave up an insistence of mine and let you iron your own husband's shirt." Rose saw the door close and smiled, remembering a frightened twelve-year-old girl's insistence that she would always iron her brother's Sunday shirt. Rose was content, but a little sad to see that Megan had given up the last vestige of a childhood that, in part, had made her what she had become.

19

"Same again, Jack?" the landlord of the Checkers Inn asked, as Jack walked up to the bar. Without waiting for a reply, he poured the liquid of Jack's desire into a glass tankard that had hung on a hook above the bar. He hadn't even asked for Jack's money, he just took threepence out of the pile of coins that Jack had placed on the bar when ordering his first pint.

Jack raised the mug to his lips and closed his eyes as he drank the frothy beer. Its hoppy taste went down his throat to join the five pints that had already made the same journey. He looked around the room where two men were playing board skittles and had been at it for over an hour. "Bloody stupid game!" he said under his breath. He looked at Peter Evans, who was sitting in a settle by the fireplace reading a newspaper. His black and white sheepdog lay at his feet gnawing on a bone.

"Hey Pete, what's the chance of me taking that bone off your dog?" Pete looked up from his newspaper and over the top of his wire-framed spectacles.

"Rather you than me," he said, "he's been carrying the bloody thing around with him for nigh on a week."

He folded the paper and placed it on the table in front of him, then stroked his companion.

"Come on, Ben, time to go." He took off his spectacles, placing them in a tin box which he slipped into his jacket pocket. Like his master, Ben got up on frail legs and walked to the door, carrying his bone. Peter placed his empty mug on the bar, bid the landlord farewell and as he passed Jack, he reached out and, in a friendly manner, shook his shoulder. "It's nice to see you made it home, Jack. A lot of men didn't and if I'd been thirty years younger, I'd have been there with you. We must have a talk sometime." With that, he followed his dog out of the door.

'Bloody old fool,' Jack thought. 'Have a talk sometime?' he mused, 'what in God's name would we talk about? He's got sod all to say that would be of any interest to me.' Jack knew he was being unfair to Peter's invitation for a talk and was also aware of his unforgiving attitude to people's concerns for his welfare. But it was the realisation that after all that had happened in the last four years, nothing had really changed. It was as though he had not been away; men still worked and women still washed, cooked, and had babies. It was as it always had been, and he hated it. He hated the predictability of the life he was about to lead.

It had been two weeks now since he had first seen again his beloved green hills and had heard the welcoming voices of family and friends. Their profound pleasure in seeing him again was evident in their gestures and their assurance that he had always been in their prayers. It humbled him to think that, for all the time he and his friends were away, their absence inspired local people to be on their knees praying for their safety, albeit that, in a lot of instances, it seemed their prayers proved fruitless. That period seemed an age ago and now, as he gazed into his half-empty mug and watched the frothy head slide down the inner surface of the tankard, he thought of the future. And not for the first time he dreaded the thought of the years ahead, stretching out like an endless ocean and knowing it was an ocean he couldn't swim. He wondered when it had all started to fall apart; when in his mind had he become conscious of this feeling of isolation?

He drank the last of his beer and asked for another which was duly served. The landlord grunted, helped himself to Jack's money then disappeared into a room at the rear of the bar. Jack, with a fresh pint in his hand, walked to the settle vacated by Pete and sat down. He looked into the flames of the fire flickering lazily over the logs. A grey plume of smoke came down the chimney and spilled into the room. It rose up the face of the chimney and spread some distance across the ceiling then disappeared. He looked again at the flames, seeing fires that burned in the desert camps of Egypt, remembering the warmth they gave on cold nights. As he stared, images of past companions, ones that he would never see again, appeared amongst the flames, their faces overlapping each other as, one by one, they ascended with the smoke. He needed again to experience the feeling of being a somebody, to be looked upon with respect as, God knows, he felt he had earned it.

The sounds of battle were still fresh in his mind and the scenes of unimaginable horror had never left his eyes. Beads of sweat formed on his forehead as he recalled, with nervous excitement, moments when he could have died, moments when the bullets and bayonets had passed within inches of his body. It was at these very times when he had experienced the ultimate sense of being alive, that this feeling outweighed any fear of death. In fact, he had sought it; not the feeling of death, but the feeling of being alive, and he had encountered this feeling many times: Times when he had run screaming like a banshee at his enemy. Warm blood had run through his fingers as he comforted a dying comrade. When he had bayoneted, without remorse or compassion, prisoners that lay at his feet. To be alive in the midst of death, to smell and to touch the afterlife, seemed an experience that was demanded of him and he had excelled in it.

He was about to reach for the 'County Times' that Pete had placed on the table when three young men came through the door. Their loud and boisterous manner irritated him and their continued shouting and swearing irritated him more. He himself had often been accused of being boisterous, loud, and a source of trouble. Drink, and too much of it, was his problem. But right now, at that very moment, their behaviour was unacceptable to him. He picked up his pint and drank the last of the beer that it held. Then, as he started to read the newspaper, a fresh pint of beer was gently placed on the table beside him. He looked up to see one of the young men who had just walked in standing before him; he half-recognised the face but couldn't put a name to it.

"Jack Davies, isn't it?" the young man asked, smiling. His brash manner had been left at the bar with his two companions, who had now stopped talking and were looking curiously at their friend as he placed the drink in front of Jack. "This one," he said, "is in memory of my Uncle Bob. He mentioned you a lot in his letters back home." Jack looked blankly at the young man that had just bought him a beer,

"Thanks …thanks," he said, his mind being confused with the name Bob. "I…I."

"It's okay," said the young man, "anyway, that's for Bob." He touched the peak of his cloth cap as he turned and walked back to the bar to rejoin his friends. Jack looked at the beer in front of him for some moments, and as he did, the name Bob swam around in his head. He reached forward and picked up the full pint, then before putting the frothy head to his lips, he said out loud, "Here's to Bob", and on his first mouth full of beer he thought, 'who the fuck was Bob?' Jack drank a further two pints, each one to the memory of Bob, before the landlord called time. Then, with two bottles of stout in his overcoat pockets, he was gently escorted off the premises and onto the dark damp streets of Montgomery.

20

Bill cursed as the rain started to fall; the breeze that swayed the treetops not half an hour ago was now getting stronger. He guessed it to be around two in the morning, maybe a little later, but time was of little consequence to him. For every morning is a Monday morning and, when daylight fades and evenings come, when darkness creeps stealthily over the horizon like a thief, his nightmares return.

From his shoulder bag, he took out a torch and a canvas sheet. The latter he placed over his head so that it fell over his shoulders and legs. At the front, just under his chin, he threaded a three-inch nail like a big safety pin to both sides of the sheet, holding them together; six inches lower he threaded another nail. The sheet would now keep him reasonably dry even in the heaviest rain. He switched on the torch, this being now the only light in which to see his way, the rain clouds having obscured any moonlight.

He was about to ascend Montgomery town hill; he had skirted part of its lower section and was now following a sheep track that snaked its way through the thick gorse bushes which had grown over that particular section.

A clap of thunder and a flash of lightning brought him to a sudden stop. He was, at this point, undecided as to what to do, turn back or carry on? Although it was raining heavily, he decided to go on. The wind swirled around him and its effect on the rain was to make it fall in all directions. Another crash of thunder was followed by more lightning and, for a split second, he could see everything around him. Clouds with their unstoppable motion rolled on, releasing their cargo of rain as they went.

It was an eerie and thrilling sight and he wondered if Holmes had felt like this as he pursued the beast of Dartmoor. He swore that if he listened carefully, he could hear the baying of hounds himself. What made him think of Sherlock Holmes at this time, he didn't know. 'It's funny how things spring to mind in the most unlikely of places,' he thought, 'but then, this is a likely place!'

Three hundred yards ahead, the gorse bushes finished. This harsh and unforgiving plant gave way to grassland that ran along the ridge and down the far side. From its crest, you could see for miles: to the north, on a clear day, the Berwyn Mountains were visible and some people have even claimed to have seen Snowdonia beyond and slightly west, but Bill never had.

He walked clear of the last gorse bush as yet another flash of lightning lit up the sky, its jagged silver thread crossing the firmament at will. Three seconds later, a thunderous cascade of noise split the heavens. All around him chaos was in progress; the wind was screaming at him, rain, the like of which he had never seen, came down in waves. He stood in awe at this spectacle about him. Time and again, thunder would seemingly shake the ground he was standing on. The lightning gave him glimpses of the night sky, each glimpse being different from the one before it. Flashes of light illuminated the onslaught of the storm and the dark angry clouds, in their perpetual motion, would have moved on and changed in shape each time the sky lit up. This was theatre at its best and he was the only one in the audience.

Bill became conscious of the danger he was in, an open invitation for lightning to strike since, apart from the charred and half burnt remnants of the centre post from the celebration bonfire, he was the tallest thing standing. These bonfires had burned on hilltops throughout the land to celebrate the end of the war. Their beacons of light could be seen from one hilltop to another. To Bill, it seemed such a long time ago. When those bonfires burned, he was still in Egypt, and now, over a year later, the scorched earth from such fires had time to heal. From its ashes, new grass had grown and, when the centre post from the bonfire finally fell, all evidence of an immensely meaningful human event would be lost.

He was about to descend the hill when, above him, another crash of thunder erupted and it was when the lightning bathed the hilltop in white light that he saw a figure moving towards him. It was some distance away on the Montgomery side of the hill. Unsure of what he had seen, he crouched down and waited for the next flash of lightning. Straining his eyes, he tried to pick out any movement; maybe it was a sheep or a cow, or a bush swaying in the wind. But he already knew what it was and when the lightning lit up the sky again there, not a hundred yards away, was a man walking towards him. He quickly made his way down the hill and hid himself amongst the nearest gorse bushes.

"It's a bloody tramp," he mused. He wore a long raincoat, and his hair, Bill noticed, was also long, its wet strands swirling around his drooping head. His arms were by his side and in his left hand he held a bottle - a drunken tramp at that, Bill thought.

Bill was intrigued as to why a tramp would be walking the hills at this hour of the night and in these conditions. He knew there was a hay barn not far away and, from the direction the tramp had walked, he must have passed it. While travelling, tramps slept the night in such accommodation. They were usually harmless, timid, and private people, but a little scary at the same time.

Rain was still coming down and the wind pursued the clouds in its attempt to win some kind of race; in doing so the gorse bushes rustled and swayed. Their whistling songs varied as to the strength of the gusts that blew through their spinney branches. A mountain ash just below him gave the orchestra an added dimension, its sound totally different to the gorse section, with its mournful wail giving depth and harmony to this beautiful symphony.

Above him, another sound cut through this natural gathering of musicians; from his hiding place, he could distinctly hear singing. This intrusive vagrant was actually singing. Although hardly audible, "Oh, I do like to be beside the seaside" came across as rather strange. As the lightning continued to turn night into day, this sad figure, now hardly twenty yards away from Bill, took off his raincoat, waved his arms skywards and started to curse. He was surely mad about something. It was then, with his head raised, that a flash of lightning lit up his silhouette and for a second, frozen in time, Bill saw his face. It was Jack. Suddenly, Bill went very cold. He sank further into the bushes unable to believe it was him. He looked again - it was definitely Jack. He was effing and blinding and shaking his fists at some imaginary something. He tried to make sense of Jack's drunken babbling, but his words were muted by the unrelenting wind. "God, why did you" and another gust of wind carried off the rest of that sentence. As he was shouting obscenities, he began to take off his clothing - his jacket, waistcoat and shirt, and then, with some difficulty, his trousers.

Bill was dumbfounded by Jack's behaviour and didn't know whether to laugh or cry. Then he got cramp in his left leg from his awkward position kneeling amongst the gorse bushes. He rolled onto his side so as to bend and straighten his leg, hoping the cramp would go away. When he looked up again, Jack was folding his clothes and placing them upon the muddy ground at his feet. With the rain falling upon Jack's near-naked body, he proceeded to take off his long johns. The man must be stark raving mad! Unable to get his long johns over his boots, he sat down, removed his boots and then rid himself of this last troublesome garment. He rolled up his long johns and added them to the pile of sodden clothes at his side. In the diffused light, he then watched Jack stand, his hands again went skywards.

"Come on then, you devils of the night!" a crash of thunder above their heads smothered more words and, when the lightning came, he looked ghostlike. His wet naked body glistened. What Bill could make out from his drunken ravings was that he wanted God to strike him down. He demanded the grim reaper do his business. Bill heard him shout, "Come on, you collector of souls, take me and add me to your greatest of all harvests". As he watched Jack pleading for heavenly intervention, Bill began to feel uncomfortable. This must be the closest to God Jack had ever been, on the top of a hill, stark naked, in the middle of the night with the rain pouring down and, to make it really interesting, some thunder and lightning thrown in. Now, Bill thought, if he were God and someone went to all that trouble to have a word with him, he would have been really impressed. Nonetheless, he was witness to a conversation which was private and it made him feel rather guilty, although now, for obvious reasons, would not be a good time to get up and leave. With his canvas cloak over his head and with his body rising up out of the darkness, Jack would be forgiven for thinking that God had indeed granted his wish and had sent the grim reaper to do his bidding. He chuckled to himself as he pictured the scene.

Jack was now sitting down, his head bent backwards. The bottle Bill saw him carry was held vertical to his lips. He drank the last of its contents, belched then threw the empty bottle in Bill's direction. It went over his head and into the darkness, falling soundlessly into the bushes. He was getting cold and his legs were getting numb from being in the same position for so long. He was hoping Jack

had said all he was going to say and would sod off. The
rain had eased and was now nothing more than a drizzle.
The thunder could still be heard but its rumblings were
some miles off, growing more distant by the minute. Bill
noticed the orchestra had stopped playing, the wind and
clouds had run their race and were replaced by a stiff breeze
and high clouds. With the clouds now having sufficient
gaps to see the stars and the moon, Bill's attention was
again drawn to Jack, his cramped legs barely holding him
as he stood again. Jack raised his arms once more, this
time from his side, stopping at shoulder height. His hands
hung limply from his wrists, there was no shouting, no
verbal abuse. Nothing, except silence.

Then Bill noticed something rather odd. A short
distance beyond Jack was the celebration post. Its profile
rose some two feet above Jack's head and, up until now, it
had played no part in this hilltop drama. But now, with
Jack standing silent, his arms outstretched at his side, the
post took on a different role from its original purpose.
There, in subdued light against a purple sky, was the
silhouette of Jesus on the cross.

Bill was now on his knees trying to get a better
view and, as he parted some bushes obscuring his vision,
the faint glow of a lightning flash many miles behind
them again caught the image of Jack. The mist-like rain
glistened on his motionless body, drips of water fell from
the fingers of his drooped hands. He then lifted his head
and, with hopelessness in his voice, shouted, "God, am
I the consequence of my own doing?"

Now, Bill had never heard Jack say such a profound statement in his life. Normally, a profound statement by Jack might be, "Is it my round already?" But although spoken by a sad and confused drunken man, those nine words did not diminish their significance for one minute. As those words swam around in Bill's head, Jack lowered his arms, put on his overcoat and gathered his clothes, and without another word or gesture, he left, walking in the direction he had come. No doubt he would spend the rest of the night in Ted Parry's hay barn, but at least he would be dry and warm.

Just how much Jack would remember of tonight, Bill could only guess. He emerged from his hiding place and walked the few yards to where Jack had made his pleading. The celebration post, in its isolation, now looked lonely and wanting, but for those few moments, it had become much more than a post in the ground. To believers and non-believers, and the people in between, it had become a symbol, one which was recognizable to all. He ran his hand down its wet and charred surface, then, with a little reluctance to let go of the night's events, he began to make his way home.

21

"Is that you, Bill?" in a hushed call Jessie responded to the sound of the back door being opened.

"Good Lord, Mother, what are you doing up at this time of the night?" She saw her son's advancing frame fill the doorway that separated the kitchen from the living room.

"Did the thunder wake you?" As he spoke, he stooped to untie the wet leather laces of his boots.

"What am I doing up at this time of the night? And no, the thunder did not wake me." She felt angry that he had deprived her of yet another night's sleep and, although Jessie had the patience of Job, enough was enough. She felt that, even at the risk of having a row, she must say something.

"What are you on about, Bill? Walking the roads and hills in the middle of the night, like a homeless tramp. Isn't it enough that I have worried about you for the last four years?"

He looked up and in the faint orange glow from the fire he saw his mother and strangely, to his shame, he felt unconcerned as to her predicament. Had it come to this?

That in the pursuit of his own sanity, he had discarded the ones that love him? *Am I the consequence of my own doing?* Jack's words would not leave him. Then as he looked into his mother's face, half in shadow and half in flickering light, he knew it to be so. She was sitting in her chair, waiting for a response to her criticism of his thoughtless behaviour. He then sat opposite her in his father's chair and answered the best way he could.

"I told you, I am finding it hard to settle." He sounded unconvincing and knew she wouldn't be content with that, so he carried on.

"And.....and I can't sleep because I have bad dreams, images of the past, that sort of thing." She looked at him with a face of cold stone. "Maybe...maybe you have a remedy?" he stammered.

Immediately, he had visions of his mother standing over a big black pot, chanting alien words as she threw in squirrels' teeth, moles' tails and rabbits' eyelids.

"Look, Mum, this isn't going to last forever so please go back to bed and don't worry so." He stood up and reached for her hand. "I'm alright, I really am."

"Sit down, Bill." He sat down; this was a demand, not a request. "So, you have bad dreams, do you? Well, I have a few of those myself. You, Bill Jones, don't have the monopoly on bad dreams. When you were a little boy, I had bad dreams. As you were growing up, I had bad dreams. In my dreams, I have been to your funeral many times. I've picked the flowers and chosen the hymns. For a long time after you went away, I would, unknown to your father, go into your room and open the drawers that held your clothes. I would take out a shirt or a jumper and hold it to my face; it was the closest I could get to you without your being there. My solace was the scent of your body on those clothes, but I paid a price even for that because in my dreams your clothes turned red with blood as I saw your body lying on the desert floor amongst the decaying flesh of others. Now, how's that for a bad dream? So, tell me, Bill, how much do my dreams differ from yours?" He was dumbfounded. For the second time that night, he had heard, from their own mouths, the secret fears of two people he had known all his life. His understanding of the one was not difficult but he was totally unprepared for the revelations of the other. She reached out and patted his knee.

"Dreams are universal," she sighed. "We all have them in some form or another and to us all they are real; they twist and turn. Situations can become exaggerated and distorted. We can fall into deep black holes with the knowledge that we will never return. We can also walk with God and drink with the Devil, but it isn't in your dreams that the problem lies, Bill. The problem lies with either your inability to accept the things you have seen and done, or to justify such scenes and actions. Either way, you can't go back and undo what has been done. I realise there may be things that you could never tell me and, to be honest, I don't want to know - I don't need more horror to feed my dreams."

As she spoke, he pulled his chair closer and held her hand; he felt it was cold. He instinctively put another log on the fire, along with some smaller kindling, the latter immediately catching fire, and a warm homely glow reached into the room. He sat down and again held her hand; her voice had become softer and compassionate, reminding him of his first recollection of her voice. As a child, he would lie in her arms as she sang lullabies, the smooth tunes that he could still recall were like a calm sea whose rippled waves lazily ebbed and flowed on sandy shores. There was no rush, just pure contentment. He laid his head on her lap.

"You are cold," he said.

"That matters little," she replied, as raising her hand, she gently ran her fingers through his hair.

"You haven't done that for a long time."

"Not since you last needed me to," she said with a smile. With that, she closed her eyes and murmured sleepily, "Stay a while, it's been so long, hasn't it?" He didn't reply; there seemed no need for conversation. Then, like her, he closed his eyes. Was this one of those moments in life that would always be remembered? On the face of it, this act of placing his head on his mother's lap was not something he had done before. Countless times her lap had been a pillow that he had cried and slept on, but he had been a child then and now, as a man, an observer may well think his action rather effeminate, or to say the least unmanly, but it seemed right and proper. In the confines of his home, he felt comfortable enough to allow himself the pleasure, even for a few moments, of abandoning this cloak of self-reliance and preservation that he had worn for so long.

"Is there anything you would like to know?" he asked.

"What about?"

"I don't know," he said, "about Egypt I suppose; did I tell you we went to Bethlehem?"

"Yes, in one of your letters."

"And that I swam in the Suez Canal?"

"I didn't know you could swim."

"In a country like that, the climate encourages you to learn."

"There is one thing I would like to know and don't be mad at me for asking." There was a nervousness in her voice that both intrigued and worried him. He was tempted to raise his head from her lap but maybe he could answer her question without looking at her face. Although she had mentioned that the need to recollect tales of horror was not her wish, he still felt apprehensive.

"Well?" he encouraged her to carry on, "and I promise not to be mad."

"I would like to know the real reason you didn't go to Ian's memorial service last Sunday. I've been thinking about it all week and for the life of me, I don't understand it. He was your friend; couldn't your religious doubts and dislike for his father have been put aside for one day?" Bill could feel tension in her body as she spoke; her hand had stopped stroking his hair and was now resting on his head. He could feel a slight trembling of fingers as she carried on.

"I made the excuse to all that you were too upset to attend but, all this time after his death, I don't think too many people were convinced. I know Megan wasn't. So, just what was it that made you so determined not to go?"

"He shot himself." He heard an intake of breath and, for a second, was unsure which one of them was the more surprised, he, at his willingness to discard a promise that he'd made regarding Ian's death, or her look of disbelief as he raised his head, looking into her face in the flickering light of the fire as he held her hands.

"It is true," he said, "and I want your word that you will never tell a living soul what I have told you, not even Father. You see, in telling you this I have broken a promise to the boys, but I would like to think that, on this occasion, your need to know is greater than my need for silence. Anyway, sometimes mothers should be exempt from the promises of silence that their children make."

"I am so sorry." Her voice was just above a whisper. "I'm so, so sorry." A tear rolled down her cheek and fell onto the back of Bill's hand.

"No doubt you're curious as to why he did what he did and the truth is, I really don't know. We reported that he had died in action on the field of battle and was buried where he lay, along with another lad in our unit. The report was true, we just omitted at whose hand he had died."

The chiming of the clock made Bill look at its scrolled hands: a quarter past four. He looked back at his mother; her eyes had followed his but she said nothing.

"There is another truth about Ian; he was a brave man. And really that's all there is ……. that's all you need to know."

As Bill climbed the stairs to his bed, he pondered on the word 'man' in the context of describing Ian to his mother. It was a word that for some years he had difficulty with, even to the point of describing himself. Ian had just turned twenty-one when he died. For just when do boys become men? He had fought with eighteen-year-old men and thirty-year-old boys. Do mother's sons, on the last day of their twentieth year, become men the following morning? Do men that have seen fifty summers think they were men when they had seen twenty-one? Now as he thought of Ian, he suddenly realised maturity didn't come with the passing of years. That distinction, he concluded, came with the collective thoughts of one's peers.

It was five hours later when he awoke, beams of sunlight coming in through his bedroom window and lying like ribbons across his bed. The dawn chorus, inspired by a beautiful early spring morning, was at its best. He dressed and went downstairs.

The house was empty. In the kitchen, he turned on the cold-water tap. Water trickled into a white enamel bowl that looked at home in a white Belfast sink that must have been installed during his absence, an improvement on the old stone one, he thought. He turned off the tap but the water didn't stop as it should have done, it slowed to a drip. Then his hands started to shake as he watched with growing anticipation; drip, drip, drip, drip; any second, he expected the water to turn white but it didn't, then the dripping stopped. His hands were still shaking when he washed his face. He looked up and, above the sink on the windowsill, a small cracked shaving mirror reflected his movements. But his gaze went beyond his reflection in the mirror.

"A shave wouldn't go amiss," he said to himself. At that moment, his mother opened the back door, the familiar sound of wood scraping flagstone was something that he had grown used to and, annoying as it was, it had its place in his home.

"What a beautiful morning," she said as she brushed past him.

"Just been up for the milk. Megan usually gets it for me Saturday mornings but she can't make it this morning." She placed the two milk cans on the table. "Your father's gone to fix a gap in a hedge somewhere, where a few sheep broke through last night. Arthur found them wandering the road on his way to the malt house first thing this morning." Bill dipped his shaving brush into a mug with a missing handle, containing the last of the tepid water from the kettle.

"That'll keep him busy for a couple of hours," he said. He felt a little uneasy at the thought of his father working while he was sleeping. "You should have woken me; I could've given him a hand," he said, trying to ease his guilt.

"You were asleep and I didn't like to wake you. By the way, I saw Jim in that garden of his, it must be heartbreaking for him to see it in the state it's in. It would be a nice gesture if you could go up and help him out; I'm sure he'd appreciate it." As she spoke, she brushed past Bill again, carrying a bundle of dirty washing. He wiped his face and followed her into the wash house, where she dumped the clothes into a basket and set about raking the ashes from under the boiler. He rolled up his shirt sleeves, then reached and took down the garden spade which hung from a nail in the wall of the wash house.

"I'll go on up, then," he said. "I'll see you later, might go for a beer before dinner."

"Don't forget Megan is coming for dinner, so don't go wandering off."

"Okay, okay," he said as he walked out of the wash house. It didn't surprise him that nothing was said about their talk the previous night but he was glad that it had happened, as much for her sake as for his own. He had slept well and that morning he felt much better and fresher than he had for a while. He decided that today was going to be a good day.

The previous Saturday morning, Jim had looked out of his bedroom window, surveying the unkempt garden of his home and was disheartened to see it in the state it was in. It had never looked like this; normally at this time of the year, it would have been dug over in readiness for the vegetables that he would plant. Then, in a month or so, the fruits of his labour would be seen emerging from the soil. The rows of King Edwards, in furrows as straight as an arrow, running parallel to bean sticks like soldiers on parade, standing motionless awaiting the long haul of the bean shoots that were to climb them. There would be rows of cabbages, lettuce, onions, beetroot and other vegetables. As it was, there was nothing except the gooseberry bushes and rhubarb to suggest the existence of any kind of garden. He groaned as he realised the amount of work needed to re-establish his patch to its former glory.

Violet had told him that dandelions and buttercups grew in profusion as if purposely planted and, from the hedges that formed the boundary of the garden, nettles and brambles grew thick and unrelenting, encroaching onto ground that had previously been denied them. The stone garden path that he had meticulously laid the summer before he went away, was now a carpet of moss and weeds.

She had tried to stem the tide of the advancing undergrowth, but her weeding counted for nothing so she gave up and let nature take its course. Jim dressed, and, leaving Violet in their bed, went downstairs. The children, already awake, were in their room. He had popped his head around their bedroom door and told them to be quiet so as not to disturb their mother. It seemed odd for him to be called Dad again, especially by children who had become strangers to him. Their suspicions of him were evident at their first meeting. The two younger ones, George and Claire, hid behind their mother's skirt, bewildered as to what was going on, whilst the eldest, Sam, with his distant memories of a man that used to live in their house, was at a loss as to what was expected of him. Then to be ushered by his mother toward him did nothing to hasten any bond that may develop between them. In fact, it was Jim who had for many weeks anticipated the moment of their meeting, and the only unforeseen prediction on his part was when Sam, now at nine years of age, stepped forward and offered his hand in friendship. As Jim and Violet laughed at Sam's sudden act of maturity, Jim privately thought that it was a smart thing to do and was rather proud of his son's good manners. Then, when for the first time in nearly four years he held Violet in his arms, his thoughts of renewed responsibility as a husband and father were a prize worth coming home to.

22

On the second Saturday after arriving home, Jim set to work in the garden. After an hour of cutting back its boundary hedge with a long-handled sickle, he stopped and lit a cigarette. He then tested the sickle's blade for sharpness by dragging his thumb across its blade. He picked up the whetstone he had previously placed on a post, then with long strokes, he drew it along both sides of the sickle's blade. As he sharpened the sickle, he thought of Bill and Jack. He hadn't seen either of them in the two weeks they had been home, but he had heard about them. Jack, he had been told, had taken to drink and Bill to roaming the hills at night. Jim wasn't surprised at Jack's need for drink and he understood Bill's need for solitude as much as he understood his own. Whereas Bill walked the hills, he sank a nine-pound axe head into oaks and elms, facing them off ready to take a crosscut saw that would sever their trunks, sending them crashing to the ground.

During his first day back at work, his workmates had, naturally, been eager to talk about the fighting he was involved in. They asked him questions about his experiences during the war. He responded as best he could, but the fire of enthusiasm had died a long time ago and, in the end, he had respectfully asked them to confine their questions to anything other than the fighting.

"Jesus," he said to a young lad holding the reins of a team of shires, "Ask Tom. He was in France and would have seen more dead bodies than ever I did."

"He won't tell us sod all," said the youngster. "Anyway, he's got shell shock and I can't understand him."

"So I've noticed," Jim said as he glanced at Tom, half-hidden among the branches of a large oak that had just been felled. His nerves were bad and his speech was affected by intermittent stammering.

The young lad let go of the reins and went to the rear of the horses. He unhooked the chains that bound the trunk of a tree that had just been dragged up from the dingle below. "I wish I had been there," the youngster uttered, as he threw the chains wide of the oak. He spoke now as much to the horses as he did to anyone that would listen. 'Well,' thought Jim, "there's no answer to that. Not one that he would understand.' Then he remembered how hundreds and thousands of the country's most able and impressionable put on a khaki uniform and went willingly to serve their country. They walked into a fog of uncertainty armed with a rifle and bayonet, obeying orders that on occasions were beyond belief, resulting in the unnecessary deaths of so many.

Politicians would have them believe it was for King and country that they fought and, in the beginning, it may have been so, but Jim knew that when in the thick of it, you fought to save your own neck. For him, King and country came way back in the line of importance, somewhere between your dog and ferrets and a good fart, he reckoned. Still, there were those who, on occasions, abandoned common sense and risked their lives to pursue actions that were, in hindsight, deemed stupid. His thoughts were that bravery and stupidity amounted to much the same thing and he was a little confused when the word hero was brought into the equation. Violet had looked the word up for him in the dictionary: "a doer of great or brave deeds". Of course, this explanation held no surprise but he felt the word "stupid" should fit in there somewhere. On occasions, he had witnessed the deaths of men attempting heroic deeds. Some achieved their objective, but most didn't. They would die and become a statistic in whatever battle they finally departed this world. As he often said, "dead heroes don't have much to live for". But of those very deeds and actions, stupid or otherwise, Jim was as guilty as the people he criticised. Of course, he didn't see it that way. The difference between him and other mortals was that his actions had nothing to do with heroism and everything to do with logic. Other men's stupidity was his calculated gamble; their bravery his natural instinct, and for a man who couldn't read, or write anything but his own name, his common sense made him exceptional in the art of survival.

"Dad." Jim turned his head. "Mum wants you to go and shoot a rabbit and she says if you don't go, I might as well." Sam stood by the back door, his father's shotgun in his hands. Jim saw his son playfully put the gun's butt to his shoulder and look down its barrel. He was pointing it across the brook and into some trees.

"I hope you haven't got any cartridges in that?" Jim's casual question got a similarly casual answer.

"You bet I have." And with that, there was an almighty bang. Instinctively, Jim let go of the sickle and dropped to his knees. Sam was on his arse; the biggest piece of an already broken pane of glass fell out of the kitchen window, screams of terror came from within the house and a dead pigeon fell from a pine tree. A plume of silver-grey feathers floated amongst the tree's pine needles, each one hanging as if suspended on a spider's thread. Slowly, they drifted clear of its branches and as raised voices could be heard, they descended on a faint breeze, not touching the ground until all recriminations, verbal reasoning and threats of a thick ear were complete.

Sam, unaware of the consequences that his action would bring, was still willing to pay any penalty that would come his way. He had asked his father a number of times to take him shooting and was aggrieved that his requests were dismissed on each occasion. It would be different, he thought, if his father had refused to take him when he went shooting. But in the week he had been home, he hadn't even taken the gun down from above the fireplace.

As he looked out of his bedroom window, with tears running down his face and an aching shoulder from the recoil of the shotgun, he could see his first wood pigeon lying where it had fallen and he felt disappointed at his father's indifference.

Jim stopped for a moment and looked at the brown angry water of the swollen brook as it rushed under the wooden footbridge. He could feel the old timbers vibrate under his feet. He shrugged his shoulders, turned around and walked to the road, changing his mind on the direction he should take. His shotgun swung loosely over his left shoulder, both barrels now visibly empty of the cartridges that Sam had placed in them. Up until the point of taking them out, he hadn't touched the firearm since his return and if not for Sam, it would have stayed above the fireplace a lot longer than it did.

He stopped and looked around. To his right, for about two hundred yards, the field he was in was quite flat. After that, it dipped sharply into a wooded dingle. In front of him, at some distance, sheep grazed unconcerned at his being there. Beyond them, the ground gradually rose, the grass then giving way to thick gorse bushes that stretched far to his left. He walked to a tree stump and sat down. From his pocket, he pulled out two cartridges and placed them into the gun's chambers. The bright red cylinders slipped in as easily as the hundreds that had preceded them, but this time it was different. This time there was no excitement. The anticipation of shooting a rabbit did nothing to hasten his heartbeat. He stood up and closed the gun, the distinct click as it locked into position reminding him of the bolt action of his army rifle and although the sound and mechanics of it were totally different, to him, both sounds were a prelude to mayhem. Slowly, he walked past the sheep, their heads lowered, gleaning from the field the best of the winter grass - grass that would soon respond to the forthcoming warmer weather that springtime would bring. A startled rabbit ran swiftly in front of him and made for the safety of a stretch of dead fern. Their brown withered fronds and broken stems provided good cover for a rabbit. This rabbit had encountered men with long sticks before. It wasn't the men as much as the long sticks that they feared, for these long sticks made a sound like thunder and did harm to their kind. Jim walked on. His mind was on other things. He was desperately sorry for ignoring his son's pleas to take him shooting but his heart wasn't in it. How could he tell him he no longer wanted to shoot anything anymore? How could he explain his need to see things live? Jim shook his head. Sam was his father's son and he would never understand. He walked for some ten minutes, then cautiously approached an embankment. He walked the length of its base until he reached the field's boundary. The hedge was ragged and unkept. Every now and then, along its length a tree, against all odds, had managed to grow, their stunted forms now void of leaves, exposed the lay of their crippled branches. The constant wind made them grow at an unnatural angle, giving them an arthritic look.

Jim held his shotgun in a position of readiness and, as he climbed the gradient, his right thumb pulled back the hammers of both barrels. He wanted to turn back and go home, but he couldn't. He would rather have dug a hundred gardens and felled a thousand trees than to do what he expected of himself. At the top of the embankment, he knelt and peered through the brambles of a blackberry bush that had ventured a yard from the hedge's base. The scene that greeted him was as he expected; twenty yards away, two rabbits were busy eating, going over the same grass that sheep had probably done earlier. One raised its head and looked around; Jim held his breath. Satisfied as to its safety, the rabbit lowered its head and carried on eating. Five yards further on, another pair were doing the same. To think that the mere act of shooting a rabbit had become distasteful to him was ridiculous. Men shot rabbits to eat, for goodness sake.

What was it that made him feel the way he did? He had always respected the sanctity of life and never shot more than was needed; why would he? Jim lowered his head and sat down, releasing the hammers on his shotgun as he did so. Then he lay the gun on the ground beside him and looked at the sky.

The sun shone from between what few clouds there were. Some lapwings caught his attention; high in the air they would tumble about, giving those who would care to watch a flying display that was unsurpassed and on a stiff wind the unmistakable call of a curlew reached his ears. Then, with some determination, he reached for his gun and again pulled back its hammers. With their tarnished barrels poking through the brambles and the stock nestled against his shoulder, he aligned the sights on the nearest pair of rabbits, who by now were feeding side-by-side. There was a slight tremor in his hands and beads of sweat had emerged on his forehead. He decided to use the right barrel on one of the rabbits and the left barrel, with luck, would take out one behind it. He blinked. His eyes were stinging from the sweat that had now run into them and he was very aware of the tremor in his hands. He inhaled deeply.... then held his breath.

His target was clear, then everything became rather fuzzy; misty shapes loomed in front of him. One rabbit stood up on its back legs, its paws raised. Jim blinked again, this time shutting his eyes tight, squeezing out the sweat that was now flowing freely down his face. On opening them, the sight that greeted him made him freeze and a shudder ran through his body. In front of him, at twenty paces, were two Turkish soldiers, one kneeling, the other standing and rolling a cigarette. Their clothes were ragged and blood-stained. In their unshaven and gaunt faces, Jim saw a haunting emptiness. He felt a tightness around his chest and found it difficult to breathe. His mind was reeling as he calculated his chances of getting out of this situation alive. Not taking his eyes off the soldiers, Jim noticed that the green field, now abandoned by the rabbits, had been replaced by a dusty, reddish landscape. A rocky outcrop lay behind and to the right of the soldiers, five paces behind them, were two more soldiers, also in a kneeling position, their dishevelled look matching those of their companions. Were the rabbits about to have their revenge? Had they come back as men to taunt and humiliate their enemy? A slight movement from the soldier standing caused a surge of blood to run through Jim's veins. This man from his past, he felt sure, had intentions of evil. The soldier slowly lowered his hands and turned his head. Jim looked into his eyes and realised that the empty coal-black eyes that stared back knew that he was there. Above them, in a clear and silent sky, the lapwings still danced.

Their flights of fancy went unnoticed. Then, as two gunshots rang out, they dispersed in mild panic, regrouping elsewhere to start again their sky dance where maybe a more appreciative audience would marvel at their antics. The echoes of the gunshots reverberated from one hilltop to another and their sound finally drifted away on the same breeze that carried off the call of the curlew.

23

Jack stood up and brushed away the hair from his naked shoulders. The cut strands fell silently onto the red quarry tiles of the kitchen floor and lay around the legs of the wooden stool he had been sitting on. His mother placed a pair of scissors on the kitchen table and then, with the tea towel that had been used as a cape around Jack's neck, she proceeded to wipe his back.

"There, that looks better," she turned him around then looked him square in the face, making sure his sideburns were both level, "and don't let it get so long next time". Jack looked at himself in a hand mirror and grunted his approval.

"I suppose you're going up to the pub now?" she said. He looked at a clock that hung on the wall.

"Why do you keep that clock ten minutes fast?"

"Because I like it that way." He turned and gave her a peck on the cheek.

"Just going up for a couple," he said with a smile.

"And when was the last time you walked into a pub and only had two pints?"

"Can't remember," he said, still smiling. "But then, I can't remember ever saying I was only going for two." He reached for the clean white shirt she was holding.

"I didn't hear you come in last night. Were you out in that storm?" she asked. Jack looked at his mother as he rolled up his shirt sleeves. "Pretty rough at one stage, wasn't it?"

"I was on my way home and just made it to Ted Parry's hay barn before the worst of the rain. Spent most of the night there."

As drunk as he was, he remembered his rendezvous with God on Montgomery Town hill. He remembered standing naked in the rain shouting his demand that God or the Devil take him. Either one, it made no difference. He looked out of the window where, in a patch of blue sky, the sun was shining. He took a deep breath and made his exit, promising his mother he would be back in an hour. 'God wasn't ready for me', he thought as he walked the three hundred yards to the pub, and maybe his approach to the Devil wasn't as it should have been. Still, they'd both had their chance and he had had his say and, at the risk of being conceited, today he felt good about himself; today he felt that a burden had been lifted from his shoulders. Now he could look anyone in the eye and with justification. He regarded his conduct as a soldier to have been acceptable, if not honourable, and any mantle that he was still to carry was now a price he could pay.

He stopped and looked over the iron railings at the swirling waters of the brook that ran alongside the road. His attention was drawn to the visible energy it produced.

It was a living thing that crashed and pushed against the straining banks that held it at bay. It was a brown ribbon of spirit that challenged every turn it made on its rush to the River Severn some two miles away. He leaned on the topmost rail and looked intently at one particular spot of the swollen stream, the swift-moving water confusing his eyes, yet he still looked. 'Children and raindrops,' he thought. Children were attracted to water and water was the nectar of the Gods, and only the Gods knew the destiny of both. He wasn't quite sure where he was going with his thoughts, and it all sounded rather silly but still, he gazed at the water; there was something familiar about its urgency. "Controlled panic, that's it. Controlled panic!" He smiled to himself as he made the connection, "I'm like this bloody brook," he said out loud. Then he thought again of children and raindrops, in themselves both innocent and harmless and raindrops on roses could even be thought of as rather romantic. But when raindrops converged with others and are then multiplied by millions, the resulting outcome was controlled panic.

As for the children of Jack's generation, a few of the boys grew up to be soldiers, soldiers that formed their own ribbon of spirit, soldiers that also rushed from one bend to another. There had been many turning points for Jack and, as poignant as some were, did any of them really make a difference? Did the bones of men that littered the ground multiply his curses, and if so, did they also divide his humanity? With flared nostrils and a beating heart, would he still slaughter the world just to take one last breath? And now, at the end of it all, and on reflection, could he take an olive branch from his adversaries and give a white dove in return? He doubted not, for he was he and they were they and, as surely as raindrops make rivers and children grow up to be villains, heroes, and anything in between, Jack had now finally found himself.

He continued to stare at the raging water, then, above the sound of its anger, a voice, almost incoherent, caught his ears.

"Don't do it, Jack- it's not worth it!" He turned. Across the road, standing at the entrance to the Smithy were Megan and her brother.

"A penny for them," David said, as Jack walked over.

"For my thoughts?" Jack replied, laughing. "You wouldn't want to get inside my head. Anyway, it's full of rubbish." He looked at Megan.

"Well, you're a sight for sore eyes; where are you going all dressed up?" He had seen and spoken to her a couple of times since he had arrived home and, on the first occasion, as she stood outside his front door to welcome him home, he hardly recognised her. He remembered the letters she had written to Bill. He also remembered how he found it difficult to picture how one so young should feel almost duty-bound to write to the boys of her village. As Bill read out her news and best wishes, his image of her changed, for these were not the words of an adolescent, not the words of a sixteen-year-old girl, at least not the one he had last seen on the village green all that time ago.

Her letters were, in the main, light-hearted and informative, but there was anxiety and a fear which she could not hide. A mother writing to her sons could not

have been more concerned. In one letter, she actually
asked Jack not to take risks. How could she have known
that, of the three of them, he was the risk-taker? The one
with that certain bravado? The one to raise his hand and
the first to step forward? He often thought that his actions
would be his downfall. Was it that because he was smaller
than most men he felt he had something to prove? He
could hit the deck and be up and running before most of
the big boys had their knees off the ground. He was fast,
he was surefooted and, as one sergeant, whose name he
couldn't recall, said to him,

"Davies, your attribute to the King's Army is that you
can run like the wind and hide in small holes so don't fuck
up your advantage by thinking that the Devil isn't out to
get you." Twelve hours earlier, as Jack had laid his weary
head on the hay in Ted Parry's barn, he had thought of
the sergeant who had warned him of this dark and sinister
image. He had chuckled to himself as he closed his eyes.

"There was no need to worry about the devil getting
me, Sergeant. He wasn't ever going to get me. Why should
he? As of tonight, he has finally got off my back."

Megan smiled at Jack.

"Bill's mum has invited me to dinner. You don't
think I'm overdressed, do you?" Her smile had given way
to a look of disappointment. She'd tried so hard to look
just right and now was Jack implying that she had indeed
overdressed?

"Not at all," said Jack. "You look lovely." He had
learned that Bill's mother and Megan had become friendly,
and the way Megan had talked of Bill, even though she

had not even met him since his return, suggested that she had some ulterior motive other than just to welcome him home. To say he was not a little bit envious of Bill would have been untrue. He had even thought of asking for her company but had had second thoughts, concluding that Bill was probably more suited to her than he was. They talked for some moments and Jack suggested David go for a drink with him, but David reluctantly declined, saying that he had too much work to do. Jack watched him as he slowly moved into the shadows of the blacksmith's shop, his movements hampered by the long and heavy leather apron he wore. They were both silent for a moment.

"A lot of horses have rested their hooves on that apron," Jack said as he watched David disappear.

Megan followed his gaze. "It was his dad's; he wears it from time to time."

They both turned and, without a word, walked into the village. Behind them, the steady ring of iron striking iron could be heard and its sound, as David's dad had told him as a child, was to stop a village from sleeping.

"So, you will be seeing Bill, then?" Jack smiled as he spoke. He wondered if Megan would pick up on his intended inference of a relationship between the both of them, but she didn't reply. She stopped walking and turned to Jack.

"Jack, would you do me a big favour?" her mind was elsewhere as she spoke. "It's about David," she paused and, as she hesitated, she bit her bottom lip. "The morning the three of you went away, David told me that he should have also gone. He didn't think it right that he should have to stay behind. He made enquiries to see if he could join up but they wouldn't have him. They said that, as a blacksmith, he was needed at home and anyway, they would have had their quota of blacksmiths in the mounted regiments. There were not many weeks when he wouldn't say that he should be with the boys. He felt very guilty for a long time and I think he still does." As she spoke, she lowered her head, her hands playing nervously with the gloves she held, threading them through one hand and then the other. "I must confess I didn't want him to go to war, I was fifteen years old Jack. He was all I had. Was I wrong? Was my not wanting him to go a good enough reason to justify a duty that he felt was more important? Guilt has also been a companion of mine. Sometimes I could handle it and sometimes I couldn't. For months, I would put it at the back of my mind, then, every time I would write to Bill, there it was again."

Jack listened to Megan's self-reproach and concern for her brother and the more she talked, the better he understood. But he wondered why she was telling him these things that had worried her so. He looked at her; he hardly knew her and she knew him even less. Did a few words in a few letters convey more than the words themselves? Was he ready for the trust he was sure she was about to bestow in him? A little confused he may have been, but daunted he was not.

"There is one thing I do know; David is not a coward." Megan, as well as raising her voice, raised her head and looked Jack in the eyes. "He would have fought shoulder to shoulder with the three of you. He would have done your bidding as you would have done his." She paused again and lowered her eyes. "But the question of what he would have done does not arise, does it, Jack?"

"Megan," Jack interrupted. "I don't know if you should be telling me these things but for what it's worth, David should not feel any guilt for not having put on an army uniform. He had proved himself long before Kitchener had pointed his finger, telling us how much our country needed us, and if the favour you are asking of me is to tell him so, then I will. Whether he takes heed of anything I say, I won't know. Look, Megan," ... Jack was now wondering if he was the right sort to convince David that there was no stigma attached to him for not joining the ranks, "there were questions asked about other men, but never once was David's name ever mentioned. We just thought of him as one of those who had to remain at home to keep the country running, like farmers. Maybe I am not the person to speak to him of such matters, as I have too many faults for my word to be credible. I drink too much, swear too much; in fact, I do too much of things I should do less of, and on top of everything, I am totally irresponsible. Responsibility has never asked anything of me and I have never sought it."

"But you will speak to him?"

"If that is what you want."

"Thank you, Jack, it would mean a lot to me."

"How could I refuse?" Jack smiled as he conceded to Megan's request. "And as for you, Megan, for whatever reason you wrote your letters, don't ever think they were of no consequence. Letters would cause us not to sleep at nights. For days, we would hang on to their words and the thing about letters is that their value is as much in the mind of the one that reads them as it is in the one that writes them." He went on to tell Megan that most men had letters in their breast pockets. That he had seen men laugh while reading them and some he had seen cry, and sometimes men who had time, would hold them in their hands as they died. Then he stopped talking and smiled and, as his thoughts started to wander, he heard Megan again thank him. He watched her as she turned and walked the road to Bill's house.

"Thank you, Megan," he replied softly, but she didn't hear him for as he spoke, Megan, in her blue-grey dress, disappeared around a corner. For a moment, he stood and looked at an empty road. She was gone and he felt alone. "A fine lady," he said to himself as he kicked a stone which bounced and rolled in the direction of the pub door.

24

On the morning of Megan's arranged dinner date at Jessie's, she did what she mostly did on a Saturday morning. She would place some of Michael's clothes, ones that she had washed and ironed, into a basket, then she would call at the shop for a portion of his favourite cheese and anything else he was short of. Mavis had offered to do his washing, but Megan insisted that she would do it, as it was no trouble to her and that her presence alone was a tonic to everyone, especially to Michael. He had mentioned to Megan some weeks earlier that the time they were spending together was something special to him. Megan had noticed that Michael's health had deteriorated sharply in the last few weeks, more so since the death of Shy three weeks earlier. He awoke and found him dead on his blanket. Michael tearfully carried him out and buried him in the field outside his home, in a spot that could be seen from his kitchen window.

Since then, Megan had called on Michael most days, just to see how he was and, as Mavis was away in London, she was getting more concerned. She had mentioned her concern to Jessie, saying that sometimes she was frightened as to what she may find on opening his door. Jessie, in reply, said that she would make a point of calling on him herself. When she did, Michael would ask about Bill and, while talking of him, Jessie sensed a kinship that existed between them. She knew that, before the war, the pair of them would sit for ages in the pub talking. Michael would talk and Bill would listen. It was common knowledge that Michael had been in the American Civil War but that was as much as most folk knew and, although Jessie had supposed that Bill was privy to Michael's life, at least insofar as what Michael wanted him to know, she didn't ask and he didn't tell.

As Megan knocked and entered Michael's home, she was surprised to see him gutting a rabbit on the kitchen table.

"Good morning, Michael," she said as she closed the door behind her, "How are you feeling this morning?"

"Not so bad," he said as he wrapped the rabbit's intestines in a newspaper along with the rest of the unwanted carcass. He then poured cold water from an enamel jug into a bowl and washed his bloodied hands. He emptied the bowl into the sink and watched the red-stained water disappear down the plughole.

"Got you some cheese," Megan said as she placed the strong cheddar on the table, "also some of Rose's bread pudding and your clothes." Michael, turning from the sink, looked up and smiled.

"Ha, Rose's bread pudding, now that's something I can eat and hold down. Jessie called yesterday afternoon," he said without stopping. "I told her I would be going down the pub today about one o'clock and to let Bill know." Michael, having wrapped the rabbit up in a tea towel, was now placing it in Megan's basket.

"What time will you be going to Jessie's?" he asked as he handed her the basket.

"Around two-thirty," she said before giving him a peck on his cheek. "Thanks for the rabbit."

"Not a problem," said Michael as he held open the door.

"Off to the Rectory now for a couple of hours," she smiled. "Will I see you tomorrow?"

"God willing," he said. Megan looked at him and tilted her head.

"Michael Gill, do you believe in God?"

"No," he said, smiling back.

"Then why did you say God willing?"

"Just in case I'm wrong," He bent down and kissed Megan on the top of her head; "Love you, Megan Davies."

"Love you, Michael Gill," she laughed as she walked through his open door and out to the road.

25

It was still early morning when Bill made his way to Jim's house. He found him outside trimming the hedges that surrounded his garden.

"Not the right time of the year to be doing that," he shouted from the road. Jim looked up smiling.

"I hope you haven't come here just to exchange pleasantries," he said as he stopped and waited for Bill to join him.

"Well, I have brought a spade if that's a clue as to why I'm here," Bill smiled back. "Mother said you were in your garden; she saw you earlier."

"Yes, I did see her; had she been up for milk?"

"Yes, and she suggested I come and give you a hand."

"Well, put that spade down and grab a sickle; there won't be any digging today as I want to finish this hedge first, hopefully before dinner. If you go on the other side of the hedge, we can work both sides together."

As they worked, Sam came out of the house and joined them.

"You remember Bill, don't you, Sam?"

"Yes sir," answered Sam.

"My, you've grown up a bit," said Bill, "and how old are you now?"

"I'll be ten at Christmas, sir. Is there anything I can do?" he asked his father.

"You can gather up the cuttings," said Jim, as he again started to swing the sickle he held. They had worked for an hour, only stopping when Violet came up the path with a tray of bacon sandwiches and three mugs of tea.

"Hello, Violet," said Bill as he took the tray from her, giving her a peck on the cheek at the same time.

"Hello, Bill. How are you?" Jessie had told Violet about her concern for Bill, about his walking the hills at night, so Violet was surprised to see Bill looking so well and she told him so. "You're looking well, Bill. Have you seen Megan yet?" knowing full well he hadn't.

"Violet," Jim said, sounding a little disappointed in her line of questioning.

"Just asking," she said, smiling at Bill, "just asking. You'll see a difference in that girl since the last time you saw her."

"No, I haven't seen her yet," Bill replied, "but I will see her."

"She's coming for dinner, isn't she?" Violet interrupted.

"Violet," Jim said loudly. "For goodness sake leave the man alone. He doesn't want to be questioned about his love life."

"My love life!" exclaimed Bill. "I haven't got a love life." The three of them started to laugh as Violet turned and walked back to the house.

"You soon will have," she muttered to herself, then without turning, she shouted, "Bring the tray into the house, Sam, when you've finished."

"Women," said Jim, as he and Bill sat on a wooden bench, both reaching for their mugs of tea. Sam sat on an upturned bucket eating his sandwich, when Jim asked him if he would go into the house to eat, as he would like to talk to Bill. Sam, looking dejected, got up from his bucket, dropping his sandwich onto the ground at the same time. He picked it up and wiped away the dirt on his trousers. As he walked up to the house, Jim called after him, "Do you fancy going shooting rabbits tomorrow?" Sam looked at his father and a beaming smile came to his face.

"Yes!" he shouted excitedly as he ran into the house. "Mum, Mum!"

"And how are things, Bill? I'm sorry about Violet," Jim said, shrugging his shoulders. "You know what women are like."

"Well, no, I don't know what women are like," said Bill with a little laugh. "You must know I do a lot of walking, day and bloody night," he continued, "although I had a good night last night – well, up until just after four this morning. And you, Jim?" he asked.

"Much the same, only I don't go for the walks in the middle of the night," he grimaced. "Anyway, it's Jack I'm worried about; he's drinking a lot."

"So I've heard."

"He's been banned from The Cottage for fighting, and he's talking a lot."

"Talking a lot?" Bill said frowning.

"Yes, talking about things that happened in the desert. I haven't seen him to talk to. He'll probably be down the pub dinner time so I think I'll go down myself for a drink. I've only been in twice myself since being home."

Bill didn't tell him about seeing Jack on the town hill; there wasn't any need for him to know, he thought.

"I'm going down there myself; apparently, Michael wants to see me."

"Not so good, is he?" Jim asked.

"No, Mum told me he's not good at all. It will be nice to see him again, though."

Just before midday, they had finished. Bill picked up his spade and looked up at the sky. "Looks like we could have some rain."

"It won't be much," said Jim, having been into the house for the trench coat he was now wearing. As they walked, Jim told Bill about the incident the previous Saturday, when Sam had shot a pigeon outside the house.

"I gave him a clip round the ear and sent him to bed. I don't know, Bill, but I just don't like shooting anything anymore."

"And what did you do after sending him to bed?"

"I went for a walk and shot a couple of rabbits," they both laughed, "but I didn't like doing it," Jim added.

"Maybe," said Bill, "but tell me, what is the difference between you and Sam when you were his age?"

"Nothing."

"Then let him be, Jim; he is what he is. Be thankful for it."

"It's just that I'm finding it hard. How could I go into the pub and tell people that I don't like shooting rabbits?"

"Maybe, but why are you telling me?"

"Because you, I thought, of all people would understand. Would you have trouble shooting rabbits?"

"No, I don't think so, but then I have my own fucking problems, Jim. I have nightmares that you wouldn't believe; they come out of the bloody walls at me."

They walked for a further few minutes, each lost in their own thoughts.

"I'm dreading taking Sam tomorrow," Jim said with a sigh.

"But you have to do it."

"Yes, I know."

"Right, I'll see you shortly," said Bill as they stood outside his home. "I'll hang up my spade and change my clothes; Mother won't want Megan seeing me like this."

"I'll see you, Bill. I hope Jack is there and thanks for giving me a hand."

"Not a problem. You still have a lot more to do to that garden to get it back to how it used to be." Jim grunted, "I know."

"How are Jim and Violet?" Jessie asked as Bill walked in.

"Fine," said Bill as took off his boots. Then, as he climbed the stairs, he heard his mother shout.

"How long will you be at the pub?"

"A couple of hours," Bill shouted back.

"Well, it's twelve now, so don't be late."

Bill, having changed, combed his hair and looked at himself in the mirror above the kitchen sink, then placing his cap back on his head, opened the back door and walked outside. On leaving the gravel path to the road, he thought of Megan and he wondered how much she had changed in the four years he had been away. He thought also of the letters she had sent him. He had kept them all, bringing them back with him. As he walked, he pulled his coat around him and pulled his cap down firmly over his brow. He looked up; it had started to rain again; he saw patches of blue sky between some rain clouds. 'Just sun showers,' he thought. As he lowered his head, he noticed a figure walking toward him. It was a woman and, as she got closer, he noticed she wore a blue-grey dress. He couldn't see her face; it was obstructed by the umbrella she carried.

'It's Megan; it has to be,' he smiled at the thought. He stopped and waited for her, all the time growing more confident the closer she got. Then, when she was a few yards away from him, he said, "Hello." The lady stopped suddenly and when she raised her umbrella, he saw a beautiful lady, one that he hardly recognised, but recognise her he did. When she saw him it was as though time and distance had been stripped away. They were again on the village green where she had touched his arm and wished him well. Then as they stared at each other, she started to cry, her tears becoming lost amongst the raindrops that fell on her wet face. He saw her having difficulty with the umbrella, then when she dropped it, she came to him with arms open wide and wrapped them around his neck.

Whilst Megan walked the road to Jessie's, the conversation she had just had with Jack was not on her mind. Her mind was on other things.... did she choose the right dress? Wear the right shoes? Were her shoes even suitable and did she use too much of the perfume that Mavis had given her?

'I can't go back and change,' she thought, 'I don't have time.' She stopped and opened her umbrella.

"This is ridiculous," she said to herself "It's raining, and my shoes would be the last thing he would look at." As she walked, she thought of what words she would use on seeing Bill for the first time. With the umbrella over her head, slightly drooping at the front and the rain dripping from its edges, her vision was somewhat limited to a few yards in front of her.

"It wouldn't be right to shake his hand, maybe I could give him a hug, maybe a kiss on the cheek would be more appropriate."

"Hello," she heard a man's voice say. Megan froze and raised her umbrella; in front of her at three paces stood Bill. As they looked at each other, Megan started to cry,

"It's you, Bill, isn't it? It's you."

"Well, I hope it's me, Megan," Bill said, looking at the lady wearing the blue-grey dress.

"Right now, I wouldn't want another man to be in my shoes." Megan stood sobbing as she fumbled with the umbrella strap around her wrist. Once free of it, she let it fall to the ground, then rushing the few steps that separated them, raised her arms and wrapped them around his neck.

"Hello, Bill Jones," she said through her sobs. "I've missed you, and now you're home." With the rain dripping from her hair, she felt as though she was drowning, drowning in happiness and, as she felt his arms around her, she knew instantly that this was the man she would love forever. She looked up and saw a rainbow beyond the trees, trees that she had just walked under. For the last twelve months, this was the moment she had longed for. This moment above all moments, when she could cast aside her past and, for the present, take whatever comfort Bill was willing to give her and she was going to wallow in it. She could feel the warmth of his body seep into the numbness that was hers.

"Don't let me go, Bill," she whispered as he moved one arm up her back, placing his hand on her head then running his fingers through her damp hair. She could feel his breath on her neck as she clung to him.

"Hello, Megan Davies," he said, even his voice sending a shiver through her. "Are you cold?" he asked, still holding her.

"No, I'm as warm as toast."

Megan was sobbing on his shoulder. In his mind, Bill remembered a fifteen-year-old holding his arm and giving him a quick kiss on the cheek before running home, the same girl that had written countless letters with no indication as to the feelings that she now showed. And now, as he held her, he felt lost, or maybe it was a feeling of being found; he didn't know and he didn't care. When she asked him not to let her go, he wasn't about to anyway; he wanted to hold her for a long time. He could smell her scented neck as he ran his fingers through her wet hair and, for the first time, he sensed that he was on the verge of a new life, a life he was to spend with the girl who wrote him letters.

When they parted, they just looked at each other, summing up the difference in their present appearance from what they looked like four years earlier. Bill was more mature in his looks, she thought. He was lean, with high cheekbones, with a defined dimple in his chin and he was taller than she remembered. Megan, having lost the adolescent look she had, was the prettiest girl he had ever seen. It was her eyes that Bill remembered: wide, almond-shaped and kingfisher blue. She was slim, with the same long black hair that she had always had. Bill bent down and picked up the umbrella and held it over them both.

"I'm sorry, Bill," she said. "Meeting you has been on my mind for the past two weeks, ever since you have been home, and I have told myself that I wouldn't cry when I met you."

"You don't have to be sorry for that," Bill said reassuringly. He reached for her hand, but as he did, Megan stepped forward.

"I want to give you a hug again," she said, "just to be sure."

"To be sure of what?" he kissed her on her forehead.

"To make sure I am not dreaming this," she said as she hugged him for a second time.

"I regret I didn't call to see you when I could have done. I think Mother is a little disappointed in that I didn't see you before you went to London with Mavis, but I needed time, time on my own, time to think and to be truthful, I didn't know whether you would think of me being anything other than a friend who you wrote letters to and me being a friend who wrote letters back."

"And now?" she said pulling away.

"Now…. maybe there could be a future for us," Bill looked at her smiling.

"The rain has stopped," she said, "and the rainbow has gone."

"Rainbow?"

"Yes, there was one behind you and now it's gone."

"Did you make a wish?"

"Yes, I did."

"Well, I hope it comes true," he said, still smiling.

"I hope so too," Megan said, still holding Bill's hand. "Are you going to see Michael?"

"Yes, I was on my way."

"He'll be waiting for you," said Megan in an anxious tone. "Has your mother told you that he is not at all well?"

"Yes, she's told me," Bill said with a frown. "I'd better go." He reluctantly let go of Megan's hand.

"It won't matter if you're late for dinner, Bill, your seeing Michael is more important and I'll see you later."

"See you later, then," Bill said as he turned and started to walk away.

"Bill" Megan shouted; he stopped and turned, "Welcome home."

"It's nice to be home, Megan," he said as he turned again, anticipating his meeting with a man who had become a little more than a friend.

Megan stood and watched him go, as she wanted to see him walk out of sight. She leaned against the high embankment of the roadside and she felt her legs tremble with the thought of him. Would he look back before he walked around the last bend? She ached for him to turn.

'Nothing matters anymore,' Bill thought. In a little more time than it took to walk to the pub, his life had changed and nothing mattered any more. The only thing that did matter was the lady he had left standing in the road behind him and he knew she was watching him. Before the corner in the road that would take him out of her sight, he stopped, would she be there, he wondered? He turned; she was there, she raised her hand and he raised his.

"Now, Michael." he said to himself as he walked the remaining short distance to the village pub.

26

Michael slowly closed the door after watching Megan leave his home. He shuffled over to the kitchen sink and was violently sick; the pain in his stomach was such that if he hadn't have held onto the sink he would have gone down. In his vomit, he noticed small clots of blood, not a lot but enough for him to notice. He struggled to his chair and sat down. A cold shiver went through his body as he closed his eyes. He slept for a long time, awaking to the feeling of Shy gently nuzzling his leg; he looked down and realised that he had been dreaming.

He sat up; the pain that was in his stomach had eased considerably. He stood up and again went to the sink, this time pouring cold water into a bowl and washing his face; reaching for a towel, he glanced at his clock. It was twenty past twelve when he left his house and started the short walk to the pub. He was hoping that Bill had got the message that he would be there and was looking forward to seeing him. The pain in his stomach had gone only to be replaced by a dull ache, an ache that he felt he could handle.

Fifteen minutes later, he was at the bar. Toby handed him his pint and he walked to the vacant chair that he jokingly regarded as his. He had just sat down when Jack walked in, followed by Jim a few moments later.

"Have you seen Bill?" Michael asked as he pulled out his pipe from his jacket pocket.

"He'll be down shortly," Jim answered. "I've just left him; he's been giving me a hand in the garden and he's just called to see his mother."

Michael lit his pipe and settled into his chair. He looked at the beer on the table by his side and doubted that he could drink it. He looked at Jack and Jim talking at the bar and, as he did so, Bill walked through the door.

As Bill closed the pub door behind him, he paused and looked around. The small porch area made him feel, for whatever reason, a little uncomfortable. In the corner behind the door stood two walking sticks, one with a horse's head handle, the other a knotted black holly. He detected the smell of fresh paint, deducing that the walls had just been painted. He smiled; fresh paint, but still the same colour. Two steps to his left was another door, behind which he could hear voices. He inhaled deeply as he turned the door handle and walked in.

"A pint for my comrade in arms, landlord," Jack's smiling face eased the apprehension that Bill had felt on entering.

"Bitter, is it, Bill?" Toby reached down to a shelf under the pumps and brought out Bill's dimpled glass pot.

"Washed it last week, thinking you might be calling."

"You mean you haven't washed it in four years?" asked Jim in amazement, now standing back from the bar on Bill's approach.

"No point," said Toby as he eased the pump handle forward, releasing the brown liquid in a steady flow into Bill's glass.

"No point," he said again, "as he wasn't here to drink out of it, was he?"

"But couldn't you have washed it at least once a year?" said Jack.

"I don't know why you are so concerned about Bill's glass; yours has had the same treatment," chuckled Toby, placing Bill's pint on the bar.

As Bill tentatively took his first sip, he looked around the room. He noticed new pictures hanging on the walls, or perhaps they were the old pictures, pictures that had always been there, ones that he had never taken any notice of before.

On entering the bar, he noted Michael sitting where he always sat, by the fireplace. His broad smile on seeing him had a warming effect on Bill and the thought occurred to him that the last time he stood in this bar with a beer in his hand, he was in the very same company as now. But unlike now, with four long years behind himself, Jack, and Jim, the anticipation of adventure that once filled their heads was now replaced by doubts and confusion. Then as Jack, Jim and Toby went on about the merits of cleanliness, Bill looked over to where Michael was sitting. His hunched posture was a reminder that Michael was now an old man, and the destiny of old men lay not 200 yards from his home. By the look of him, it wouldn't be too long before his destiny was realised. Bill didn't like to think it but think it he did.

Michael looked up as Bill ambled over, dragging a chair.

"And how are you, Michael?" he said as he sat down.

"Well I'm still here," Michael replied with a smile. "Nice to see you again," he said as he reached out and shook Bill's hand.

"Have you seen Megan yet?" Michael asked, still smiling.

"Just met her on the road and we said hello. Mum has invited her for dinner."

"And you just said hello?" There was surprise in Michael's voice.

"Well, I was giving her a hug as I said it," Bill said, laughing as he spoke.

"Now that sounds better. It's a fine young lady you have there, Bill, a fine lady."

Bill was about to ask Michael to explain himself about Megan being a fine lady but thought not to.

"Got yourself a new pipe, Michael?" Bill said, changing the subject. Michael laughed. "Never seen you smoke one like that before; it's an American corncob, isn't it?" Michael looked Bill in the eyes, wondering how he knew about an American corncob pipe.

"Saw an American newspaper reporter smoke one in Alexandria; he told me all about them."

"Is that one from America, Michael?" Michael shook his head. "Jesus, Bill, I was looking forward to asking you questions about your time away and all you want is to know about my pipe! Stuff that happened over fifty years ago."

"No offence Michael, but it seems I've got all the time in the world to talk about my shit and you haven't. So, let's talk about your shit first." They both laughed. Michael loved this kind of banter. Bill was right of course; his 'tell it as it was' approach was something Michael had missed; this man to man thing. He revelled in the way in which, to some people, Bill's questions may seem trivial and of no importance but was delighted that he had asked him about his corncob pipe, as no one else would even have thought about it.

"I'm not sure what day it was," said Michael. Bill suddenly placed his hand on Michael's shoulder and rose from his chair.

"Hang on a minute, Michael, let me buy a round."

"Jack, Jim, I have a coin in my pocket that needs spending." Jack and Jim turned as Bill came between them.

"Drinks for the four of us," said Bill as he slapped a shiny shilling on the bar.

"Are you going to spend it? The sacred shilling! Never thought I'd see the day," said Jack in a somewhat triumphant manner. He had been trying to get Bill to spend his shilling for the last four years but to no avail.

"Not for me," said Michael, "but I charge you, Toby, not to take that shilling. I will exchange it for one in my pocket."

"As you wish," said Toby, not caring who paid for the drinks.

"Are you sure you won't be having one, Michael?" Bill asked.

"No, still got pretty much a full pint, but I could still raise a glass to whatever you boys will be drinking to."

"And to that, may I propose a toast?" said Jim. "To all those that are still breathing."

"I'll drink to that," agreed Michael. Jim and Jack drank their pints and left.

"As I said, I'm not sure what day it was," Michael reiterated, "but from the 11th to the 15th of December 1862, we were fighting in Fredericksburg, Virginia. We marched with fixed bayonets up Hanover Street that December morning, with sprigs of green in our caps. Just ahead was carried our regimental flag, bright green with a gold harp and the ancient Gaelic words, *Riamh Nar Dhruid O Spairn lann,* emblazoned on it."

Michael looked at Bill as he spoke in his native tongue. "And it's meaning?" asked Bill, smiling. Michael took a deep breath and closed his eyes.

"Never retreat from the clash of spears."

"A nice day to die," said a soldier on my right; his name was Jimmy McGill. We had been marching since sunrise. There were hundreds of us marching to Fredericksburg; the Unionists were up ahead, and we were going to shift their ass; well, that was the idea." Michael stopped talking, had a drink of beer, drew on his pipe then carried on with his story.

"In front of us was an open plain and two hills known as Mary's Heights which were covered with Confederate artillery. Shot and shell exploded all around in a blaze of flashes, and the sound, the sound was enough to awaken the dead. At the base of the hills was a stone wall and behind that, a sunken road. We paused to regroup behind a slight rise on the plain. Jimmy was still there at my side when the command to advance came through. We double-quicked across the plain toward the stone wall and were now under the range of their artillery. Our lines staggered and slowed as men were blown away like they were never even there. Next, we were met by a blaze of fire as the Confederates behind the stone wall let go with their muskets and canister and that's when it happened. Jimmy was in front of me, running like the rest of us toward the wall. Anyway, he caught a bullet in the chest and stopped suddenly, coming back and knocking me into the fellow behind. He dropped his musket, the bayonet of which entered my inner right thigh and came out the other side. I fell against a tree stump, hitting my head and knocking myself out. When I came to, Jimmy was lying on top of me. I managed to pull the bayonet out of my thigh, then sat with my back against the tree stump. I held Jimmy in my arms and could see he was done for, but he was still breathing. I started talking to him, telling him things would be alright and he started talking back to me. He asked if I could take his pipe out of his coat pocket because he fancied a smoke, so anyway, I did so and stuck it in his mouth - and that's when he died. He was the second person to die in my arms." Michael looked up.

"And the cob pipe?" Bill asked.

"I asked him if I could have it; he didn't answer so I put it in my pocket. I couldn't let him go without there being at least something to show that his existence on this earth was worth something, even if it was only a corncob pipe," Michael paused. "You know something, Bill? This is the first time I've smoked it in all these years."

"And the reason you've decided to smoke it now?" Bill raised his eyebrows as he spoke. Michael chuckled, looking up and answering as much with his eyes as he did with his lips.

"Coming to terms with my life, laying a few demons, so to speak. And you, Bill, how many ghosts have you got, hiding away in some dark corner of your mind, a mind that isn't the one you had before you went away?"

Immediately, Bill thought of things that kept him awake at night.

"I'm trying to understand the demons I'm left with," he said, gazing intently at the floor. For a moment, neither spoke, Bill's mind on other things, flashing between the moment he held Megan to visions of dead men. He looked at his fingers, fingers that had held and pulled the trigger on a rifle sending out bullets in defence of the realm. The same fingers that had gently stroked the jet-black hair on Megan's head, whose scented skin still lingered in his nostrils from when he kissed her on the cheek. He turned his hands over; were these the hands that held aloft his rifle with its bayonet glinting in the sun as it sank into the hearts of men? Michael was aware of the silence between them; he looked at Bill and could see he was in another place.

"Is there anything you would like to tell me, Bill?" his voice just above a whisper, almost goading an answer.

"You can lay your demons on me. As I have said, I have a few of my own so a few of yours isn't going to make any difference to me." He paused; "but it may help you to talk about it." Bill wrung his hands as he looked up.

"It seems we have a lot in common, Bill. We have seen and done much the same things and there is nothing I can say that will erase all the shit that you don't want in your mind. My guess is that when you gave Megan a hug, a lot of that shit came bubbling to the surface and if it didn't, it soon will. You held your Megan after events marred your life and I held my Megan - you remember me telling you about my Megan?"

"Yes," said Bill, "a long time ago."

"Well, I held mine before such events marred my life."

"And the difference?" said Bill, raising his eyebrows.

"Over fifty years and a lot of soul-searching." Michael paused for a moment; "not that your demons matter to anyone other than yourself," he added. "When I die, my ghosts will die with me, as God knows I have had them for long enough." He paused then held his pint at arm's length, passing it through a shard of light that beamed through the window. "Not the best pint I've had in here," he said with some dissatisfaction.

"It happened in the Sinai Desert," Bill said, looking around at the same time, just to make sure that he couldn't be overheard by Toby.

"We were on a reconnaissance walk," he smiled when he said walk, "just to see what was out there." He went on to tell briefly of the circumstances and outcome of the exercise, of Tom and Ian's deaths and the deaths of the nine prisoners.

"It was when I stood up on the ridge after seeing the Phoenix take Ian's soul. You may think it strange that I should make such a claim, of seeing the Phoenix I mean, but it's what I needed to see at the time and see it I did."

"Anyway, I happened to look up and, away in the distance on a section of flat plain, I could see a line of men heading our way. They were about two miles away. I couldn't make out who they were, but I thought that if I could see them, they could see me. Behind me, the terrain, gently rising and dipping, stretched out at much the same distance, then it finished at the foot of some rocky outcrops rising to a hundred feet or so."

"I left Ian and ran to tell the boys. As you can imagine, there was a bit of a panic. Jim shot off, climbing to the ridge to see for himself, the rest of us getting our things together ready to leave. When Jim got back, he said we had an hour, maybe a bit more, to get out of there. We would take the camels up to the ridge where Ian lay and head for the rocky outcrop which was in the direction that we were going, and hopefully come across the railway line."

"And the prisoners?"

"Demons, Michael, you wanted demons. Well, there are plenty of them lying in a graveyard in the Sinai desert. I suppose graveyard is the wrong word as a graveyard is a place where people are buried; these were left in the open as we didn't have time to bury them; we didn't have a choice to take them with us either.

"The decision was taken to kill them. I could see Jack getting agitated as he picked up his rifle - suddenly he started screaming, which triggered everyone else to do the same. Well, everyone except Jim, who stood motionless, then through the mayhem, he could be heard shouting something about doing it in an orderly fashion.

"Everything happened in a frenzy; we took it to an obscene level of slaughter. The prisoners, at this point, started to scream themselves as they began to realise what was happening.

"Jack, screaming his head off, ran to a man kneeling and thrust his bayonet through his chest, then everyone, including me, followed suit.

"We all rushed at the prisoners, even going to the point of pushing each other out of the way to get to them. I killed a man who just stood there looking at me, my bayonet entering his heart as he shouted "Allah Akbar!" David ran past me, his face so contorted with the curdled screams of a man possessed that it stopped me in my tracks. I saw Jim remove his bayonet from a man's back and saw a fountain of frothy blood gushing from his mouth. It was madness.

"Trevor plunged his bayonet into a man with such force that the guard on the bayonet handle entered his chest and got stuck under a rib. On pulling it out, his rib broke and could be seen exposed on his bare chest as blood pumped out.

"They were bayoneted sitting down, standing up, crying and begging. It was worse than a nightmare.

"Then it all went quiet. In under a minute, all nine prisoners were dead. I sat down, my mind a blur. There was blood on my hands and arms. I looked around but no one said a word, then Jim shouted, "Right lads, let's get the fuck out of here!"

"We were all in shock as we led the camels to the ridge where Ian lay. We tried to dig some sort of grave for him and Tom, but the sand kept running back in and we didn't have time. So, we left them exposed to the elements, and that was a hard thing to do, Michael. Looking over the far ridge, we could see the line of men getting closer and if they didn't see us before, they certainly saw us now. We left that accursed place. Two and a half hours, Michael," Bill shook his head, "two and a half hours, that's all it took, from the moment Jim first saw them to the moment we left. It seemed like forever.

An hour later, we looked back. Nothing, in fact, we never saw them again. It was getting dark when we got to the railway line; we followed it for another hour before we got to El Arish. Not surprisingly, our boys were there, asking us how we enjoyed our little walk before realising that, in the dark, two of us were missing. Jim made his report and that was it."

Bill stopped talking and looked at Michael, "There are more demons, but this was different and just to say they were the enemy and war is war doesn't lie easily with me. Well, Michael," Bill said sitting upright in his chair, "you now have some of my ghosts, what, pray, are you going to do with them?" A broad grin spread across Michael's face, "I'll just add them to mine and take them along with me," he said, laughing. To see Michael laugh brought a smile to Bill. They were both silent for a moment, Michael digesting what he had heard and Bill realising that this was the first time he had told anyone about the demons that haunted his mind.

"And Megan," Michael said changing the subject; "it may be none of my business, but I like to think that the welfare of that lady is my business. I've got to know her very well in the last two and a half years. In fact, her presence in my life has made it more fulfilling and less complicated than it used to be and I love her for that."

He stopped speaking then raised his head, looking Bill square in the face. Bill noticed how much older he looked; wrinkled skin now covered a face that, with the passing of time, had only stories to tell. He was shaved and wore a clean shirt under an old but well-kept tweed jacket.

"She loves you, Bill" Michael's words engendered a warm feeling within Bill; he wasn't surprised at the announcement, but for Michael to utter them……. Bill thought for a moment.

"Did she tell you that?" Bill said softly, looking into Michael's cloudy blue eyes. He noticed a sparkle in them, a sparkle that wasn't there a minute ago.

"No, she didn't, well, not in so many words, but I know a woman in love, Bill, believe me."

"Why are you telling me this? Do you think people can fall in love by just writing letters, although there was nothing in them to suggest any kind of involvement one way or another?" "Well," he said, reaching for a paper quill that lay on the floor beside the fireplace, "it seems that you can, and don't think she knows nothing about you; she knows everything about you."

"From Mum?" Bill said with a sigh.

"Yes," Michael interjected, "plus, I told her that I thought you were a good enough sort of chap. Bill, there's no conspiracy going on here. I just told her my thoughts regarding you and I think I am a pretty good judge of character. Do you remember the day when you brought me that wild duck and a rabbit when I was poorly and I couldn't get to the shop on account of the snow? You were twelve or thirteen at the time. Tell me, was it a suggestion of your mother that you brought those things? I often wondered about it and would like to know." Bill shifted in his seat, feeling uncomfortable that Michael should bring up a good deed that he had done when he was a kid.

"It was nothing, Michael. I just asked Mum if I could take you some stuff. She added some other things, but clearly it was nothing."

"Nothing to you, Bill, but it was something to me. And the future, Bill, what of the future?" Michael said changing the subject.

"I'm going to marry Megan!"

"Are you really?" Michael said with a broad grin spreading across his face, "and when did you decide this?"

"Two minutes before I walked through that door," Bill nodding his head toward the door of the bar.

"My God, Bill, that's rather sudden isn't it? Obviously, you haven't told her of your intentions," Michael paused, "but what makes you think she will have you?"

Bill smiled, "You've just said that she loves me."

"Well, that's a good enough reason!" Michael said as he slapped his knee with delight.

"And what about you, Michael, I hear you have a lady friend yourself?"

Michael nearly choked on his beer and a shooting pain went through his stomach as he heard Bill speak of Mavis. He turned with a grimace that distorted his rugged face. Bill stood and tapped his back.

"Are you alright, Michael?" he asked with some concern.

The pain in Michael's stomach went almost immediately as he took some deep breaths. Then, with a broad grin spreading across his face, Michael answered, "Yes, I suppose I do have a lady friend, but sadly, love has come too late in my life."

They spent another half-hour talking about Michael's past and Bill's future. Then Michael got to his feet, saying he was tired and needed a little nap and that Bill was already late for his dinner reunion with Megan.

Outside, Michael put on his overcoat and shook hands with Bill, again congratulating him on his decision to ask Megan for her hand in marriage. As they still held their handshake, Bill asked if Michael would consider standing in for Megan's father and give her away at their wedding. His response was that it would be a privilege and an honour.

They parted, Michael with unsteady feet walking away to his right and Bill, with a heavy heart, knowing that Michael may never be at their wedding. Turning left, he walked around the corner of the pub and had only gone a few paces when he stopped and turned around; he didn't want Michael to walk alone on his way home. It didn't take but a few moments for Bill to catch up with Michael. He could see that he was struggling even on level ground and he still had a steep hill to climb before he could have that sleep that he needed. As he fell into step with Michael, he said he thought he would see him to his door.

"It's all right," Michael said, "I can make it on my own."

"I know you can, I am just doing what Megan would do."

"Yes," said Michael, "Megan has walked me home many times."

As they started to climb the steep incline to Michael's home, he stumbled and fell to his knees. Bill helped him up. "Can I make a suggestion?" he said as Michael brushed his trousers, "I'll give you a piggyback." And that was how Michael arrived at his door.

As Michael slid off Bill's back, he slapped him on the shoulder.

"Thank you, Bill, you are very kind," he said as he opened his door.

"No, Michael, being kind is carrying someone on your back up a hill to their house." Michael looked bewildered.

"Isn't that what you have just done?"

"No, Michael, I didn't carry someone, I carried my friend. Be seeing you and have a good sleep."

27

Euphoric - that was the only word Michael could use to describe his feelings. He sat at his table drinking a cup of tea, a drink that quenched a thirst a beer couldn't. He was overjoyed at meeting Bill again. Sliding his hand into his trouser pocket, he pulled out the shilling, Bill's shilling, the one that Toby had exchanged for one of his. Bill, he thought, didn't understand the significance of the coin he held but, one day, Michael felt sure he would.

"I have things to do," he said to himself. He left the table and went into his bedroom. Opening his wardrobe door, he reached in and, from an array of boots and shoes, he brought out an old cardboard shoebox. Tucking it under his arm, he walked back and placed it on the kitchen table. He removed the rubber band that held the lid in place and opened the box. Inside were two round tin containers, ones he had found outside the burnt-out remains of a cotton plantation owner's mansion in Virginia. He held one, took off its lid and emptied its contents onto the table. Four coins spilled out, one rolling halfway across the table and onto the floor. He picked up the gold double eagle coin, turning it over in his hand. On one side was stamped the date 1861 with the Liberty head above it. On the other, an eagle behind a shield; in one of its talons were three arrows and, engraved around the coin's edge, the words 'United States of America Twenty D'.

He placed it back on the table then opened and emptied the other. He looked at the eight gold coins and smiled. There used to be nine, he thought, but the ladies and publicans of Shrewsbury had that one over thirty years ago. Three days of drunken debauchery, some might say, whereas he would say he'd had a good time. The landlords were obliging and the ladies catered for his every need. He never repeated the experience and, as he looked at the small fortune in front of him, he wondered why not.

He stood with his hands on the table, one each side of the shoe box. He looked in again, hesitating, then took out another smaller cardboard box; this one fitted into his hand and was tied with brown string. It was given to him by Nell three days after he had buried his Megan, all those years ago. It was a box he had never opened and never really wanted to, but now was the moment. He picked up a knife that lay beside a half-eaten loaf and cut the string. Inside was a crumpled piece of brown paper that filled the box. He placed the crumpled paper on the table and started to unravel it. At its centre was a gold wedding ring; his hands were shaking as he flattened out the paper. Under the ring and on the paper, in childlike writing, were the words: "May this ring be placed on another girl's finger". It was signed by Megan. Michael had never read these words before and, as he clutched the ring, his shoulders shook and his faint sobbing grew louder as he lowered himself to his knees. After a while, he rose and placed the coins back in their metal tins, reading again their faded green labels: F Joyce and Co, London, England, percussion caps. He then placed Megan's ring back in the brown paper and crumpled it in his hand before putting it back in its own little box, saying in a soft voice, "She'll understand." Michael had decided some months earlier that he was going to bequeath all his possessions to Megan and Bill. To Megan, because he loved her as much as any man would love a daughter and to Bill more so now, having revealed his intention to marry and look after Megan. At ten past eight, Michael started to tidy up his home. He swept the floor and washed the two cups and dinner plate that had been in the sink since Megan came that morning. He put away the bread, along with some butter, jam and the piece of cheese that Megan had brought with her. Potato peelings, which were in a cardboard box, he placed in a bin outside his door. He built up the fire, then went again to his bedroom. He opened the bedside drawer that held his mother's handkerchief and, from the drawer, took some sheets of white paper, envelopes, a bottle of ink, pen and a pencil. As he sat at his table, he glanced at Shy's blanket by the fireplace, groaning as he thought of how he missed Shy's company.

Michael wrote two short letters in pencil, one to Megan and one to Bill. To Megan he spoke of his love, his encouragement towards her aspirations and dreams, wishing her well for the future and thanking her for her company over the last few years, adding that she had become a wonderful companion and comfort towards the end of his life. He ended his letter with a Latin phrase, one that he remembered as a kid, one the Catholic priest would always say on leaving their home in Ireland... *amor est vitae essentia.*

In Bill's letter, he mentioned in no uncertain terms that if he didn't look after Megan and treat her well, he would bloody well come back and haunt him. He also wished him well for the future and thanked him for his friendship and the piggyback ride he gave him up the church pitch; he also ended this letter with a Latin phrase ...*vale mi amice.*

Michael placed both letters in envelopes, writing their names on each, then placed them in the shoe box. He decided to leave the box on the table until his passing, as one day soon he feared his time would come. He hoped he would live long enough to see Megan and Bill married and the thought of giving Megan away on her big day, if indeed that were her wish, thrilled him.

His thoughts then turned to Mavis and the short time that they had had together. He looked at the white, flat glove box on the table, containing a pair of gloves that he had asked Megan to buy for him. They were a little present for Mavis on her return from London, her solicitor having sent word that he needed to see her regarding her signature on papers, so as to settle the affairs of her estate. He was looking forward to seeing her as he never thought that he would ever have loved again, but he did.

Satisfying himself that everything was in order, he picked up his pen and dipped it into the ink bottle. As he lifted it out, he ran the nib along the edge of the bottle ridding it of excess ink. Again, he looked around the room, then with a clean sheet of paper in front of him, he wrote in bold black ink.

"Michael Barry Gill
My last will and testament" ....

That night Michael Barry died.

The following morning, Megan decided to give Michael an early call; she hadn't slept well on account of her mind being full of the evening before. She was oblivious to thoughts other than Bill. She wanted to tell Michael all about her feelings and thoughts regarding Bill, but her world fell apart as she entered Michael's home. Megan suddenly went cold as she knocked on his bedroom door; there was silence as she entered. For a moment, she thought he was sleeping, but deep down she knew he was dead. The memory of her father came flooding back. Nine years ago, another world was lost to her and now, for the second time, death had taken away a relationship that she held so dear.

She sat on his bed and looked at the man who had taught her so much. She wanted to tell him about the new man in her life and that's what she did. She lay beside him and held his cold hand, then told him of her dreams.

Mavis was notified of Michael's death by telegram and arrived back in Llandyssil the following day. Mavis spent an hour with Michael and, as devastated as she was, she later said that the six months that they had together was heaven. She added that finding Michael was like finding something you had lost, not even knowing it was something you were even looking for.

The passing of Michael, although expected, left a void in the community; few people really knew him, but everyone knew of him. His funeral was a big event, curtains were drawn as his coffin was carried through the village and onwards up the hill to the cemetery, where he was laid to rest. Mavis wore the white gloves that Michael had Megan buy for him some weeks before his death and, taking them off in her room at the Rectory, she placed them back inside the white glove box that Megan had given her. Mavis slowly placed the box in the bottom drawer of her wardrobe and, as she closed it, she wondered if she would ever wear them again.

Four months later, Bill and Megan were married, and as Megan walked back down the aisle, married and blissfully happy with Bill by her side, she looked up to where the rafters met at the apex of the church roof and whispered her thanks to Michael. In doing so, she shed a tear, a tear that was gently wiped away by a hand that bore the ring that was destined to be placed on another girl's finger.

Thirteen months after their marriage, Megan presented Bill with a son.

Three weeks after that, their son was christened; his name - Michael Barry Jones.

28

Jim had been home four weeks when he went to see Skinny Steve's mother, wanting to fulfil the promise he had made and his conscience would not let him renege on that promise. He may not have written a poem, but she welcomed him with open arms. They spoke for an hour or so before he left, calling in at Montgomery Church. He didn't really know why he was there, but he was there. He opened the big oak doors; they creaked as he walked in, then closing them behind him, the noise echoed throughout the building. He stood for a moment looking at the altar and stained-glass window, thinking that he had more reason to go than to stay. He was about to leave when the door opened and the Vicar of Montgomery walked in.

"Hello," he said with a smile. They exchanged pleasantries for a while then he surprised Jim with a statement.

"I'm always intrigued as to why people visit churches other than on a Sunday."

"To pray?" said Jim with some hesitation.

"You would think so, wouldn't you?" he answered thoughtfully, "but I believe that many people enter church for reasons other than to pray."

"Take yourself, sir."

"Jim, my name is Jim."

"Alright, Jim, take yourself. I'm curious as to the reason you are here; could it be the architecture? Or the Church's history, or maybe some other reason?" Jim looked at the man with the white collar around his neck and decided that he liked him. He was easy to talk to, unassuming, with the ability to make him feel at ease.

"The reason I am here," said Jim, "is because I have just told someone a lie."

"Look, perhaps you would feel more comfortable talking outside, Jim, as I know these places can be intimidating sometimes," he said as he looked around the church. Jim followed him outside and, as they walked around the church, Jim told him about his visit to Skinny Steve's mother and the lie he had told her.

"And the reason you lied?" he asked Jim.

"Because I wanted her to know that he didn't die alone, that he was being held by someone he knew."

For a moment, they walked without talking, then the Vicar stopped and asked Jim if he had actually held Steve.

"Oh yes," said Jim, "I held him like I'd have held my own children, but he was already dead."

"And your purpose in visiting the church?"

"Well," said Jim, "it wasn't to ask for forgiveness. I suppose I went in to explain my lie."

"And did you?"

"No, I'm afraid I find churches…. what was the word you used, intimidating?"

"Yes", replied the Vicar, "and where do you go when you feel the need to talk to God?" Jim smiled.

"Into the fields."

"My God," exclaimed the Vicar, "that's where I go sometimes. So yes, if you feel closer to your God in a field, then so be it. As for the lie you have told, I can understand, you had nothing to gain from it other than to give some comfort to a lady who had lost her son. I cannot speak for God, but I think your actions are commendable as it's you that will have to live with the lie, but please don't lose sleep over it. What is done is done and let that be an end to it. Now, Jim, I must leave you as I have to visit a lady who is not well and is expecting me." He extended his hand and, as Jim shook it, he knew that they would meet again.

"Thank you, Jim, it's been a pleasure to meet you."

"Thank you for listening," Jim said as the Vicar turned and walked away. He had gone some distance when he turned and shouted to Jim.

"Come and see me sometime; maybe we could arrange a meeting in a field somewhere." Jim smiled and shouted back,

"I would like that, Reverend; I would really like that."

"So be it!" drifted back the reply.

29

Four months after returning home, Jack went to visit the lad from Crescent Street, Newtown. He had been committed to a mental asylum in Forden, some ten miles from his home. Jack was taken to a door on the first floor of the building. This he knocked.

"Enter," said a voice. Jack opened the door and walked in.

"Take a seat," said a chubby man who sat at a large desk and was in the process of putting a stamp onto an envelope. Jack sat down in a chair opposite him. He gave the stamp a thump with his fist, then looked up.

"And what can I do for you?" he asked, looking over the thin wired spectacles he wore.

"I'm looking for a man," Jack said.

"His name?" answered the man, not taking his eyes off Jack.

"Robert, Robert Pugh."

"Ah, Robert. And what, may I ask, is your interest in this man?"

Jack sat upright. "I, err, I found him," said Jack not really knowing what to say.

"You found him?" asked the man, raising his eyebrows

"Yes, I found him in a shell hole in Egypt during the war."

"Ah," said the man whose smile widened on hearing of Jack's explanation.

"And you are, don't tell me," he said getting a little excited, "you are Jack, are you not?"

"Yes, I'm sorry I didn't introduce myself before, but yes, I'm Jack. How did you know?"

"You are the man that saved him."

"Well, I don't know about that," said Jack, a little bewildered.

"He thinks you did," the man said as he pushed his chair back and stood up. He left the desk and walked to a window, one that rose from floor to ceiling.

"Have a look," he said. Jack stood by his side and looked out of the window. In front of the building was a gravelled area and, beyond that, a large well-manicured lawn surrounded by flower beds full of rose bushes.

"The man sitting on the bench, the one with his back to us, that's him." Jack looked and saw the bench; it was on the edge of the lawn. The man sitting on it wore a blue jumper and was motionless.

"That's him?" said Jack.

"That's him," the chubby man replied as he walked back to his desk. "He sits there most days. He doesn't say much, he's no trouble. His mother comes and visits him twice a week; would you like to see him?"

"No, no I don't think so. I wouldn't know what to say to him. I just called to see him, that's all."

The chubby man didn't say a word as he stood by his desk, he just looked at Jack, then, taking off his glasses he spoke;

"Jack, can I give you some advice? All across this country, there are hundreds, if not thousands, of men like Robert in institutions such as this and they are where they are as a direct result of the war. As you must know, there are some men living in the community who are not as bad as Robert and are cared for by their families. But nonetheless, it was the war that made them what they are." The chubby man again walked to the window and gazed out.

"I think," he said with a sigh, "that you should for your own benefit consider going to see Robert. You may wonder how on earth you're seeing him could possibly be of any benefit to you and the truth is" he said, walking back to his chair, "I don't know if it will. I have been here many years and I have seen what war has done to the minds of men and you can take it from me there isn't a man that came back from that war that hasn't been affected by it in some form or other. They may not even be aware of it but, believe me, they are not as they should be. I understand that you don't need the likes of Robert to remind you of the fighting and killing that you may or may not have done, but, in some respects, it may help you understand your good fortune. You, Jack, don't have a wooden cross with your name on it, stuck in the ground somewhere with your body lying beneath it and you are not in a place like this, suffering with a troubled mind. So yes, Jack, go and see him and say hello and if you don't get any benefit from seeing him, remember you are in a far better place than he is."

With some apprehension, Jack crossed the gravelled area between the asylum building and the bench where Robert was sitting. On his approach, Robert turned his head. There was a vacant look in his eyes, Jack thought, as he sat next to him. Robert smiled; Jack recognised him immediately and, although it had been over two years since he had found him in a shell hole, he hadn't altered at all.

"Hello," Jack said.

"Hello," Robert replied, pausing for a moment, "and what is your name?"

"My name is Jack." Jack was anticipating some kind of reaction when he mentioned his name but there was nothing.

"My name is Robert," he said, the smile not leaving his face. Jack never mentioned the war, so they talked of other things and when he mentioned how nice the garden looked, especially the roses, Robert went into a world of his own. He knew every goddammed rose that bordered the lawn.

"That one there," he said pointing to a red and white one, "that's a Jacques Cartier, and the next one to it is a Madame Alfred Carriere, then we have Reine Victoria, a Crepuscule." Jack was amazed at Robert's knowledge of roses and was lost after the Variegata Di Bologna, but Robert carried on and after he had named the last one, he looked at Jack and at the same time his smile was back.

"Well," said Jack, "you certainly know your roses." At the mention of the word roses, Robert was off again, naming every one of them for the second time. Jack waited until he had finished then, standing up, he told Robert that it was time for him to go. Robert also stood up and informed Jack that he must go too as he mustn't be late for tea. It was those last words from Robert that held Jack's attention.

"And what will happen if you're late for tea, Robert?" asked Jack, already knowing the answer

"My mother will …."

"Box your ears?" interrupted Jack, laughing.

"How did you know that?" asked Robert, looking surprised.

"A good guess, I suppose," answered Jack.

As they stood facing each other, Jack held out his hand. Robert took it firmly in his and as they shook hands, Jack, with a lump in his throat, said "Goodbye."

"Goodbye, Jack," Robert said, looking deeply into Jack's eyes, then without letting go of his hand he said, "I knew a man called Jack once, a long time ago; he saved my life." Robert let go of Jack's hand, then turning, he walked away.

Jack was overcome with emotion; he couldn't remember the last time he had cried and it took a man in a mental asylum to do what a sane man couldn't.

As he walked home, he thought of Robert and his talk with the chubby man about men being unaware of how the war had changed them. The irony was that maybe we are all lost and are only now beginning to find our way back. For some it will take many months, others it may take years and a few, like Robert, are unlikely ever to return. He thought of his drinking; did he drink to forget the war, or did he drink to remember it, or indeed, did he drink because of it?

Then, as he walked through Montgomery and with no answers coming to mind, he called in at the Checkers. Maybe the answer was there.

Epilogue

One midsummer's day, seven years after the war had ended, Bill, inch by inch, let the hemp rope slip through his fingers as he and his fellow pallbearers lowered the oak coffin containing Jack's body slowly into the grave. Then, standing back, he watched the gathered mourners shuffle forward to pay their last respects to one of their own.

Jack had been found in Ted Parry's hay barn the week before, drunk and in a bad way. He had been taken home and put to bed. Two days later, he died of pneumonia. He was thirty-two.

Bill could hear the church bell strike one o'clock as people, with heads bowed, filed past, gazing into the hole that had been dug the day before. The sun cast its shadows on nearby headstones, some of which were of Jack's forebears that had long been forgotten. The Very Reverend Jacob Thomas mumbled words, throwing onto the coffin a handful of soil as he spoke. That done, he turned and without another word, walked away, fully aware that the people he had just addressed felt nothing but contempt for him.

Jack would have loved his funeral service. The Reverend Jenkins had retired, moving back to London, and had been replaced by the Reverend Thomas. His presence after only four months had left many disappointed. They were not used to his condemnation of any heathen, even a dead one, entering his church, nor his fire and brimstone rhetoric from the pulpit. At Jack's funeral, he said there were two sure ways of going to hell: not believing in the existence of God and succumbing to the evils of drink. Jack, he hinted, was a prime example of one to be condemned and in not so many words, condemn him he did.

During his ranting, Bill stood up, his anger at how the Reverend Thomas was portraying Jack was more than he could stand. Without acknowledging the presence of the man in the pulpit, Bill ushered his family up the aisle of the church and out through the church doors. Jim, having a mind to do the same, stood with his family and followed Bill, both families waiting outside until the service was over. Undaunted by their leaving, the Reverend Thomas spoke of their insensitivity in walking out of the House of God during the proceedings.

It was at this point that Isaac James, Jacks' uncle, rose from his seat to stand before the bier on which Jack's coffin rested. Facing the vicar, he said,

"This is the funeral of Jack Davies and we do not need you, Sir, to tell us of his failings. Some years ago, like many others from this village, he went away and fought in a war that was sanctioned by the government and we were told, by God. Jack was a good man, Sir, and for you to speak of him and my friends in such a manner is wrong. So, I too will leave this Church. You may be a man of the cloth, Sir, but you are not a man of the people." He had taken three steps up the aisle when he slowly turned and, again facing the vicar, said,

"Let he who is without sin cast the first stone."

Others joined Isaac as he slowly walked out of the Church; they waited as he stopped opposite Mavis who, sitting in an end pew, smiled on his approach and, offering his arm, calmly asked if she would care to join him. Mavis, still smiling, stood up too and, linking her arm through his, said softly, "I was wondering how long it would take you to walk out."

After the death of Michael, Mavis stayed on at the Rectory, spending less and less time in London. Michael had bequeathed his cottage and worldly possessions to Megan and Bill. Soon after moving into Michael's cottage, Bill set to work, adding two extra rooms, one for his growing family and one for Mavis. Isaac had become a constant companion of Mavis. He did not replace Michael, but they enjoyed each other's company. It was partly this and the opportunity to become a live-in grandmother, fulfilling a wish that she had expressed many times before, and it was to these ends that Mavis came to stay, saying that life in London for her had changed and that now she felt more at home in the little village that she first visited all those years ago.

Eighteen months after Jack's funeral, Mavis died in her sleep. She was found as Megan took her a cup of tea one morning. She was buried at Michael's side and wore the white gloves that he had kissed years before.

Bill still had bad dreams but nothing like the ones he used to have. He still walked the fields but not at two o'clock in the morning. On the Sunday afternoon following Mavis's funeral, he was out walking with Jim's son, Sam, now a young man of eighteen years and the image of his father. Bill, being conscious of Sam by his side, thought of the young men of his age that had gone to war some twelve years before. The thought of Sam in army uniform and carrying a rifle sent a shiver through him. On reaching the brow of a hill, they both turned to look at the view behind them. Sam, not looking at Bill, suddenly asked him if he ever thought of the war. Bill, a little taken back by the question, didn't answer immediately. He just gazed at the valley in front of them. Casting his mind back, he thought of Jim and Jack and of how the three of them would wander over the land ferreting for rabbits. He remembered the last time they did it before going away.

'Those rabbits,' he thought, 'the ones that lay dead in the snow.... like the three of us, they had known what fear was.'" Bill smiled as he turned and looked at Sam.

"You ask if I ever think of the war?" Stepping forward, he answered, "It never leaves me, Sam. It never leaves me."